FROM PURITANISM TO THE
AGE OF REASON

FROM PURITANISM TO THE AGE OF REASON

A STUDY OF
CHANGES IN RELIGIOUS THOUGHT
WITHIN THE
CHURCH OF ENGLAND
1660 TO 1700

BY

G. R. CRAGG
M.A., PH.D.

CAMBRIDGE
AT THE UNIVERSITY PRESS
1966

PUBLISHED BY

THE SYNDICS OF THE CAMBRIDGE UNIVERSITY PRESS

Bentley House, 200 Euston Road, London N.W.1
American Branch: 32 East 57th Street, New York, N.Y. 10022
West African Office: P.M.B. 5181, Ibadan, Nigeria

First printed 1950
Reprinted 1966

First printed in Great Britain at the University Press, Cambridge
(Brooke Crutchley, University Printer)
Reprinted by photolithography in the Republic of Ireland
by Browne and Nolan Limited, Dublin

PREFACE

RELIGIOUS developments in the later seventeenth century form, by common consent, a neglected phase of English history. Most of the general works on the subject are old, and very few of them can now claim to be satisfactory. Nowhere has the neglect been so conspicuous as in the field of religious thought. The present work owed its origin to a conviction that the importance of this period far exceeded the attention it has received.

In its original form, this essay was submitted for the Archbishop Cranmer Prize, and its scope has been largely determined by that fact. The regulations stipulate that dissertations must be concerned with changes in the life and thought of the Church of England. I have deliberately restricted myself to changes in thought, since only a limitation of this kind could keep the study within manageable bounds. I have said nothing about the organized life of the Church, or about its government or liturgy. I have even avoided any mention of changes in the favoured style of preaching, though this was closely related to the thought of the Restoration period. I have not attempted to assess the influence that the Church exerted, though it is nearly a century since Macaulay pointed out that the pulpit was one of the most formative of all the forces moulding public opinion. I have not been concerned with the history of religious thought in general, but only with those aspects of it in which changes can clearly be discerned. Consequently, the relatively static forms of Anglican theology have been deliberately ignored.

My obligations are too many to be mentioned in detail. I am indebted to the adjudicators of the Archbishop Cranmer

Prize for the favourable consideration they gave this work, and also for comments and suggestions which have been incorporated in the text. Professor E. R. Adair of McGill University has given me very useful counsel and advice, and many friends have helped by reading the manuscript, preparing the typescript, and correcting the proofs. As in duty bound, I gratefully acknowledge the encouragement originally given me by the authorities of Trinity College, Cambridge, when they elected me to the Stanton Student-ship; in the continuance of my studies, I have been indebted at every point to my wife.

G. R. C.

December 1949

CONTENTS

CHAPTER I

INTRODUCTION

'WHEN the Lord turned again the captivity of Zion, we were like them that dream.' The words came often and naturally to the men who had waited for the Restoration and known the bitterness of hope deferred. It is small wonder that the text was a favourite with Anglican preachers, both eminent and obscure. Throughout the Interregnum they had known prolonged frustration; now their humiliation was turned to triumph and their sorrow to joy. A wave of relief surged over the people; after the years of upheaval—years in which exhilaration and disillusionment had been so strangely mingled—they were returning to settled and familiar ways. After war they would have peace; after the experiments of the Commonwealth, they would have the tested constitution of king, lords, and commons; after the intensity of Puritan religion, they would revert to the sober and orderly ministrations of the Church of England. 'The old ways', they said, 'are better', and they returned to them with relief.

The Restoration era began with innovation at a discount. The cry was for stability, and stability was equated with the order which existed before the war. Most people doubtless believed that they could really return to the ways they had remembered so long and so fondly. Many of these hopes were disappointed, but the clergy were more successful than most of the gentry in making their expectations come true. They could resume possession of the benefices they had lost; they could revive old claims to preferment;[1] they could

[1] The Calendar of State Papers, Domestic, for the early months of Charles II's reign is filled with the pleas of clergy for advancement.

restore the interrupted usages and customs of the past. But they themselves had changed. Many of them had suffered severely during the Interregnum, and the mark of their trials was upon them still. The vindictiveness which crept into much of the early Restoration persecution of dissenters was the result of suffering in the past. Those who had gone into exile were also different men when they returned. Cosin and Morley and Sancroft had lived in Catholic countries as representatives of a defeated cause and pensioners of a dependent king. In the anti-Roman works of Bramhall we see with unusual clarity the situation in which the Anglican exiles found themselves. The tendency to discuss Catholicism in an atmosphere aloof and slightly unreal disappeared in the face of Catholicism as actually practised abroad. The point should not be pressed too far; if in Cosin's works there is no record after 1660 of the ritual controversies of earlier years, it may be because his opponents had been overthrown and did not need to be defeated in debate. But at least the steady and settled opposition to Rome—so decisive a factor in frustrating the plans of Charles II and of his less adroit and less successful brother, James—was strengthened and confirmed by the experiences of the exiles. The Restoration era proved that the High Churchmen were as zealous Protestants as the Puritans, and in time of need both could sink their differences in order to oppose the Papists.

Many of the returning clergy were not aware that they themselves had changed, and they had no desire for and saw no need of alterations in the system they upheld. The Savoy Conference and the Act of Uniformity showed that there would be no changes in church order, and it was tacitly assumed that the system of Christian belief was eternal and never changed. Loyal Anglicans would have been deeply shocked if they could have foreseen how many influences would play upon the thought of the Church of England, and how profoundly it would be affected by them. As one by one these forces became apparent and the nature of their effect was seen, they were vehemently denounced by those who believed that Christian thought could not—or at least should not—change. The champions of the old order were often less able and usually much less interesting than the advocates of the new, and their importance is consequently overlooked. But changes presuppose a departure from some accepted norm; indeed, they are changes only because they deviate from the standard which has hitherto prevailed. The new trends in the religious thought of a period can only be understood in relation to the old ways which they attempt to supersede. A reformer is unintelligible except against the background of the abuses he proposes to remove.

When the Restoration clergy attempted to return to the old and settled ways, it was no simple task for them to define in precise terms their theological ideal. Indeed, the character of that ideal was one of the issues which had been involved in the recent struggles. The victory they had recently won was the final stage in a battle which had raged for many years, and whose origins went even beyond the Elizabethan settlement. In the early days of the Reformation the theology of the English Church was profoundly affected by continental thought, and the first half of the seventeenth century witnessed a bitter struggle with the Calvinism introduced in Elizabethan days. This struggle had seemingly been lost and now had apparently been won. The issues might seem clear enough; many were concerned with points of order, but important theological questions had been raised as well. Predestination and free grace were battle-cries in many a fierce debate, but actually the struggle, though undoubtedly important, was very much confused. Many of the clergy might support Laud's ritual reforms and yet be Calvinists in their theology. Puritans could uphold the execution of the King, and yet be essentially Arminians. It would be easier if we could identify a certain political position with a corresponding theological emphasis. But, though any such attempt inevitably involves an over-simplification, the events of the Interregnum made it much easier to draw such inferences without seriously distorting the truth. With few exceptions the Roundheads were Calvinists, and the Cavaliers increasingly became Arminians. This is a development which, with its antecedents and its consequences, will require detailed study, but it may be noted in passing that when the restored clergy reaffirmed the basic teachings of the Church of England, they were hardly likely to state them in Calvinistic terms.

One of the notable features of the period from 1660 to 1700 is the steady persistence of an Anglicanism of moderate and non-controversial type. At the time of the Restoration its most distinguished representatives were men like Hammond and Walton and Sanderson. They stood in the tradition of Hooker and Andrewes; by going behind the recent controversies for their inspiration, they were able to go beyond them in their teaching. Though Jeremy Taylor's iridescent genius made him difficult to classify, he belonged essentially to the same school, and there were many others, less distinguished but still influential, who shared this point of view.

The general outlines of their position do not need to be stated in detail, but it is necessary to notice certain points at which it was challenged during the period which the Restoration ushered in.

Its cosmology was pre-scientific; it was apparently sanctioned by the Bible and for centuries had been woven into the substance of both academic and popular theology. The earth was the centre of the universe, and at a relatively recent period had been created in six days. The celestial bodies revolved around the earth, and were expressly intended for the service and delight of man. Heaven was situated above the sky, and hell beneath or within the earth. The orderly functioning of nature was subject to frequent and unpredictable interruptions, and malign agencies were always at work. Devils might not actually appear, but their personal representatives—witches and sorcerers—were always near at hand. The old science seemed in a general way the authority for this view of the world, but this kind of cosmology was firmly believed by people who had never heard of Ptolemy or Copernicus. It was part of the ordinary person's conception of life; it was his understanding of the stage on which he spent his days. Because it was so generally accepted it usually passed unscrutinized. It found its way quite naturally into treatises and sermons; it was as likely to be assumed in learned works of controversy as in the pulpit of the village church. To question it raised issues with which religious discussion had not hitherto been seriously concerned; men were so preoccupied with discussions of 'foreknowledge absolute' that they were imperfectly aware of the emergence of a new cosmology. Those who had heard of Copernicus were apt to dismiss his theory as a dangerous attempt to overturn the teachings of the Bible.

This traditional view of the world was often an unexamined presupposition—a part of the furnishing of the mind that men took for granted—but it had its corresponding scientific formulations. With these theology was vaguely but tacitly allied. Scholasticism, with its picture of the world

derived from Aristotle through the Arabs and the schoolmen, controlled the outlook and method of the older science.
For all its brilliance and importance, the Baconian outlook
displaced the older view with surprising slowness. In the
universities, scholasticism, whether in theology or science
or philosophy, was still supreme, and at the Restoration
seemed likely to enjoy a further span of influence. The study
of Descartes had been introduced at Cambridge by John
Smith and encouraged by Henry More, but these men were
brilliant innovators, and the average teacher still subscribed
to the scholastic outlook. Locke found little at Oxford to
suggest that a new era was opening in philosophy. But the
relation between University and Church was so intimate
that the outlook which dominated the one largely controlled
the views which prevailed in the other. The vehemence with
which the Anglican authorities reacted to James II's ill-
considered effort to force his Catholic nominees upon the
colleges shows that contemporaries had no doubt of the
decisive influence of this connexion.

Both in its outlook and its method scholasticism encouraged a reliance on authority. Your presuppositions
usually determined your result, and it was desirable,
especially in debate, to support them with the most formidable names available. Christian origins were eagerly studied
and uncritically used. The Fathers were quoted at tedious
length, and the shapeless conglomeration of extracts which
disfigure the pages of most religious works proves they
were expected to carry weight with the reader. The Bible,
of course, possessed an unapproachable authority, and it
only failed to be decisive because it could be quoted in support
of such diverse propositions. Biblical criticism had not yet
been born; all portions of Scripture were treated alike, and
every passage possessed an authority equal to that of any

other. The search for texts that would be conclusive in debate encouraged a minute familiarity with the Bible. It developed infinite ingenuity in those engrossed in the intricate battles of text and counter-text, but it still remains a marvel that men could know the Bible so well and understand it so little.

The structure of traditional theology was generally accepted, and there was little tendency to question its essential adequacy and truth. The pronouncements of the General Councils and the works of the great theologians supported it; in that authoritarian age such commendation was enough. It is quite true that the interpretation of particular doctrines was heatedly debated; but all parties claimed to be the true expositors of a standard accepted by them all. In recent years the doctrine of the Holy Spirit had been set forth in strange and disconcerting ways, but almost all the sectaries claimed to be Christians in the accepted interpretation of the word. The nature of the Atonement might be a matter of dispute, but the traditional view of the Person of Christ was generally accepted. The doctrine of the Trinity was no doubt a mystery, but few were willing to dissent from it on that account.

The accepted norm of religious thought was not often stated, because it was generally taken for granted. It was always in the background; at the end of our period, as at the beginning, it commanded the adherence of most members of the Church of England. And yet throughout the generation following the Restoration, it was under attack at almost all the points we have mentioned. Its cosmology was confronted with the discoveries of Newton as well as those of Copernicus and, by the opening of the eighteenth century, the new world view was accepted as a matter of course by large numbers of clergy and laity. The new physics found its exponents among scholars like Bentley and essayists like Addison, and educated men, as they surveyed the stars at night, were reassured to know that

> In Reason's ear they all rejoice,
> And utter forth a glorious voice;
> Forever singing as they shine,
> 'The Hand that made us is divine.'

But the theme of this song was really the wonders of the new cosmology.

Meanwhile scholasticism was becoming more and more a synonym for obscurantist ignorance. It had obstructed the progress of science and had distorted the true character of philosophy. Its method was wrong; how then could its results be right? Hand in hand with the challenge to scholasticism went an attack on authority in almost all its forms. But if one court of appeal is discredited, another must be found. Against the dead weight of tradition, whether of the classics or of the Fathers, men set the authority of reason. Different thinkers might use the word in different senses, but all alike appealed to it as the living alternative to a lifeless authority. The Bible alone seemed to hold its unique position. Those who protested against the intricacies of dogma always appealed directly to the sacred text. When Locke wished to prove the essential simplicity of Christianity, he expounded, verse by verse, large portions of the New Testament. This, he manifestly believed, would blast the arguments of his opponents. But there were already premonitions of change. The Bible also was brought, though subtly, to the bar of reason. The principles of literary criticism were emerging, and before long would be demonstrated with consummate brilliance by Bentley in his *Dissertation on Phalaris*. Though the outward protestations of deference were maintained, the Bible was beginning to lose that inward and constraining authority which had made it so great a power throughout the seventeenth century.

Even the traditional system of Christian belief was called in question. Socinianism challenged the orthodox view of the Person of Christ, and the Restoration period was acutely aware that at this point a serious issue had been raised. The Socinian was often refuted, and still more often abused, but he is the most conspicuous example of the questioning spirit as it was applied to theological belief. The Arian was a near relation of the Socinian, and illustrates the trend toward Unitarianism which had already set in. To some people a theological system that abandoned the doctrine of the Trinity appealed as a simpler and more reasonable form of belief, and simplicity and reason were establishing a virtual tyranny over men's minds. Some felt that it would make it easier to reconcile Christianity with the new discoveries of science. In due course Unitarianism virtually swept English Presbyterianism away, and it made deep inroads into the lay theology of the Church of England. It made it necessary, moreover, for the defenders of orthodoxy to restate their own belief, and the seventeenth century ended with the indecisive intricacies of the great Trinitarian controversy.

The history of religious thought from the Restoration to Queen Anne consists largely of successive attempts to modify the accepted standards of Anglican theology. Very little of this assumed the form of direct attacks on the traditional beliefs. Every innovator claimed that he was merely recalling the Church to the simplicities which had been obscured with time. Only at the very end of the century do we begin to suspect, as with certain of the Deists, that they are consciously changing the meaning of terms while retaining the familiar phrases as a screen against attack.

Since all thought was still closely related to religious thought, the account of changes in theology inevitably includes the names of many of the most brilliant and influential figures of the age. But it must be borne in mind that though Locke and Newton focused on themselves the attention of posterity, there remained the great mass of slightly inert and inarticulate belief that still largely corresponded to the ancient ideal. Nor should the contribution of the conservatives be overlooked. An 'anchor out of the stern' may help to forestall disaster, and often those who are slow to change preserve values which neither they nor their more brilliant critics fully comprehend.

The important changes are often impalpable and consequently impossible to describe in detail. The explicit content of belief may change; so may the spirit in which men approach it. The Restoration succeeded an age in which religion had been discussed with an unparalleled intensity, and the new era bore all the marks of a period of reaction. Men were distinctly wary of the enthusiasms which had made the Interregnum so great and yet so difficult a period. There was a deliberate attempt to moderate the intensities of belief. Religious discussion neither rose so high nor sank so low as it had done before. It avoided extravagance because it was unwilling to risk any passionate commitment, but the price it paid was a gradual decline toward mediocrity. Many of the influential figures were second-rate in their ability, and made no striking contribution because they had no original insight. Tillotson's ponderous folios are a cogent demonstration that where there is no vision the people perish. Men went forward into a sober and colourless age. Debate could still be virulent, but the grander notes had disappeared. Earlier in the century the pamphlet warfare had engaged the ablest minds and called forth some of the most notable writings of the period. Few Puritan pamphleteers could rise to the level of Milton's great prose passages, but many of them at least revealed a moral earnestness which commands respect. After 1660 controversy could still be noisy, but much of it was intolerably trivial, and in retrospect appears as sordid and inconsequential as an ale-house brawl. In its more serious writings, the Restoration period possessed both the strength and the weakness of moderation, but as time went on the failings tended to predominate. Even the appeal to reason lost its dignity and degenerated to the level of a pedestrian common sense. The closing years of the seventeenth century produced a theological literature dispassionate in tone and almost wholly lacking in distinction.

This kind of verdict may seem to damn the period with faint praise. But in spite of its shortcomings, the theology of the age has an attraction and an importance entirely its own. It is true that many of the men were commonplace and most of their writings dull; it is equally true, and vastly more important, that they contributed to a change whose far-reaching consequences are not exhausted yet. The early years of the seventeenth century may be inspiring, but they are unquestionably remote. The prevailing outlook is unfamiliar and the spirit of the age is alien to our own. By the beginning of the eighteenth century we are already on the threshold of modern times. We recognize instinctively the importance of the issues raised in the religious discussion of the Restoration era. The place of reason, the character of morality, the limits of authority, the nature of the universe, the reign of law—these are all questions which we still debate. What is more, we discuss them in essentially the same spirit as that which first emerged in the latter part of the seventeenth century. The same canons of directness and simplicity hold good. This does not suggest that thought has not moved rapidly and far since the beginning of the eighteenth century. It merely indicates that Tillotson and Locke and Toland belong to the modern age in a way that Andrewes and Hooker and Laud do not. Eighteenth-century writers can be perverse and unimaginative, and the terms in which they think are often remote, but there is no gulf between their age and ours such as divides the present day from the times of Charles I or Cromwell. The period of transition is the generation which followed the Restoration, and during those years the new lines of thought were marked out. The rôle of reason in religion claimed the attention of the Cambridge Platonists and the Latitudinarians, of John Locke, the Deists, and the representatives of the new science. At a great variety of other points, the theology of the eighteenth century took shape during the closing years of the preceding age. No one arose for many years to challenge the prestige of Locke and Newton. These men moulded the outlook of succeeding generations; with their immense authority they reinforced tendencies already at work, and so created—in theology no less than in philosophy and physics—a new standard to which the ordinary educated man was anxious to conform. For good and ill, the end of the seventeenth century decided the tone and character of religious thought for many years to come.

CHAPTER II

THE ECLIPSE OF CALVINISM

THE second half of the seventeenth century saw many changes in English religious thought, but none more striking than the overthrow of Calvinism. By 1660, Calvinism in England had passed the peak of its power, though at first contemporaries scarcely recognized the fact. Throughout the following generation, the character of the change became increasingly apparent, and after the Revolution all the dominant forces in public life combined to hasten yet further the decline of Calvinism. At the beginning of the century, it had dominated the religious life of England; by the end its power had been completely overthrown. In that process, the Restoration was as decisive as any political fact can be in altering the character of a people's thought. In the seventeenth century, religious developments were so closely related to political affairs that changes in one area inevitably produced important results in the other. The return of Charles II was at once the overthrow of the Puritan party and the defeat of the Puritan theology. The Restoration meant that all the political forces in the nation added their pressure to the various influences which were discrediting Calvinism. To understand the change we must follow its results during the Restoration period, but to grasp its causes we must first glance backward to the beginnings of the struggle against Calvinism. The change is so important and so closely related to national life in the seventeenth century that it is impossible to consider the new day without relating it to the old.

The conflict with the Puritans was not at the outset an

attack on their theology. Those who withstood Cartwright disliked his church polity but not his doctrine. Whitgift was no less a Calvinist than his opponent. The theology of the English Reformation had been strongly influenced by continental Protestantism, and the experiences of the Marian exiles had made them more than ever dependent on the form of doctrine that seemed best able to withstand the attacks of Rome. There was an unquestioned element of strength in Calvinism; it was a fighting creed, and it met the needs of the sixteenth century. The leaders of the Elizabethan Church were Calvinists almost to a man.

The struggle over ritual and church order raised other and more searching questions. Early in the seventeenth century, the champions of Catholic order were beginning to challenge the entire Calvinistic system. As an alternative they advanced Arminianism. In Holland it had established itself in conflict with Calvinism, and in England it provided the theological undergirding for the attack on the order and polity of the Puritans. Its emergence promised to make the breach complete. Under Abbot, the last Calvinist archbishop of Canterbury, the cleavage between the two parties was becoming increasingly clear. In his *Appello Caesarem*, Montague had boldly declared that he was 'no Calvinist, no Lutheran, but a Christian'. He did not always draw the distinction with tact or circumspection, but at least he indicated the grounds on which he ⊢and a growing body of able scholars with him—rejected the doctrines both of Geneva and of Rome. Popular opinion, however, would not admit that the new position was equally opposed to Popery and Calvinism.[1] Antagonism to Arminianism was

[1] Cf. the title of a pamphlet published in London in 1626: *A Dangerous Plot Discovered: by a Discourse wherein is proved that Mr. Richard Montague in his two books...laboureth to bring in the faith of Rome and Arminius under the name and pretence of the doctrine and faith of the Church of England.*

rising on every side.[1] But in Laud the Arminians had a resolute and able, though certainly not a conciliatory, leader. In him their views first found an exponent possessed of far-reaching authority and upheld by the highest power in the realm.

Laud was an Arminian, but he was not primarily a theologian.[2] He was concerned with church order rather than with Christian belief. He wanted to restore what he considered the primitive and rightful order of the Church of England, and he tacitly assumed that the kind of order he wished to see enforced was derived from principles which no true Anglican could oppose. But because Laud's approach was that of the administrator, it did not follow that his opponents would consent to meet him on his chosen ground. Differences in the sphere of order ran back to differences in the realm of belief; raising the level of the chancel meant exalting the position of the priest. Because Laud attacked the ritual practices of the Calvinists, they retorted by attacking his theology.

In the early seventeenth century, a disagreement of this kind quickly spread beyond the bounds of either church order or Christian belief. The Calvinists attacked the powers and prerogatives of the bishops, and this proved to be the prelude to a struggle in a yet wider field. Charles I supported Laud; the king's opponents upheld the Calvinists, and the political significance of the cleavage rapidly became apparent. Arminianism had been caught up in the tide of great

[1] Cf. the letters of Montague to Cosin, *Cosin Correspondence* (Surtees Society), vol. 1, pp. 79–100.

[2] On occasion, however, Laud could speak emphatically enough against the theology of the opposing party. Cf. his summary of the Calvinistic view of predestination in his reply to Lord Saye and Sele: '...which opinion my very soul abominates. For it makes God, the God of all mercy, to be the most fierce and unreasonable tyrant in the world.'

national issues. To the supporters of the king, it seemed increasingly apparent that the Calvinists were rebels. 'Predestination', wrote Dr Samuel Brooke to Laud, 'is the root of Puritanism, and Puritanism the root of all rebellion and disobedient intractableness and all schism and sauciness in the country, nay in the Church itself.' Arminianism, on the other hand, was rapidly becoming a loose term of abuse, and was proving a useful weapon in political warfare. In January 1629, Sir John Eliot clearly showed that the rising party in the House of Commons was committed to the interpretation of Anglican doctrine contained in the Lambeth Articles of 1595. 'We do reject', he added, 'the sense of the Jesuits and Arminians.'[1] Even more emphatic was the resolution passed during the turbulent session of 2 March 1629. 'Whoever shall bring in innovation in religion, or by favour seek to extend or introduce Popery or Arminianism, or other opinions disagreeing from the true and orthodox Church, shall be reputed a capital enemy to this Kingdom and Commonwealth.'[2]

In a struggle of this kind, the doctrine of the losing side was inevitably involved in the overthrow of its political forces. The situation was complex; many clergy who supported Laud's reforms were Calvinistic in their general theological position, but nevertheless it was Arminianism that was branded as the characteristic view of the Royalist party. As a result of the Civil War, it suffered virtually complete eclipse, and Calvinism was everywhere in the ascendant. The Westminster Assembly of Divines symbolized its triumph and furnished it with authoritative statements of its belief. For twenty years the men most

[1] Forster, *Sir John Eliot*, vol. II, p. 210, where the speech is given in full.
[2] *Parliamentary History*, vol. II, p. 491.

prominent in English religious life—the writers most widely read and the preachers most eagerly heard—were Calvinists. John Owen, one of the most influential figures of the period, first attracted public notice by an intransigent exposition of the prevailing views, and in his position and his outlook he was only representative of Stephen Marshall, Thomas Goodwin, Philip Nye and many others.

This does not imply that the Calvinists always agreed among themselves. Within the dominant theological school there were innumerable shades of opinion, and the various sects could fight bitterly enough among themselves, in spite of the Calvinism common to them all. The triumph of their creed was so complete that they could afford the luxury of disagreement. Thus, at the very moment when the citadel of Calvinism seemed to be impregnable, fissures began to disfigure its walls. The unanimity was deceptive because it was superficial.

It is as a 'Puritan dissenter' that a man like John Goodwin demands attention. He may not have been a popular leader, and the extent of his influence is hard to gauge, but the significance of the man is beyond dispute. The whole character of his thought stood out in sharp contrast to that of John Owen, and no man of his period held such enlightened views regarding civil government and religion. It is true that he was the only Puritan theologian of the first rank who repudiated Calvinism, but at least he proves that the prevailing views did not go unchallenged. It may be that Goodwin helps us to understand the secret of the weakness of Calvinism in the critical years before and after the Restoration. Calvinism had been indelibly associated with the Puritan party; it was the religious variant of what in the political sphere was the Commonwealth. The identification of Arminianism with Laud's form of church order and

Charles I's version of absolutism had led to its eclipse; Calvinism suffered from a corresponding identification with political forces, and was similarly involved in their overthrow. But when that day came, the apparent unanimity of Calvinism had been already broken. It was no longer the theology of a unified and disciplined party. In the days of its prosperity its adherents had allowed themselves the luxury of quarrelling about many things. Whereas formerly they had drawn together to oppose Laud, they had now drifted apart because of differences regarding baptism, church order, toleration, and the proper forms of civil government. Some, like John Goodwin, had abandoned the theology they formerly held, and challenged its fundamental presuppositions. When the Calvinists stood in greatest need of unity, they had lost it.

The ascendancy of Calvinism ended as abruptly as did the rule of the saints. The change, of course, declared itself more gradually, because transformations in theology are more difficult to date than events like the return of Charles II to his throne. In retrospect, however, it is clear that the Restoration definitely marked the end of an era in English religious thought. It drove from power the exponents of Calvinism, and by the same token it restored to positions of influence men who on the whole were favourable to Arminianism. In this respect, as in most others, Archbishop Juxon was chiefly important as a symbol; he was best remembered as the friend of Laud and the confidant of Charles I. He was not a great scholar or an influential theologian, but events had made him the most conspicuous survivor of those who had been committed to the principles of the school of Laud.

Though the Calvinist ascendancy was over, the true character of Restoration theology did not immediately appear. The struggle against the Puritans had often left men's loyalties curiously intertwined. The Interregnum had vastly increased the homogeneity of the Royalist party, but even after the Restoration there were still men of considerable importance whose thought reflected a condition common thirty years before. Dr Gunning, who replaced Dr Tuckney as master of St John's College, Cambridge, and who rose to be bishop of Ely, was still, as far as we can judge, a Calvinist. Bishop Morley of Winchester, who in earlier days had coined the well-known epigram about what the Arminians held,[1] remained in all essentials a Calvinist until he died. Nevertheless, a significant change had taken place. These men may have been too old to refashion the framework of their theological system, but their sympathies had completely altered. Though they might still be Calvinists when it came to quoting text-book terms, in outlook they were wholly in agreement with the general aims of the restored Church of England. Their Calvinism was a survival from the past, and bore no real relation to the interests and ideas of the new day. Morley, remarks Burnet, 'was a Calvinist with relation to the Arminian points, and was thought a friend of the Puritans before the wars; but he took care after his promotion to free himself from all suspicions of that kind'.[2] In the disputes with the Nonconformists, these men were not a whit less vehement than their colleagues on the episcopal bench. Baxter's account of the Savoy Conference makes it quite apparent that Morley and Gunning felt no kinship whatever with the Calvinists who had been men of influence during the Interregnum.

---

[1] When asked what the Arminians held, Morley replied that they held all the best bishoprics and deaneries in England.

[2] Burnet, *History of My Own Time* (edited by Osmund Airy), vol. 1, p. 314.

In the early debates, however, the crucial issues concerned church order, and here the differences were so clearly defined that the antagonists were often willing to concede agreement in other areas. Indeed, one of the remarkable features of the controversies of the early Restoration period is the explicit assumption that in doctrine both Puritans and Royalists were at one. Baxter affirmed this on behalf of the Presbyterians, and his claim was not disputed. On occasion, the same plea proved useful to the other side, and as late as 1680 Stillingfleet could reinforce his attack on Nonconformist schism by asserting that in doctrine churchmen and separatists were not divided.[1] When John Owen answered Stillingfleet, he agreed that as regards belief, 'the sober Protestant people of England were of one mind'.[2] But in neither case is the claim convincing. Theological controversy often drives men to use arguments which are effective rather than to search for judgements which are true, and any one who reads the works of Stillingfleet and Owen is more conscious of the difference in tone than of the agreement in principle. When the necessities of debate demanded it, the Restoration Anglicans were quick enough to accuse their opponents of heresy. In his *Friendly Debate*, Simon Patrick boldly identified Calvinism with Antinomianism, and charged all Puritans with both errors.[3] In fact, the day had passed when Conformists and Puritans were agreed on doctrine, and an element of Jesuitry creeps into the claims that there are no essential differences between them. The Anglican writers who are most characteristic of the Restoration Church seize every opportunity to attack predestina-

[1] Edward Stillingfleet, Sermon on *The Mischief of Separation* (1680).
[2] John Owen, *Vindication of the Nonconformists from the Charge of Schism, Works*, vol. XIII, p. 305.
[3] Simon Patrick, *A Friendly Debate* etc., 3rd ed., p. 47 (misnumbered 74); also pp. 12, 145, 153, 238.

tion, yet this question of 'decrees' had become the hall-mark of Calvinism. The Arminians had always challenged absolute and unconditioned predestination on the grounds of its ethical incompleteness; the divine will, they said, is absolutely supreme, but its supremacy is moral. God is as free to forgive as he is to punish. This is only one of the five principal subjects around which the struggle of Arminian and Calvinist raged,[1] but in England none of the others arrested to any comparable degree the attention of the average theological writer. Predestination had caught the popular imagination, and there is no shadow of doubt that those who spoke for the Restoration Church of England opposed it.

On this point, then, they were perfectly conscious of their differences, but it was only gradually that men recognized in what profound and far-reaching ways the Restoration had changed the character of English religious thought. This was due in part to the fact that Arminianism had become primarily a political question, and hence its full theological significance was never recognized as clearly in England as in Holland. Moreover, in the first instance, the reaction had been more against the temper in which Calvinism had been maintained than against the views which it advanced. Popular feeling had been more exasperated by the political and ecclesiastical forms which Calvinism had assumed than against the doctrines it asserted. That was why 'a High Church Calvinist'[2] like Morley could accept the change in government and church order without realizing its full doctrinal significance. But during the reign of Charles I the Calvinists had been quick to see that the two areas could not

[1] The others were the Atonement, Depravity, Conversion, and Final Perseverance.

[2] Dr Hook, quoted in J. Hunt, *Religious Thought in England*, vol. 1, p. 327n.

be divorced, and, though under Charles II neither side was so prompt to admit the fact, its truth became increasingly clear. For one thing, the men who exercised the greatest influence in theology were committed to Arminianism in one form or another, and were emphatic in denouncing Puritan politics, theology and church order. Cosin had fought against the Calvinists in the days before the Civil War, and he still believed that their creed was a menace in all its manifestations.[1] He could be surprisingly generous to individual Puritans, and was anxious to persuade certain of them to conform,[2] but this did not lessen his opposition to their theology. Thorndike was equally hostile to Calvinism, and though Hammond barely survived the Restoration, his influence lived on, and was strongly anti-Puritan in tendency. As bishop of Chester, Brian Walton enjoyed his new dignity only a few months, but he represented the chief opposition to the narrow Scriptural literalism of most of the Puritans, and his more liberal view of the Bible prevailed. Sheldon was perhaps more representative of the Restoration period than any of these men. He was an ecclesiastic, not a theologian, but he attacked every manifestation of Calvinism, whether in Church or State, in doctrine or polity.

The change which was taking place in English thought can best be studied in the works of a single writer. Robert Sanderson was an influential figure both before the Civil War and after the Restoration. The parliamentary authorities ejected him in 1648 from the Regius Professorship of Divinity at Oxford; Charles II elevated him in 1661 to the see of Lincoln.

---

[1] John Cosin, *Correspondence* (Surtees Society), vol. II, pp. xxv–xxvi, 97, 106, 197–205, 238, 254, etc.

[2] Cf. E. Calamy, *The Nonconformist's Memorial* (abridged, corrected, etc., by Samuel Palmer), 2nd ed. (1802), vol. II, p. 178.

Sanderson himself gives us a number of illuminating glimpses into the history of his thought. He began, where many of his contemporaries began, as a Calvinist. As a student he read the *Institutes*, 'for that book', he tells us, 'was commended to me, as it was generally to all young scholars in those times, as the best and perfectest system of divinity, and fittest to be laid as a ground-work in the study of that profession'.[1] As time went on, he modified his judgement of the work, but even in later years he conceded the immense vitality and power of the book. So great was the prestige of the *Institutes* that even the errors of Calvin were vested with authority. Sanderson, however, had also been introduced to Hooker; he read the *Laws of Ecclesiastical Polity* 'to his great profit', and found in it the necessary corrective to the rigours of Calvinism. He was still willing to accept Sublapsarianism on Calvin's authority, but Supralapsarianism he always rejected.[2] This proved an untenable compromise; the pressure of the Quinparticular controversy drove him to abandon Sublapsarianism,[3] and Sanderson was already moving steadily away from the Calvinism of his early years. In the process he modified, even if he never wholly abandoned, his antipathy to Arminianism. When he first printed his sermons, he had, by means of a footnote, accused the Arminians of holding false doctrine; when he reissued the same sermons on the eve of the Restoration, the charge was silently withdrawn.[4]

Sanderson had already moved to an intermediary position which is difficult to define. He clearly saw the weaknesses

[1] Sanderson, letter to Hammond, published in 1660. *Works* (Oxford, 1854), vol. v, p. 297.

[2] Ibid. vol. vi, pp. 352f.

[3] Ibid. vol. vi, p. 315.

[4] Cf. Walton's *Life of Robert Sanderson*, from Sanderson, *Works*, vol. vi, p. 316.

of both parties to the theological debates which raged around him. He admitted more and more frankly 'the harshness of that opinion which Calvin and Beza are said to have held, and many learned men in our Church have followed, concerning the Decrees of Election and Reprobation'.[1] He was not prepared to admit that 'the inconveniences which either do ensure or seem to ensure upon that opinion' can only be avoided by becoming an Arminian.[2] He believed that this kind of logic, with its attempt to enforce an exclusive alternative, was responsible for the divisive spirit so prominent in the Church; the simplicities of either-or were merely destructive of unity.[3] Sanderson could recognize the essential greatness of Luther and Calvin; these men were worthy instruments of God, but they were not the lords of our belief.[4] Nothing could justify the bitterly partisan spirit which the Calvinists displayed whenever they were drawn into controversy. 'Do not they [the Puritans] usually in their sermons fall bitterly upon the Papists and Arminians, but seldom meddle with the Socinians? scarce ever mention the Turks?'[5]

To a candid mind, however, the Arminians were no better. Their system was plausible, and appealed strongly to the unregenerate instincts of the natural man. It had a dangerous 'congruity...in sundry points with the principles of corrupt Nature, and of carnal reason. For it is a wonderful tickling to flesh and blood to have the powers of nature magnified,

[1] Sanderson, *Works*, vol. v, pp. 262–3.

[2] Ibid. vol. v, p. 263.

[3] Ibid. vol. iv, p. 63.

[4] Ibid. vol. iii, p. 289: 'And is it not also blameworthy in us, and a fruit of the same carnality, if any of us should affect to be accounted rigid Lutherans or perfect Calvinists. Worthy instruments they were ...of God's glory, but yet...men.'

[5] Ibid. vol. ii, p. xxv.

and to hear itself flattered as if she carried the greatest stroke in the work of salvation, especially when these soothings are conveyed under the pretence of vindicating the dispensations of God's providence from the imputation of injustice'.[1] Even more disconcerting to him was 'the manifold cunning of the Arminians to advance their party'.[2] With discernment yet with great cogency he exposed the practices to which controversy drove them. He noted with dismay the threat of schism which lurked in Arminian methods. Since Montague had raised the issue, there were many circumstances which had fostered the growth of Arminianism, but none of a kind to compensate for the dangers it raised.

Both sides alike, however, were at fault in confusing the issue by resorting to indiscriminate abuse. How could clear thinking survive when beclouded with recrimination? With the Puritans, it was a favourite device to dispose of an opponent's arguments by blackening him with the name of Arminian. The other party was just as bad. Sanderson gives examples of people who were accused of Puritanism even when the questions under debate gave no excuse for raising the cry of Calvinism. To show the absurdity of this proceeding, he appeals, significantly enough, to Hooker. Those who agree with Hooker in matters of doctrine are classed as Puritans, but what would Hooker think of so glaring an anomaly?[3]

While thus drawn between contending parties, Sanderson gradually evolved an intermediate and thoroughly characteristic position. By 1660 its essential outlines were clearly visible, and it found expression in all Sanderson's works

[1] Ibid. vol. v, p. 262.
[2] Ibid. vol. v, pp. 263–4.
[3] Ibid. vol. v, p. 265.

published after that date.[1] Moreover, it became representative of a non-controversial type of Anglicanism which was widely held after the Restoration. It is neither Calvinist nor Arminian, and it contributed to the creation of a point of view which stemmed directly from neither the one nor the other. Its essential characteristic was a humility willing both to change its views and to acknowledge that it had done so. 'And let me here tell the reader also', remarks Izaak Walton, 'that if the rest of mankind would, as Dr Sanderson, not conceal their alteration of judgement, but confess it to the honour of God and themselves, our nation would become freer from pertinacious disputes, and fuller of recantations.'[2] It is the part, moreover, both of humility and of wisdom to recognize the proper limits of debate. The bounds within which it can profitably be conducted are strictly fixed; once they have been passed, prudent men will desist from arguing. There is a note of wondering sorrow in the exclamation of Sanderson which Dr Pierce has quoted—'And yet to see the restless curiosity of men!'[3] As Hammond remarked in the last letter he wrote to Sanderson, 'God can reconcile his own contradictions', and Sanderson would have agreed with the general advice that all men should 'study mortification, and be wise to sobriety'.[4] All the weary wrangling of recent times was due, said Sanderson, to the refusal to accept the proper limits of discussion. When men are not content that mysteries should remain so, the world is 'filled with endless disputes, and

[1] Though most of Sanderson's later works appeared in the years directly after the Restoration, some were not published till as late as 1678.

[2] I. Walton, *Life of Robert Sanderson*, from Sanderson, *Works*, vol. VI, p. 317.

[3] Sanderson, *Works*, vol. VI, p. 353.

[4] Ibid. vol. VI, p. 317.

inextricable difficulties. And all the heat on both sides in the Arminian controversies, which hath begotten such intricate and perplexed difficulties, as neither side can clearly acquit itself from the inconveniences wherewith it is charged by the adverse party, had its rise from the curiosity of men, who, not content to believe those clear truths which are consented to on either side...must needs be searching into the manner, how the Grace of God and man's will do co-operate, and how far forth, and in what order'.[1]

With the diffidence that sees and accepts the limits of argument went a greater sensitiveness to the temper proper to theological debate. The arrogance of some contro-versialists, said Sanderson, led straight to their undoing. In their self-assurance they ventured to bring any mystery 'within the comprehension of reason', and found themselves 'enwrapped unawares in perplexed and inextricable diffi-culties'. In attempting to extricate themselves they had rashly pressed forward instead of drawing back, and found themselves 'driven to devise and maintain strange opinions, of very perilous and noisome consequence, which hath been the original of most heresies and schisms in the Church'.[2]

It is consequently prudent as well as necessary to recognize and allow for legitimate differences. Experience had shown Sanderson that they would be neither few nor unimportant. Lutherans and Calvinists disagreed, and even within the Roman Church there were varying schools of thought. Each of these, again, was subdivided, sometimes on issues of great consequence—'predestination and reprobation, the power of man's free will, the necessity, efficacy and extent of free grace, & etc.' Yet having honestly faced this wide

[1] Ibid. vol. VI, p. 388 (letter to Thomas Barlow, at Queen's Coll., Oxon., 17 September 1657).
[2] Ibid. vol. V, p. 256 (*Pax Ecclesiae*, 1678).

divergence of opinion, Sanderson was satisfied 'that there may yet be preserved in the Church the unity both of faith and charity'.[1]

A confidence of this kind is only saved from self-delusion if it observes certain necessary conditions. The first requirement is that men should rest content with definitions which might fall short of logical completeness. When terms are too strictly defined or pressed too remorselessly to their conclusion, the inevitable result is division. Men can only agree to differ so long as a certain liberty of individual interpretation is allowed, and this becomes impossible unless latitude is permitted. Consequently, it is the part of wisdom and of charity to insist only on the simplest and most comprehensive standards of belief. The kind of controversy which had destroyed the unity of English religious life was not necessary. There was no need to demand a uniform interpretation of debated articles. Both Calvinists and Arminians could follow their own consciences, and the kind of issue on which they had disagreed need not divide the Church. It was right, Sanderson thought, to insist on the Articles and the Book of Common Prayer; beyond that it was expedient to allow liberty.

The position which Sanderson reached and which he commended to others admittedly lacks clear and explicit definition. It solves many of the debated issues by evading them, and asks for charity instead of giving reasons. After the fierceness of religious argument, a characteristically Anglican position was emerging. It may appear more a plea for comprehension than a contribution to current discussions, but it goes back to characteristically English sources of authority, and substitutes Hooker for Calvin or Arminius. It is willing to allow a certain flexibility and a measure of

[1] Sanderson, *Works*, vol. v, p. 257.

indeterminateness in definition. It deprecates the intolerance of debate, and in sober accents pleads for a reasonable attitude to religious questions.

It is hard to estimate the contemporary influence of a man like Sanderson; he may have helped to mould the thought of the new day, or he may simply have reflected its character. At all events he is a figure of unusual interest. He had been a Calvinist but had rejected the rigidities which marked Calvinism in the days of its full-blown development. The position he ultimately reached is scarcely defined in theological terms at all. He had less confidence in reason than the typical Restoration writers; otherwise they could often have used both his arguments and his phrases to serve their purposes.

In an important respect Sanderson was representative of the new day. The debates which had developed such fierce loyalties were over, but men were not immediately concerned to define a precise alternative position. In a sense the fight between the Calvinists and the Arminians was a dead issue. Here Sanderson helps us to recognize the true character of the new day. He had reached an intermediary position which was neither Calvinist nor Arminian. But the very fact that it was a mediating position brought it in effect into line with Arminianism. The characteristic feature of Arminianism is its conditionalism, and 'moderation is the mark of its method'.[1] It is in this sense that the theology of the Restoration can be described as Arminian. The way in which Arminianism had become a political issue had tended to dilute its theological distinctiveness, and as the Restoration period progressed the results were increasingly apparent. There was no longer any deep concern with the doctrine of grace; men

[1] F. Platt, article on 'Arminianism', in *Encyclopaedia of Religion and Ethics*.

emphasized the beneficial example which Christ had left us, not the atoning work he had wrought on our behalf. Arminianism survived chiefly as a negation of what Calvinism had stood for, but, since their opponents were now so weak and scattered, there was less need for the Arminians to develop their own characteristic insights. Even their relations with Arminians abroad did nothing to bring them back to the distinctive affirmations with which Arminianism began. Burnet and Tillotson corresponded with Limborsch, and Locke and Newton with LeClerc, but Dutch Arminianism was subsiding into Socinianism even while English Arminianism was drifting toward Deism. It was consequently a shrunken and attenuated form of Arminianism that persisted throughout the Restoration period. The delicate equilibrium between Calvinism and Pelagianism was sacrificed, and English Arminianism lost its distinctive note as it merged imperceptibly with Latitudinarianism and Rationalism.

Steadily the decline of Calvinism continued. When, early in the eighteenth century, an enthusiast [1] attempted a revival, it had, as an effective force in English life, virtually disappeared. Seldom has a reversal of fortune been so complete. Within fifty years Calvinism in England fell from a position of immense authority to obscurity and insignificance. The causes of so striking a collapse are closely related to the development of English life and thought in the last half of the seventeenth century, and they require brief consideration before this chapter ends.

Calvinism had a magnificent opportunity, and for a brief period wielded wider powers than its popular support would probably have warranted. It prepared its own undoing; it failed to use its great advantages to win the sympathies of

[1] Dr John Edwards. Cf. his *Preacher* (1st vol. 1705; 2nd vol. 1706; 3rd vol. 1709).

ordinary Englishmen. With a reckless lack of moderation, the extremer sects multiplied extravagances until reasonable men were utterly antagonized. The undisciplined exuberance of certain Calvinists discredited the whole system of thought, and brought about its undoing. Writ large upon the Restoration period is the record of the dread and horror of 'enthusiasm'. Joseph Glanvill tells us that his first work was an attack upon fanaticism (a 'Corrective of Enthusiasm' he calls it), but adds that 'his Majesty's much-desired and seasonable arrival' made it less necessary than it had been when he wrote it.[1] It was a general assumption that any man of open mind would see the errors of Calvinism and forsake them. Tillotson was brought up a Puritan, 'yet even before his mind was opened to clearer thought, he felt somewhat within him that disposed him to larger notions and a better temper'.[2] In other words, the excesses of Calvinism had made it synonymous with obscurantism. This was true in many areas; the political programme of the wilder sects awakened fear, and even the current religious vocabulary aroused contempt. Robert South, who never missed a chance of ridiculing his opponents, described the Puritan preachers as charging 'all their crude incoherences, saucy familiarities with God, and nauseous tautologies, upon the Spirit prompting such things to them, and that as the most elevated and seraphic heights of religion'.[3]

Even moderate Calvinism was swept away in the reaction against everything that the Interregnum stood for. It had been, after all, the official theology of the Commonwealth. It might not have been responsible for the excesses of

[1] J. Glanvill, *The Vanity of Dogmatizing* (1660). Epistle Dedicatory.
[2] [Burnet], *A Sermon Preached at the Funeral of...John...Lord Archbishop of Canterbury*...by Gilbert, Lord Bishop of Sarum (1695), p. 10.
[3] Robert South, *Sermons*, 3rd ed. (1704), vol. IV, p. 48.

Ranters and Fifth Monarchy men, but its adherents had supported the execution of Charles I, and the Royalists found it impossible to conceive a more abominable atrocity than that.[1] It had framed the documents that had been used as tests, and had been the substance of what the great Puritans had been concerned to say. Calvinism had blessed and sanctioned the whole cause which the Restoration had irrevocably overthrown. The reaction which set in swept away the personalities and parties of the Interregnum, and with them vanished the prestige of their chosen theology. Over against this is the fact which we have already noted, that the opponents of Calvinism came back with the halo of recent martyrdom and the authority of present success.

Even the king threw his weight against the Calvinists. He did not perhaps deliberately oppose their theology, and he showed himself genuinely concerned—whatever may have been his motives—to secure them some measure of toleration. His whole outlook, of course, was far removed from theirs, and his past experience of Presbyterians had not been happy. But it was for other reasons that his influence tended to undermine the prestige of Calvinism. He was strenuously opposed to religious debate. Theological controversy would sow the seeds of restiveness and insubordination in the nation's life.[2] Struggles among theologians would end as fights between factions, and Charles II did not intend to see the peace disturbed. But a moratorium on theological debate was not favourable to Calvinism, which flourished best in the bracing atmosphere of eager discussion. Moreover, the official regulations of the Restora-

---

[1] For the strength of the cult of Charles, King and Martyr, even at the beginning of the eighteenth century, see Lecky, *England in the Eighteenth Century*, vol. 1, pp. 70–3.

[2] Burnet, *History of My Own Time*, vol. 1, p. 329.

tion ruled that many of the subjects dearest to the Calvinist could no longer be discussed in public. The Act of Uniformity was reinforced by the king's letters to the archbishops, containing directions concerning preachers. 'None are in their sermons to bound the authority of sovereigns, or determine the differences between them and the people; nor to argue the deep points of election, reprobation, free will, etc.'[1] The injunctions may have been designed to promote peace by curbing debate, but they did so by condemning the one side to silence on precisely the points it was most anxious to expound. The first clauses forbade the Puritans to justify their political creed; the last prohibited them from preaching on the subjects most characteristic of the Calvinists' theology.

Neither political failure nor official discouragement could have seriously weakened Calvinism if other forces had not been working to discredit it in subtler and more insidious ways. The character of national thought was changing in ways that made the stern affirmations of Calvinism unpalatable. The old antithesis of Calvinist and Arminian was too simple to describe the situation which had arisen. New movements of thought were profoundly influencing theology. There was a new trust in reason and a new willingness to follow its lead. When John Hales, having seen the triumph of Calvinism at Dort, returned disillusioned and 'bade goodnight to Calvin', he did so in the interests of a reason free to seek the truth. Relatively few of his contemporaries were ready to agree with him, but after 1660 he would have found a much larger following than he did before 1642. A new spirit was at work, and showed itself in many ways. That little band of brilliant teachers, the Cambridge Platonists,

[1] 14 October 1662. Calendar of State Papers, Domestic, Charles II, 1661–2, p. 517.

were ceaselessly affirming the dignity of reason, and all the weight of their influence was used to discredit dogmatism. Both explicitly and by implication they attacked everything that Calvinism represented. Closely associated with the new Platonism but developing along different lines was Latitudinarianism. This became unquestionably the dominant theological school of the new era. Among its members it numbered the most famous divines of the age, and more than any other it prepared the way for the characteristic outlooks and attitudes of the eighteenth century. At almost every point its assumptions stood in sharp contrast to those of Calvinism. Tillotson, who became almost a symbol of the later Restoration period, was emphatic in repudiating all the most characteristic dogmas of Calvinism. 'I am as certain', he wrote, 'that this doctrine [eternal decrees] cannot be of God as I am that God is good and just, because this grates upon the notion that mankind have of goodness and justice. This is that which no good man would do, and therefore it cannot be believed of infinite goodness. If an Apostle, or an angel from heaven teach any doctrine which plainly overthrows the goodness and justice of God, let him be accursed. For every man hath greater assurance that God is good and just than he can have of any subtle speculations about predestination and the decrees of God.' The cool sanity of Tillotson and the pedestrian common sense of his sermons were fatal to many of the high-flown enthusiasms of the early seventeenth century. To none of them were they so damaging as to Calvinism.

The whole temper of the times was hostile to the old forms of dogmatic certainty. People were tired of extremes of every kind. They had grown weary of the fierce intolerance with which their fathers had fought about many things. In philosophy the spirit of the time found peculiarly exact expression in the writings of John Locke. His work was at once an epitome of the latter part of the seventeenth century, and a forecast of the character of the eighteenth. Locke himself had grown up in a Calvinistic atmosphere, but 'early in life he conceived theology in a latitudinarian sense, and later on, under the influence of the Arminians and the Socinians, he developed those ideas in his own peculiar, very able and original way, which was, however, entirely non-Calvinistic'.[1] His conception of freedom of thought embraced 'freedom for philosophy and theological interests and security for freedom of thought outside the churches'.[2] Though Locke's authority in the future was to prove to be virtually unparalleled, many of his contemporaries—some of them men of great eminence in their own fields—exerted an influence even more definitely hostile to the attitudes and assumptions of Calvinism.

Indeed, the whole tone of intellectual life in England was changing. Interest in religion was steadily declining. The repeated complaints about atheism and the concern about indifference to religion are the recognition among churchmen that the nation's thought was in danger of losing all effective contact with religion. In sermons and treatises the note of anxiety grows steadily clearer;[3] even in the midst of the pamphlet controversy, antagonists could pause for a moment in their internecine warfare to notice the growing power of an adversary common to them both. In the new day even the adherents of Calvinism found their confidence

[1] E. Troeltsch, *The Social Teaching of the Christian Churches*, vol. II, p. 637.
[2] Ibid.
[3] Cf. Glanvill, *Seasonable Reflections and Discourses, in order to the Conviction and Cure of the Scoffing and Infidelity of a Degenerate Age* (1676), passim. There are many examples of the same note in preachers as different as Tillotson and South.

shaken.[1] In its pristine strength, Calvinism would have been a force to reckon with, but it had wasted its resources in futile controversies, and men now dismissed it as a crabbed affirmation of such sterile mysteries as predestination. It had become an abstract Scriptural dogmatism. In its statements 'the negative polemical side of almost every truth is set forth in clearer and sharper definition than its positive substance. Dogmas are rigorously carried out to their consequences; and the intellect and conscience alike are assailed by the coercive authority with which these consequences in their most theoretical relations are expressed and enforced.'[2] From such a system reaction was inevitable; at the end of the seventeenth century the reaction was bound to be decisive. Even in its former strongholds, the grim and militant faith from Geneva steadily lost its hold.

[1] *Memorials of the Life of Ambrose Barnes*, pp. 85–7.
[2] J. Tulloch, *Rational Theology and Christian Philosophy in England in the Seventeenth Century*, vol. 1, p. 66.

CHAPTER III

THE CAMBRIDGE PLATONISTS

UNTIL the later years of the seventeenth century, the intensity of party feeling encouraged neither impartiality of mind nor detachment of spirit. One of the problems of the age was to find a method of affirming the truth as each man saw it which would not disrupt both individual serenity and public peace. The eighteenth century met the difficulty by repudiating enthusiasm, but this evaded the problem, it did not solve it. There was, however, a genuine alternative to factious wrangling and a studied moderation. A brilliant group of thinkers, known collectively as the Cambridge Platonists, proved that zeal and charity could dwell together; they showed that religious conviction was not the necessary counterpart of a closed mind. They offered a solution which at that time not many were ready to apply. It may be that it presupposed a strain of genius which few religious thinkers possess, and which the succeeding generation conspicuously lacked. But if the Cambridge Platonists had found a larger following, the theological developments of the next century might have been less sterile than they were.

This does not imply that the Cambridge Platonists failed to influence subsequent religious thought. They profoundly affected men eminent as theologians and ecclesiastics, but it was not their distinctive quality which they transmitted to others. They conceived of reason as a divine light and of morality as the fruit of a divine life; by the beginning of the eighteenth century the one had become another name for common sense, and the other had been equated with utility.[1]

[1] Cf. F. J. Powicke, *The Cambridge Platonists*, p. 213.

The subsequent history of English thought merely emphasizes the distinctive but slightly isolated position of the
Cambridge Platonists.

Even in their own day they defied classification by most
of the accepted standards. They lived a cloistered life in the
midst of a turbulent age, but they thought in terms of its
problems and were not divorced from the main stream of its
life.[1] They belonged neither to the world of the Commonwealth nor to the new society which replaced it. They grew
up in the home of English Calvinism; they became its most
discerning critics, and yet they carried into the Restoration
period something of the best of the tradition in which they
had originally been trained.

For our purposes, however, they belong to the Restoration era. Most of them were at the height of their powers
when Charles II came to the throne. Though Whichcote lost
the provostship of King's, he was an influential London
minister for over twenty years. Cudworth remained undisturbed in the mastership of Christ's, and More continued
uninterrupted his placid ways. Their teaching was bearing
fruit in the university,[2] and the men on whom they had set
their mark were rising to positions of importance both in
Cambridge and beyond it. During the new period their
ideas attained their widest currency. Whichcote's sermons
at St Lawrence Jewry attracted discerning and influential
congregations, and many of the most important works of
the Cambridge Platonists were published after 1660.

Moreover, the Cambridge Platonists, by contributing to

---

[1] Cudworth preached his most notable sermon before the Long
Parliament, and Cromwell looked to him for advice. Whichcote, also,
was a man whose judgement the leaders of the Commonwealth sought
and valued.

[2] John Tillotson, *Sermon Preached at the Funeral of Dr Benjamin
Whichcote*, p. 7.

the decline of Calvinism, helped to give the Restoration era
one of its most characteristic qualities. The whole trend of
their teaching was directed in subtle ways against the foundations of the prevailing theology. It was an attack on Calvinism from within; it was all the more significant because
made in Cambridge and by men for the most part educated
at Emmanuel. Though it was far removed both in tone and
character from the usual forms of theological debate, the
Calvinists were quick to grasp its implications. The illuminating series of letters which Dr Tuckney of St John's wrote
to Whichcote is chiefly important as reflecting the uneasiness
of earnest Puritans. This was a new form of criticism—
criticism which ignored the polity of Calvinism, but shook
the whole system by questioning its basic conceptions. In
effect the Cambridge Platonists turned from the familiar
theological picture altogether. The old and oft-repeated
version of the sacrifice for sin had no place in their teaching,
and they conceived of salvation in a form and spirit entirely
different from the vivid pictorial imagery of the Calvinists.[1]
Bunyan was perfectly right in objecting that Edward
Fowler's 'Design of Christianity' had completely altered the
familiar conception of justification by faith,[2] but it did not
necessarily follow (as he thought it did) that the foundations
of Christianity were thereby removed. The prevailing
theology had become dogmatic and theoretical to an intolerable degree, and the Cambridge Platonists attacked it
chiefly by indicating that a broader and simpler system was
necessary. Whichcote declared that one verse in the Bible[3]
was a summary of all necessary divinity, and he added that

[1] B. Willey, *The Seventeenth Century Background*, pp. 136–7.
[2] John Bunyan, *Defence of the Doctrine of Justification* (1672).
[3] 'The grace of God that bringeth salvation hath appeared to all men,
teaching us that, denying ungodliness and worldly lusts, we should live
soberly, righteously, and godly, in this present world.' Titus ii. 11–12.

a saved state was a morally sound state. The Puritans had not only emphasized the importance of doctrine, but had dwelt with particular fondness on the mysteries of belief. The Cambridge Platonists never fell into the facile rationalism which repudiates mysteries simply because they are mysteries, but they deprecated too great a preoccupation with obscure and unintelligible doctrines.[1] But there was one of the dogmas of Calvinism which they directly and unequivocally attacked. Predestination, they claimed, was neither intellectually nor morally defensible. More bluntly called it 'the black doctrine of absolute reprobation', and Whichcote declared that 'it is not worth the name of religion to charge our consciences with that, which we have not reconciled to the reason and judgment of our minds, to the frame and temper of our souls'.[2] It is not surprising that a rigid Calvinist like Thomas Goodwin regarded the Cambridge Platonists with horror.[3]

At certain points the Puritans might be clearly wrong, but it was the spirit of their theology rather than its content that the Cambridge Platonists chiefly attacked. A narrow, abstract and dogmatic approach to religion seemed certain to pervert its character and lead ultimately to its downfall. The weakness of current theology was clearly demonstrated by the kind of discussion it inspired. The fierce faction fights which disfigured the life of contemporary English Christianity not only condemned the spirit which prompted them, but threatened the survival of all the values which they

[1] 'We cannot put a greater abuse upon God than to say he is obscure.' Whichcote, *Aphorisms*, 37.

[2] Whichcote, *Aphorisms*, 315; note also Smith's emphatic protest in *The Nature of Legal and Evangelical Righteousness* (in *Select Discourses*, pp. 299 ff.). Cf. Patrick's tribute to Smith, *Autobiography*, p. 18.

[3] *Extracts from the Papers of Thomas Woodcock* (Camden Miscellany, vol. XI), p. 66.

ostensibly defended. Something was manifestly and seriously at fault. 'The more false any one is in his religion, the more fierce and furious in maintaining it; the more mistaken, the more imposing.'[1] In this atmosphere of ignoble wrangling true religion could not survive; the life of the spirit was perishing 'in the spent air of polemic.'[2] It was necessary to find some conciliatory statement of the true principles of Christian theology. In no other way could the desolating and interminable disputes of that period be checked.

The Calvinists had been the chief offenders, but their greater guilt was partly due to their greater opportunity. The spirit of both Puritans and Laudians had been bitter and combative, and the Cambridge Platonists tried to find a middle course between the two.[3] Against the party committed to the ideals of Laud, they held that conduct and morality are more important than church polity; against the Puritans who were dominated by the rigidity of Calvinist theology, they urged that reason must not be fettered; against both they maintained that the legitimate seat of authority in religion is the individual conscience, governed by reason and illuminated by a revelation which could not be inconsistent with reason itself.[4] They hoped to reconcile all save the utterly intransigent by means of a twofold approach to religion. On the one hand they emphasized the importance of the moral element in Christianity, on the other

[1] Whichcote, *Aphorisms*, 499.

[2] Willey, op. cit. p. 133. Cf. Whichcote: 'There is nothing more unnatural to religion than contentions about it.' *Aphorisms*, 756.

[3] Cf. 'S.P.' (presumably Simon Patrick) on the 'virtuous mediocrity' of the Church of England ideal upheld by the Cambridge Platonists. He contrasts it with 'the meretricious gaudiness of the Church of Rome and the squalid sluttery of fanatic conventicles'. *A Brief Account*, etc., p. 11.

[4] Campagnac, *The Cambridge Platonists*, p. xiii.

they explored 'in a way not hitherto attempted the foundations of religious belief'.[1] They summoned the divided
parties of their day to unite on the common ground of the
great essentials of religion. On minor points, the con-
testants could agree to differ, with the assurance that 'the
maintenance of truth is rather God's charge, and the
continuance of charity ours'.[2] The essentials of belief are
contained in the Scriptures, and are so clearly set forth that
any one using his reason can scarcely miss them.

The appeal to reason is the most conspicuous characteristic
of the Cambridge school. In the exercise of reason they saw
the distinctive quality of man;[3] in its repudiation they
recognized the mark of all rebellion against God. 'To go
against reason is to go against God; it is the selfsame thing,
to do that which the reason of the case doth require and that
which God Himself doth appoint; reason is the divine
governor of man's life; it is the very voice of God.'[4] Even
the structure of the universe compels us to pay attention to
what reason says. In the external framework of the created
world God has planted an order and method—the 'Reason
in things'—which the 'deiform seed' within us can appre-
hend. 'The judgment of right is the reason of our minds
perceiving the Reason of things.'[5]

A term so constantly invoked needs to be carefully defined.
Reason had a twofold meaning for the Cambridge Platonists.
On the one hand it meant the discipline of thinking exactly

[1] W. R. Inge, *The Platonic Tradition in English Religious Thought*, p. 43.
[2] Whichcote, *Letters to Tuckney*, p. 118.
[3] Cf. Whichcote: 'There is nothing proper and peculiar to man, but
the use of Reason, and exercise of virtue.' *Aphorisms*, 71.
[4] Ibid. 76. Cf. also More's description of reason as the sacerdotal
breastplate. To take away reason is 'to rob Christianity of that special
prerogative which it has above all other religions in the world, namely
that it dares to appeal unto reason.'
[5] Whichcote, *Aphorisms*, 33.

and philosophically about the things which were Real. On the other hand it involved the unification of the whole personality in the pursuit of truth. Each of these requires separate consideration.

From the first emphasis it followed that the Cambridge Platonists were committed to an examination of the structure of belief different from anything which had recently prevailed. Religion and philosophy, so far from being divorced, were brought into the closest and most intimate relation. This was their alternative to the prevailing Protestant scholasticism, and it ran counter to the one conclusion on which the leading representatives of English thought were then agreed. 'Bacon and Hobbes, Puritans and Prelatists'[1] united in treating philosophy and religion as wholly different in kind. But the Cambridge Platonists insisted that it was precisely this separation which was vitiating the theology of the day. A new approach was necessary, and additional material needed to be used. So they turned naturally even to the pagan philosophers for light on the essential problems of the Christian faith. Because religion is reasonable, the 'best thoughts of the best men of all ages and faiths' cannot help but illuminate it. The cumbersome mass of classical learning which burdens the pages of Cudworth and More is not a result of the affectations of the academic mind; it represents an honest attempt to make available the evidence of Greek and Roman philosophy. The contemporary need, as Cudworth saw, was 'a philosophy of religion confirmed and established by philosophical reasons in an age so philosophical'.[2]

It likewise followed from their definition that the Cambridge Platonists exalted a reason which wholly transcended

---

[1] B. F. Westcott, *Religious Thought in the West*, p. 367.
[2] Cudworth, *True Intellectual System of the Universe*, Preface.

the usual limits of rationalism. It is true that they claimed for religion the entire intellectual life,[1] but their appeal was to 'the inner experience of the whole man acting in harmony, not to mere logic chopping which may leave conduct and even conviction unaffected'.[2] Reason can only be given this expansive character because of the distinctive relationship in which man stands to God. The inner light which shines in the heart of man is sent of God, but it is actually the same as reason purified and disciplined.[3] The real presence of God in the soul can sublimate reason into what More calls a 'divine sagacity'.[4]

.In the writings of the Cambridge Platonists there emerges clearly a problem which concerned all progressive thinkers of the Restoration era. If reason is given its proper place, will it not conflict with faith? What happens when there is an apparent discrepancy? But, said the Cambridge Platonists, no conflict can arise, except through ignorance or misunderstanding; religion is committed to the honouring of reason, and reason enlightens the material of faith. There is a self-illuminating power in divine truth which satisfies the human mind. 'Do I dishonour my faith', asks Whichcote, 'or do any wrong to it to tell the world that my reason and understanding are satisfied? I have no reason against it; yea, the highest and purest reason is for it.'[5] With a single voice the Cambridge Platonists declare the unity of faith and reason. Not so much as a hint escapes John Smith that the place of reason in religion should be circumscribed. Faith anticipates and completes the findings of reason, and philosophy

---

[1] Inge, *Christian Mysticism*, p. 287.

[2] Inge, *The Platonic Tradition in English Religious Thought*, p. 52.

[3] Cf. John Smith, *True Way or Method of Attaining to Divine Knowledge* (Campagnac's edition of *The Cambridge Platonists*), pp. 92–3.

[4] H. More, *Philosophical Writings*, Preface General.

[5] Whichcote, *Letters to Tuckney*, p. 48.

is the handmaid of religion.[1] It is reason, said Cudworth, that confirms the assurance of faith.[2]

If reason plays so large a part in religion, is there any place for revelation? It is at least quite clear that there can be no revelation which contradicts the evidence of our minds. A good man, remarked More, cannot believe that anything which conflicts with 'natural truth' can have its origin in God.[3] But there is still need of revelation. Reason in man is 'a light flowing from the fountain and father of lights', but since man's fall, 'the inward virtue and vigour of reason is much abated', and as a supplement to 'the truth of natural inscription God hath provided the truth of divine revelation'.[4] Truth, though of one nature, may be offered to man in various forms, but it is always reason that apprehends it. The truths of morality, of physical science, of natural religion, or of the will of God as disclosed in Scripture—all are ultimately grasped by reason. There is no conflict between faith and reason or between revealed and natural truth. 'Our reason is not confounded by our religion, but awakened, excited, employed, directed, and improved.'[5]

The significance of this constant emphasis on reason becomes apparent as soon as we remember the course of subsequent religious discussion. Earlier in the seventeenth century, the prevailing tendency had been to depreciate reason and to minimize its rôle in religion. There had been protests—from Hales and Chillingworth, for example—but in no sense did they represent the general attitude of their time. During the middle years of the century, the whole weight of Calvinism had been thrown against any exaltation

[1] J. Smith, *Select Discourses*, p. 442.
[2] Cudworth, *True Intellectual System of the Universe*, vol. II, pp. 517 f.
[3] H. More, *True Grounds of the Certainty of Faith*.
[4] J. Smith, *Select Discourses*, p. 61.
[5] Whichcote, *Select Sermons* (ed. 1698), p. 298.

of what seemed a part of man's corrupt and unregenerate nature. But in the closing period of the century, the place of reason was so magnified that it became customary in religious discussion to concede its unquestioned authority. Protestant theology in England was steadily returning to an emphasis on reason which had been inherent in its original position, but which had become obscured with time. In this development the Cambridge Platonists played a notable part. Ultimately the progress of 'enlightenment' saw reason conceived in narrow, unimaginative terms, which were far removed from the position of the Cambridge men, but it is impossible to understand the emergence of eighteenth-century theology if we ignore the development which runs from the early pioneers of a liberal theology through the Cambridge Platonists, the Latitudinarians and the Deists.

For other reasons also the preoccupation of the Cambridge Platonists with reason is important. They asserted its significance because they believed it kept religion abreast of current intellectual developments and prevented it from subsiding into superstition.[1] They regarded it as equally necessary in checking the contemporary trend toward atheism.[2] Reason made it possible to hope that the bitterness of controversy could be resolved into the mutual self-respect of intelligent men.[3] Because of reason, they said, we can hope that men will grasp the resplendent truths of God;[4] above all, it is our assurance that we can achieve a moral and spiritual independence. We can see for ourselves what is

---

[1] Cf. S.P.: 'Nor will it be possible otherwise to free religion from scorn and contempt, if her priests be not as well skilled in nature as the people, and her champions furnished with as good artillery as her enemies.' *A Brief Account...*, p. 12.

[2] More developed this subject at length in his *Antidote to Atheism*.

[3] Whichcote, *Aphorisms*, 58.   [4] Ibid. 28.

good, and we can appropriate it as good because our own insight has recognized its essential worth.[1] In an authoritarian age this was the charter of the liberty of the Christian man. The period which ensued saw the question of authority raised repeatedly; it never saw it answered with such luminous discernment or with such reasonable hopes that, after the tyrannies of spiritual compulsion, men would find a freedom which was above licence because it was never beyond reason.

'In the use of Reason and the exercise of virtue we enjoy God',[2] and these two activities, so closely associated in Whichcote's words, together represent the most characteristic affirmations of the Cambridge Platonists. Their opponents, who resented the 'crying up of reason', also reproached them with advocating 'a kind of moral theology'. What was intended as a censure would have been accepted as the highest form of praise. They constantly revert to the good life and to the factors in experience which weaken or confirm it. The detailed exposition of their ethical theory is no part of our present task,[3] but it is necessary to note why their emphasis was important in seventeenth-century thought. To begin with, it is essential to notice that the intimate relation with religion, so characteristic of the treatment of reason, is just as pronounced in the case of morality. The Cambridge Platonists wrote much of the good and the beautiful, but these led, not to abstract virtues, but to the Christian graces. Morality, indeed, was seen as the manifestation of the present energy of the spirit of God.[4] Equally significant was their treatment of moral ideas.

---

[1] Ibid. 40.   [2] Ibid. 121.

[3] This has been done in painstaking detail in de Pauley, *The Candle of the Lord*.

[4] Cf. Raven, *John Ray, Naturalist*, p. 37.

Descartes had suggested that true and false, right and wrong, depended for their validity upon the will of God. They were so because He had decreed it thus. The Cambridge Platonists vehemently objected. Right and wrong belonged to the eternal nature of things; they were part of the law of the ideal world.[1] The distinction between them was essential, not arbitrary, and even the will of God could never change it. These eternal and immutable ideas governed the mind of God and the minds of all His rational creatures. Because these moral ideas are imprinted on the will of man, each of us has within himself a guide to conduct both more complete and more dependable than the authority of either Church or Scripture. Morality, then, was regarded as an integral law of man's being and not as an arbitrary imposition from without. The relation of this emphasis to contemporary thought is immediately apparent. The Platonic tradition is laid under contribution to correct not only the dangers detected in Descartes, but the errors blatantly proclaimed by Hobbes. The claim that right and wrong depended on the will of God might have seemed to guarantee the permanence of ethical distinctions, but the suggestion that they could be determined by the dictates of a human ruler left them at the mercy of an autocrat's caprice.

But if these eternal ideas are really to determine our conduct, man must have some genuine liberty of choice. Any kind of fatalism[2] is certain to destroy even the possibility of moral life. To guarantee the freedom of the will, Cudworth reverted to the idea of reason. The free man was guided by reason, and to be ruled by its dictates was to follow

[1] Cudworth, *True Intellectual System of the Universe*, vol. II, p. 533.
[2] Cf. Cudworth's division of fatalists into three kinds: (i) atheistical fatalists; and theistical fatalists, who either (ii) consider that God's will is the ultimate sanction of morality (e.g. Descartes), or (iii) identify God with the course of nature.

what was most real in one's self. This is the origin of true self-determination, and Cudworth in particular insisted that it was fundamental to any genuine morality.[1] It was crucial to his refutation both of Descartes and Hobbes. If you accepted Descartes' 'spurious form of absolute liberty of choice', what became of the power of habit and disposition? It was Cudworth's notable achievement that he realized that the nature of the will and the meaning of freedom had to be carefully examined, not casually assumed. He recognized both the scope of the problem and the method by which it must be solved, but his own answers remained either un-published or buried amid the formless erudition of his massive works.

In the seventeenth century all philosophy had some re-ference to theological problems. In the case of the Cam-bridge Platonists the pressure of the prevailing attitude united with their own absorbing religious interest to direct their attention constantly to theological issues of the most fundamental character. They were philosophers, but their subject-matter was religion. Immortality was constantly in their thoughts; although both natural and revealed religion testified to its reality, it seemed to be endangered by the materialism of Thomas Hobbes. But more important than the destiny of the soul is its conviction that the true source of its life is in God, and that His eternal reality stands un-shaken. Again and again they reverted to the question of the divine nature, and usually they modified the Puritan em-phasis on the power of God by stressing His goodness. It is in Cudworth's major work—the vast and unwieldy *True Intellectual System of the Universe*—that we have the subject

[1] Cf. J. H. Muirhead, *The Platonic Tradition in Anglo-Saxon Philosophy*, p. 63. In this and the succeeding paragraph I am largely indebted to Professor Muirhead's work.

discussed with some approach to philosophical precision. Cudworth was convinced that he was dealing with issues of the first importance for his day, and it is with the relation of his argument to the thought of his time that we are primarily concerned. He affirmed the being of God;[1] first he defended His reality against those who currently denied it, and then set forth the positive grounds of his own belief. In his day the critics attacked the idea of God partly because it seemed incomprehensible, partly because of the difficulty inherent in the idea of the infinite. In refuting both these arguments, Cudworth revealed at once the character of contemporary assaults on religion and the quality of his own belief. He agreed that what is inconceivable is void, but he refused to concede that the incomprehensible could be identified with it and similarly dismissed. There are some things which we imperfectly grasp because of the greatness of the subject and the limitations of our minds. But even the idea of God does not really fall within this category. 'As where there is more of light there is more of visibility, so where there is more of entity, reality and perfection, there is more of conceptibility and cognoscibility.'[2] Moreover, the sense of awe and wonder are not without significance. 'A kind of ecstasy and pleasing horror...seems to speak much to us in the silent language of nature, that there is some object in the world so much vaster than our minds and thoughts that it is the very same to them that the ocean is to narrow vessels.'[3]

The attack on the idea of infinity could be met by defining more exactly the true nature of the term. Similarly the charge that religion sprang from 'fear, ignorance of causes, and the fictions of politicians' called forth an exposition of

[1] Cudworth, *True Intellectual System of the Universe*, vol. II, pp. 513 f.
[2] Ibid. vol. II, p. 519.
[3] Ibid.

the sense in which religion is rational and the sense in which it is not. It may be reasonable, and yet fall short of—or go beyond—the exactitudes of formal logic. In man there is an awareness of God which is part of the relevant evidence, and with a sure instinct Cudworth recognized that nothing can explain the phenomena of religious experience except the sense of the infinite within the heart of man.

The arguments which Cudworth refuted indicate the direction taken by anti-religious writers in his time. It is equally important to notice the positive considerations that appealed to him. The ontological argument as revived by Descartes had become part of the theological armory of the age, but Cudworth used it with discrimination, recognized its need of restatement, and finally admitted that the urgent task is not so much to establish the existence of *some* necessary and eternal being as to determine His character. Is He perfect in wisdom and love?—or merely the apotheosis of inert matter? The hierarchy of values convinced Cudworth that the world is unintelligible except in terms of a wise and holy God.

In the later seventeenth century the trend of religious thought was steadily toward rationalism and 'enlightenment'. At certain points the Cambridge Platonists fostered this tendency and contributed to it, but in one respect they stood aside from the main current of contemporary thought. As the seventeenth century drew to a close, the growing trust in reason led increasingly to a veneration of clear and distinct ideas. But the Cambridge Platonists were all, in some degree, mystics. With loving care they brooded over the obscure passages of the neo-Platonists, and something of the same quality is reflected in their own work. Their writings prove both their familiarity with the literature of mysticism, and their ability to examine it with critical

discernment.[1] There are, they said, some forms of knowledge—and those the highest—which cannot be grasped in
conceptual form; they are the product of a personal relationship with God, and we enjoy them in communion with
Him. This is what Scripture means when it speaks of 'seeing
God', and the intellectual satisfaction which it offers is above
anything our unaided reason can achieve.[2] 'But how sweet
and delicious that truth is, which holy and heaven born souls
feed upon in their mysterious converse with the Deity, who
can tell but they that taste it? When reason once is raised, by
the mighty force of the Divine Spirit, into a converse with
God, it is turned into sense; that which before was only
faith well built upon sure principles (for such our science
must be) now becomes vision.'[3] For the same reason, More
hinted that the knowledge of God can only partially be
explained by reason or in the terms that it commands. There
are no words adequate to convey what in the last resort is
indescribable. How can you explain what happens when the
life of God is disclosed within the limits of our life? We have
only one resource; we can suggest its meaning as we are able,
and then affirm that our human life can ascend to the divine
because God has descended and drawn us to Himself.[4]

These men are manifestly not describing an experience
common to most theologians in the second half of the
seventeenth century. But if in one respect it set them apart
from their contemporaries, in another it emphasized a
development of great importance in the intellectual and
religious life of the period. The Cambridge Platonists were
mystics, but when touching esoteric matters, they did so
with a degree of sanity which many continental mystics

[1] Cf. John Smith's criticism of the 'via negativa' in *Select Discourses*,
pp. 426 f.
[2] Smith, op. cit. p. 166.   [3] Smith, op. cit. p. 17.
[4] Cf. Inge, *Christian Mysticism*, p. 294.

conspicuously lack. There is a complete absence of that
atmosphere of oppressive extravagance which is unfortu-
nately so common to mystics. Their writings are never
reminiscent of bizarre regions wholly beyond normal human
experience. The reason is that the Cambridge Platonists rose
to the direct apprehension of God in and through nature,
not in spite of or beyond it. 'God made the universe and all
the creatures contained therein as so many glasses wherein
He might reflect His own glory. He hath copied forth
Himself in the creation; and in this outward world we may
read the lovely characters of Divine goodness, power and
wisdom.'[1] This explains the sanity so characteristic of the
Cambridge Platonists, but it also coincides with an important development in seventeenth-century thought. The
Puritan was not, as a rule, greatly interested in nature; he was
apt to see the world as a vale of tribulation, the present scene
of his testing and temptation. Certainly it had little direct
religious significance. But the notable feature of seventeenth-century intellectual life was the development of
natural science. The detailed study of the physical world was
preparing the way for a wholly new understanding of its
character. One of the tasks confronting religious thought
was to meet the consequences of this new knowledge and to
weave its findings into the fabric of a spiritual view of life.
The attitude which merely renounced the world could never
have faced this problem in a constructive way, but there is
no lack of indications that a definite and reasonably successful attempt was made to bring together the new knowledge
and the old faith. By the end of the century, physical science
was already proving to be an armory from which apologists
could draw formidable weapons to defend the faith.[2] There

[1] John Smith, op. cit. p. 438.
[2] Cf. notably in Bentley's *Confutation of Atheism*.

is no need to exaggerate the contribution of the Cambridge Platonists to the creation of this outlook, but it should certainly not be overlooked, and in at least one instance its results can be clearly seen. The Cambridge Platonists, says Dr Raven, profoundly influenced the outlook of John Ray; they gave him 'a theology in which reason and science could find full exercise, and the highest kind of mysticism go harmoniously with observation and exact knowledge'.[1]

In the years which immediately followed 1660 it was probably a general belief—though a foolish one—that changes in religious thought had been arrested. It was natural for the leaders of the Restoration Church to revert to the systems they had known in younger days, but this instinct, so natural in itself but so reactionary in its tendency, took no account of the contemporary forces which it faced. It might be possible to control the manifestations of irresponsible sectarianism, but these no longer represented the influences most likely to affect religious thought. Social and intellectual forces of tremendous power were altering the outlook of Englishmen on many subjects. In such an atmosphere, how could theology remain unchanged? New situations were arising, and a new temper had appeared; it was necessary for theology to speak to the point of view which prevailed in the reign of Charles II, not in that of his father of hallowed memory.

Their part in this process of adjustment and restatement emphasizes the importance of the Cambridge Platonists. In the days before the Restoration they had begun to set forth an interpretation of the Christian faith which undermined the authority of the prevailing theology, and prepared the way for important subsequent developments. For twenty years after the return of Charles II, they continued,

[1] C. E. Raven, *John Ray, Naturalist* (Cambridge, 1942), p. 37.

by writing, teaching and preaching, to present their characteristic point of view. Their attitude to reason, their view of morality, their conception of God, their mysticism, their interpretation of Scripture—all these raised issues with which every important thinker of the Restoration period was concerned, because these were the subjects to which men's minds were irresistibly drawn. But it is well to notice that the Cambridge Platonists reflect, sometimes an attitude likely soon to change, sometimes the actual results of the new outlook.

Throughout the century there had been periodical efforts to bring Christian theology into closer touch with prevailing systems of thought. We have noted the presence of those who were opposed to any change, but most of the independent thinkers of the century were interested in religious restatement. The remarkable feature of the age, however, is the extent to which this effort to find a new expression of Christianity was prompted by a desire to preserve intact the central affirmations of the historic faith. It was generally assumed that Christianity was true; where it might seem open to question, the fault was wholly due to misunderstandings in the past. Hales at the beginning of the century and Toland at the end both reflect this determination to preserve the essentials of belief, but there is no better example of this outlook than the work of the Cambridge Platonists. They assumed that the central affirmations of the faith are beyond dispute. Christianity is true; men only need to see it as it really is to recognize its value and accept it. What they themselves provided was restatement from within; they criticized the misconceptions, not the underlying truths. It would be futile to try to illustrate in any detail a conviction which so thoroughly permeates their work. But before the century ended there were already protests against what Mr Willey has called the conservative character of seventeenth-century rationalizing.[1] A new attitude had been developing in society. It was natural for Restoration courtiers to scoff at religion; by the time of the coffee-house wits a destructive attitude was still more widely held and its results were yet more extensive. This was reflected even in serious theological discussion. Toland might loudly profess his loyalty to the Church and its faith, but both those who anticipated his position (e.g. Blount) and those who developed it revealed a spirit at once critical and hostile.

The kind of reinterpretation which the Cambridge Platonists offered is in itself important. The contrast between the writings of John Bunyan and John Smith is only due in part to the different character of the people they addressed. Bunyan wrote in vivid pictorial terms because he thought in them. In this he was true to his Puritan tradition. To speak of the 'drama of salvation' was not to use a figure of speech, for nothing else could adequately suggest the forms in which the subject was presented to the believer's mind. But the Cambridge Platonists set forth ideas, not pictures. Everything is less concrete, and consequently tends to be more abstract. Each doctrine, as it reappears, assumes a more generalized form. To Cudworth the Incarnation signifies not so much the Word made flesh in a historical sense as the eternal incarnation of the Logos. The sin we are saved from is 'nothing but straitness, poverty, and non-entity'. Where the Puritan had affirmed facts, the Cambridge Platonists emphasized values. This resulted both in loss and gain. It curbed the extravagant literalism—even materialism—of certain kinds of doctrine. It brought men back to the purposes which had often been obscured by the distorted dumb-shows on which their minds had dwelt. But by the

[1] Willey, op. cit. p. 138.

end of the century it issued in a form of theology which steadily lost in vitality as its abstract character grew more pronounced.

The seventeenth century saw the beginning of the modern movement in philosophy. An age which produced the works of Bacon and Descartes, of Locke and Leibniz might well claim a distinguished place in the history of thought, but even among such contemporaries the contribution of the Cambridge Platonists is too distinctive to be ignored. They represented a return to Greek philosophy which had important consequences. They asserted the essential congruity of Christianity and Platonism, and re-established an association between the two which in many quarters still persists. They claimed that the nature of God should be interpreted in terms of the Idea of the Good; wherever belief is not associated with a faith in the supremacy of truth and goodness it ends, they said, either in formalism or in superstition.

Closely parallel was their statement of the principles of idealist philosophy. In Cudworth we have a serious attempt to express in modern terms a satisfactory alternative to the naturalism of Hobbes and the empty spiritualism of Descartes. In so doing he presented the essential elements of idealism. It is not necessary to recapitulate them here, but the alliance between theology and idealism has been so persistent and often so fruitful that its first appearance in seventeenth-century thought requires at least passing notice.

Few motives inspired the Cambridge Platonists so constantly as their dread of superstition. They had seen what its consequences might be, and much though they feared any repetition, they realized that the reaction from blind incredulity might drive men into atheism. John Smith wrote with these twin dangers always before his mind. The same appalling alternatives inspired More to produce his *Antidote to Atheism*. In opposition to superstition and unbelief, they set forth the claims of 'religion...in truth and power'. In their opposition to superstition, the Cambridge Platonists struck a note echoed by almost all their contemporaries and successors. One of the unvarying features of later seventeenth-century religious thought is its attack on all the distortions which ignorance can introduce into the domain of faith. In many cases, this was only a shallow pose, dictated by nothing more profound than subservience to the ruling conventions of the age. Superstition was regarded as the mark of the sectaries; everything connected with the sectaries was repugnant; therefore superstition ought to be attacked. But the whole atmosphere of the age encouraged the same tendency. The steady trend toward greater confidence in reason made superstition seem particularly abhorrent, and as 'enlightenment' increased there was a real danger that anything beyond the narrow limits of common sense would be repudiated as a superstition. In the Cambridge Platonists the protest was all the more effective because they both attacked the abuse and suggested its remedy. They advocated a rational theology which was both devout and penetrating, and they did not overturn the forms of popular belief without offering an alternative that would satisfy both the intellect and the emotions.

With unusual clarity the Cambridge Platonists set forth the serious responsibility which Christianity lays upon the individual. Every man must apply his own reason to the problems of belief and action. Hobbes, they felt, had threatened all ethical realities by subordinating good conduct to obedience to the ruler, and this lent added emphasis to their protest against anything that imperilled each man's sense of his responsibility. This explains their insistence on the importance of personal religion and their steady preference of reason to authority and of altruism to self-interest. Similarly they opposed centralization in Church or State; in religion it imperilled the judgement of the individual, in politics it endangered his freedom of action. But in stressing the importance of the insight and responsibility of the instructed man, the Cambridge Platonists stood virtually alone. No one else recognized so clearly the dangers of authority, or emphasized with equal discernment the importance of the truth which each man grasps for himself and then uses as the foundation of good conduct.

Given such an attitude to the individual, toleration followed as an inescapable obligation. If a man did not see the truth, he must be shown it by the methods of persuasion; if he did, no amount of coercion could justify him in forsaking it. The whole philosophical position of the Platonists was a foundation for their doctrine of toleration. Their view of the place of reason in religion and their conception of morality and its implications led naturally to the belief that toleration was not a concession granted because expediency demanded it, but a right inseparable from the inherent dignity of man.

There is no satisfactory measure of the relative importance of religious writers, but the extent of their influence at least indicates to what degree they moulded later thought. In this respect the Cambridge Platonists occupy a peculiar position. They did not found a school, and yet they profoundly affected their successors. Because of their distinctive and inimitable qualities they seem slightly isolated from contemporary thought, and yet subsequent developments in theology are unintelligible if we ignore their influence. The record of those who acknowledged a debt to the Cambridge Platonists in itself suggests their importance. The thought of Glanvill and Norris was so coloured by the writings of the Cambridge men that they are sometimes treated as members of the group. Cumberland also stood on the vague frontier between the Latitudinarians and the Cambridge Platonists. Stillingfleet, Tillotson, Patrick, Fowler, and Burnet—the Latitudinarians in fact— might modify the teachings of the Platonists, but the imprint of the older men was upon them to the end. In ethics, the Cambridge Platonists established a tradition which determined the character of English moral philosophy for a century and a half. In political theory they interpreted the idea of sovereignty in a way which Locke expanded, popularized, and established as the ruling principle in English political thought. But the Cambridge Platonists are not important simply because of the nature and extent of their influence. They represent as profound a restatement of Christianity as English theology has produced, and their unswerving conviction of the grandeur and scope of the divine activity gives to their writings a dignity and a persuasive power which neither the changes of fashion nor the passage of time have obscured.

CHAPTER IV

THE LATITUDINARIANS

A NAME given in contempt is often retained for the sake of convenience. 'Latitudinarianism' was coined as a designation for the Cambridge Platonists,[1] but it has held its place because there is no better term to describe the liberalism of the latter part of the seventeenth century. A feebler nickname never achieved success. From the very first it was found to be long and cumbersome, and 'the cholerick gentlemen' who used it had to teach 'their tongues to pronounce it as if it were shorter than it is by four or five syllables'.[2] It started as a term of abuse;[3] because it was comprehensive it proved to be permanent and ultimately became a designation which implied respect.

The circumstances surrounding its rise explain the persistence both of the name and of the phenomenon it described. A pamphlet[4] published shortly after the Restoration ostensibly contains the reply of a Cambridge man to the inquiries of a friend from Oxford. Wherever he goes, remarks the friend, he meets this word, at once so popular and so ill-defined. He has heard it used both from pulpits and in taverns, but never by anyone who could adequately

[1] G. Burnet, *History of My Own Time* (ed. by O. Airy), vol. 1, p. 334.
[2] S.P., *A Brief Account of the New Sect of Latitude Men; Together With Some Reflections on the New Philosophy* (1662), p. 4.
[3] 'A Latitude-man, therefore...is an image of Clouts, that men set up to encounter with for want of a real enemy; it is a convenient name to reproach a man that you have a spite to; 'tis what you will, and you may affix it unto whom you will; 'tis something will serve to talk to, when all other discourse fails.' *A Brief Account...*, pp. 4–5.
[4] S.P., *A Brief Account....* The author is usually identified as Simon Patrick, though the attribution has been questioned.

explain its meaning. This fleeting glimpse of public opinion in the years immediately following the Restoration is the most important thing the pamphlet contains. It enables us to sense the eagerness with which people would seize on any alternative to the familiar forms which theology had recently assumed. The Calvinism of the Puritans was defeated and discredited, but many Englishmen had no great relish for the high churchmanship of Laud. They did not wish to choose between the bigotry of the one and the rigidity of the other. Moreover, Latitudinarianism had the specious appeal of being a new theology for a new day. The Restoration had been an important change, and men were interested in a new system of thought that gave promise of keeping in touch with the temper of the age. Before the period was over, the Latitudinarians had proved decisively that they understood the mentality of their time. Whether they really met its needs is a different question; they certainly sensed its temper and spoke in terms it could understand. Before the Revolution the Latitudinarians were the most influential preachers in London,[1] and after 1688 their ascendancy on the bishops' bench was unchallenged.

Latitudinarianism was a term originally applied to the Cambridge Platonists, but it was soon transferred to a much more inclusive group than a band of teachers from one university and of one philosophic school. In seventeenth-century literature it is a word which needs careful watching; contemporaries had seen its usefulness as a name for the vague liberalism which was increasingly prevalent, and the term is often inexactly used. Sometimes it refers to the

[1] Patrick was at St Paul's, Covent Garden; Lloyd and Tenison successively at St Martin-in-the-Fields; Tillotson at Lincoln's Inn Chapel and St Lawrence Jewry; Burnet at the Rolls Chapel; Stillingfleet at St Andrew's, Holborn, and St Paul's Cathedral. Glanvill, whom I have included with the Latitudinarians, was rector of Bath, and consequently not a Londoner.

Cambridge Platonists; more often it does not. Subsequently it has, by general consent, been applied to the progressive theologians of the Restoration and Revolutionary periods. The boundaries of the group are ill-defined; it was claimed, said Bishop Fowler, that a Latitudinarian was 'a gentleman of a wide swallow',[1] and the same may be said of the term itself.

The Latitudinarians can be clearly distinguished from the Cambridge Platonists, but the relation of the one group to the other is unusually close. Most of the leading Latitudinarians were Cambridge men; they had been taught by Smith or Cudworth or More, and had doubtless listened to Whichcote preach in Holy Trinity Church. Patrick was a friend and avowed admirer of John Smith; he preached the sermon at his funeral, and the tribute, though slightly extravagant, is manifestly sincere. Tillotson and Stillingfleet and Tenison were all educated at Cambridge, and, to put the matter beyond doubt, Burnet has assured us that the main influence in moulding the thought of the Latitudinarians was the teaching and example of the Cambridge Platonists.[2] At many points this influence can be traced in the mature writings of the younger group of men. They emphasize reason and exalt morality, but the differences between them are as important as the similarities. There is a vein of genius in the Cambridge Platonists which their able but pedestrian successors lack. In Smith and Whichcote there is a depth which is missing in Patrick and Stillingfleet. You can transmit a certain kind of rationalism, but mysticism

[1] E. Fowler, *Principles and Practices of Certain Moderate Divines of the Church of England, Abusively Called Latitudinarians...In a Free Discourse Between Two Intimate Friends* (1670), p. 10.

[2] 'The most eminent of those who were formed under these great men were Tillotson, Stillingfleet and Patrick.' Burnet, *History of My Own Time*, vol. 1, p. 335. Cf. also [Burnet], *A Sermon Preached at the Funeral of...John...Lord Archbishop of Canterbury...*, pp. 11, 12.

is a subtler and more elusive matter. Something of incalculable value had faded into the light of common day.

It was natural for the Latitudinarians to stress the rôle of reason in religion. That, as we have seen, was one of the characteristic contributions of the Cambridge Platonists to seventeenth-century religious thought, and for Stillingfleet and Tillotson an emphasis on reason was an integral part of their heritage. It was in keeping also with the temper of the day. The recent excesses of certain of the Puritan sects had left all sober men with an ingrained horror of 'fanaticism'. They reacted against the 'enthusiast' and all his ways. Over against unregulated inspiration—a force unpredictable and beyond control—the Latitudinarians set the authority of reason. But the Puritans were not their only foes. At times the struggle with Romanism flared up into fierce activity, but guerrilla fighting was constantly in progress. Here also the Anglican case was solidly based on reason. The Roman Catholics believed they could impale their Protestant opponents on the horns of a dilemma. There were only two alternatives, they said; you could accept the authority of an infallible church, or you could subside into deism. It was of no avail to appeal to Scripture; unless authenticated by a church which could not err, the Bible had no decisive voice in religious controversy. The authority of the Bible, retorted Stillingfleet, is firmly established; it rests not on a single irrefutable argument, but on the sum of many considerations. By itself none of these may be conclusive, but taken together they provide the moral certainty which is all that rational men can ask or need.[1] The appeal, that is

[1] Cf. especially the discussion which arose out of Romanist resuscitation of the Laud-Fisher controversy (*Labyrinthus Cantuariensis*, 1663). Stillingfleet's answer was entitled *A Rational Account of the Grounds of the Protestant Religion. Works* (1709), vol. v, especially p. 195.

to say, is to considerations which an intelligent person can value and assess; to weigh the sum of evidence and reach an enlightened conclusion is a rational activity. Against atheism also the consistent appeal was to reason and its authority.[1] It was 'the great unreasonableness' of the unbeliever's attitude that Stillingfleet undertook to prove,[2] and he triumphantly concluded that, judged by reason, 'all the pretences of the atheist' are 'weak, ridiculous and impertinent'.[3]

The Latitudinarians were more ready to praise reason than to define it. As a rule they used the word to signify, in a rather general way, the exercise of all the mental faculties. Imagination, of course, was thoroughly suspect, and reason was apt to be equated with orderly processes of thought. They refused to limit it to 'the logic of the schools', which a rigid Aristotelianism had made odious to progressive minds. Perhaps the nearest approach to a definition was given by Burnet when he claimed that the leadings of the divine spirit do not supersede reason, if by reason we mean 'the clear conviction of our faculties'.[4] It was the avowed purpose of the Latitudinarians to eliminate the irrational from religion; the use of our mental powers, they said, can only advance the cause of faith. What they advocated, indeed, was a restoration of reason to its rightful place. A disorderly and chaotic 'enthusiasm' cannot lead us to an intelligent comprehension of the truth, and to grasp the truth is 'the most natural perfection of the rational soul'.[5] It was to this

[1] Cf. Glanvill, λογουθρησκεία, *or a Seasonable Recommendation and Defence of Reason in the Affairs of Religion, Against Infidelity, Scepticism, and Fanaticism of All Sorts* (1670).

[2] Stillingfleet, *Origines Sacrae*, p. 375.   [3] Ibid. p. 392.

[4] Burnet, Essay on *The Beginnings and Advances of a Spiritual Life* (appended to Scugal's *Life of God in the Soul of Man*).

[5] Stillingfleet, *Origines Sacrae*, pp. 1–2. All references to this work are to the 3rd ed., 1666.

end that man was made, and one of the curious features of the religious discussion of the period is the free appeal to an hypothetical Adam, an ideal creature in complete possession of perfect rational powers.[1]

The exaltation of reason places a correspondingly high value on the kind of religion that reason can discover for itself. Most of the Latitudinarians were careful to emphasize that natural religion must be supplemented by the disclosures of revelation, but they dwelt with real satisfaction on the fact that the mind, without appeal to any extraneous authority, could grasp in broad outline a religion which included the essentials of belief.[2] In his essay on *The Agreement of Reason and Religion*, Glanvill enumerated three points which he regarded as necessary to true religion: (i) the existence of God; (ii) the providence of God; (iii) the reality of moral distinctions.[3] At times, indeed, Glanvill was content to expound a very general form of theism, which showed little apparent relation to the doctrines of Christian theology. Stillingfleet was more cautious, and Tillotson left the whole question in a much more nebulous condition, but all of them accepted with alacrity the testimony of reason to a natural religion.

From the witness of reason, the Latitudinarians drew three important inferences. The first concerned the importance, both practical and speculative, of immortality. On this subject the evidence of natural religion had always

[1] Glanvill, *The Vanity of Dogmatizing*, pp. 2, 70 f.; Stillingfleet, op. cit. p. 2.

[2] Cf. Stillingfleet's repeated claim that 'the idea of God is most consonant to Reason', op. cit. pp. 367, 371 et seq.

[3] Glanvill, *Essays on Several Important Subjects in Philosophy and Religion* (1676), Essay v, p. 3. Glanvill adds (p. 4) four subsidiary points (also very general in character), but even when so augmented this stands in striking contrast to what earlier writers would have accepted as an outline of religious essentials.

been accepted as particularly clear, but wherever they turned the Latitudinarians saw the importance of immortality called in question. It was attacked by the theoretical atheists, and Stillingfleet gravely remarked that this was a tendency which would 'degrade the rational soul so far below herself as to make her become like the beasts that perish'.[1] It was ignored by those who disregarded the imperatives of the Gospel; faced with Restoration morals, Patrick maintained that 'eternal rewards in the life to come' are 'the great motive to well doing'.[2]

The second inference was that reason, by recognizing the limitations latent in our knowledge, is the true corrective to dogmatism. So far from making us overconfident, reason encourages diffidence and humility. The first step in all rational activity, whether in religion or in science, must be 'to destroy the confidence of assertions and establish a prudent reservedness and modesty in opinions'.[3] We are surrounded by such unfathomable mysteries that any form of dogmatism is intolerable·arrogance. Even when he has outlined the extent of human ignorance and proved that confidence is only folly, Glanvill feels that he has 'drawn but a cockle shell of water from the ocean. Whichever way I look upon, within the amplitude of Heaven and earth, is evidence of human ignorance; for all things are great darkness to us, and we are so to ourselves. The plainest things are as obscure as the most confessedly mysterious; and the plants we tread upon are as much above us as the stars and heavens. The

[1] Stillingfleet, op. cit. Preface to the Reader. Cf. Glanvill, Essays..., IV, p. 8.
[2] Patrick, A Friendly Debate Between a Conformist and a Non-Conformist (1668), p. 27.
[3] Glanvill, Essays..., I (Against Confidence in Philosophy and Matters of Speculation), p. 1. Cf. also Essays..., II (Of Scepticism and Certainty), pp. 39f.

things that touch us are as distant as the poles, and we are as much strangers to ourselves as to the people of the Indies.'[1]

In the light of reason, superstitious beliefs and practices, whether in religion or elsewhere, are seen to be utterly indefensible. This was the third inference drawn from the authority of reason. 'I never found a disposition to superstition in my temper', remarks Burnet; 'I was rather inclined to be philosophical' (i.e. to explain things scientifically) 'upon all occasions.'[2] 'I have ever hated and despised superstition of all sorts', he says elsewhere, 'and have found a great deal of it even among those that pretend to be the farthest from it.'[3] Even Glanvill, though fierce in denouncing the 'sadducees' who deny the reality of evil spirits, rejoices at the decline of superstition; we are no longer at the mercy, he says, of fanciful explanations of meteors and other natural phenomena.[4]

The cult of reason increased the authority of natural religion, but the Latitudinarians were anxious to prove that it accorded very closely with revealed Christianity. Their tendency was to frame a reasonable system of belief and then demonstrate that it was actually the same as the traditional faith. This process was constantly at work; natural and revealed religion were summoned each in turn to reinforce the prestige of the other. The status of the first was established by proving its essential identity with the second, while the validity of the second was sustained by the witness of the first. Stillingfleet was continually defending revelation by

[1] Glanvill, *Essays . . .*, I, p. 32.

[2] Burnet, quoted in Clarke and Foxcroft, *Life of Gilbert Burnet*, p. xlv.

[3] Quoted in Clarke and Foxcroft, op. cit. p. 248.

[4] Glanvill, *Essays . . .*, IV (*The Usefulness of Real Philosophy to Religion*), p. 8. In *Philosophia Pia*, Glanvill explains how science helps religion against her four chief enemies, of which one is superstition. He recognizes two kinds of superstition; either kind is more dangerous to religion than atheism is. Op. cit. pp. 13 f.

an appeal to reason. He proved that the Mosaic history must
be true because it was reasonable, and he established the
credibility of the whole idea of revelation on purely rational
grounds. Yet, though willing to show that revelation has
the support of reason, he was careful to insist that its
authority is ultimately greater. He offered 'several grounds
for divine revelation from natural light', but in defining the
relation of the two he laid down the general principle that
'the immediate dictates of natural light are not to be the
measure of divine revelation'.[1] Step by step he disclosed the
nature of God's purpose as revealed in His dealings with
mankind. From the remotest beginnings God has unfolded
His plan and declared His will.[2] But how are we to know that
these things are really true? Though reason can support
revelation, by the very nature of things it cannot prove it.
No arguments that the human mind alone can advance are
able to establish the truth of what revelation declares.
How, then, do we know that we are not deceived? Miracles
supply the answer. They are the proof of what revelation
proclaims. When Moses declares the law of God he is to be
trusted because he confirms his claims with miracles. When
Christ manifests 'the sweetness and grace of the Gospel',
miracles again afford the demonstration of its truth. 'Now
what conviction can there be to any sober mind concerning
Divine Authority in any person without such a power of
miracles going along with him, when he is to deliver some
new doctrine to the world to be believed, I confess I cannot
understand.'[3] Consequently we reach the conclusion that
the relation of faith and reason is close and intimate, but
ultimately the authority of faith is greater. It can vindicate

[1] This principle is enunciated and expanded in Book II, ch. v of
Origines Sacrae.

[2] Cf. de Pauley, *The Candle of the Lord* (London, 1937), p. 200.

[3] Stillingfleet, op. cit. p. 143; cf. also pp. 147–8.

its claims by arguments which, though sufficiently rational
once they have been advanced, can never be supplied by
reason alone. The certainty of faith, says Stillingfleet, is as
great as that of reason, but its grounds are stronger.[1] The
Latitudinarians, it is evident, did their utmost to make the
best of both worlds. Against the 'fanatics' they maintained
the essential congruity between reason and revelation;
against the pure rationalists they insisted on the supreme
importance of the truths which, because they are beyond the
reach of unaided reason, God has disclosed. But the Latitudinarians were more conscious of the challenge from the
first group than from the second, and consequently the
characteristic features of Christian doctrine were generally
overlaid with a veneer of natural morality.

In the seventeenth century the question of authority had
been raised in so many forms that no group of progressive
thinkers could evade it. The Latitudinarians were quite
satisfied that the authority of antiquity was overrated, and
had often been seriously abused. The practice of silencing
discussion with a quotation was detrimental both to enlightenment and to learning. The elaborate parade of
authorities had combined with an infinite ingenuity of
structure to make preaching almost unintelligible to the
common man, and Tillotson's type of homiletics represented
the most popular and effective protest against smothering
the sermon with quotations. A superstitious reverence for
the past is one of the perversions to which authority is always
subject. 'We adhere to the determinations of our fathers as
if their opinions were entailed upon us.'[2] Quite apart from
other serious consequences, this regard for antiquity had
cramped the development of natural science, which had
advanced most rapidly where the past had been least able to

[1] Stillingfleet, op. cit. p. 345.   [2] Glanvill, *Essays*..., I, pp. 25-6.

bind it.[1] In due course this protest against authority was carried a great deal further than the Latitudinarians would have approved. They rebelled against the use to which the classics had been put, but they believed there was a legitimate authority which should be carefully conserved. Glanvill did not intend any protest he had made to be twisted to disparage Christian antiquity. He refused to be party to any attempt 'to gain credit for new conceits in theology....No, here the old paths were undoubtedly the best...and I put as much difference between the pretended new lights and old truths, as I do between the sun and an evanid meteor; though,' he adds, 'I confess in philosophy I am a seeker.'[2] This difference of approach he justifies by an appeal to the different nature and history of the two disciplines; theology began with full brightness, but science in obscurity.

The Bible consequently retained its sovereign and unchallenged place. It teaches us, said Stillingfleet, what we should believe and it shows us how we ought to act. The grand conclusion toward which the chief theological work of the Latitudinarians moves ponderously forward is the assertion of 'the divine authority of the Scriptures'. Six hundred closely printed pages were not too much for such a task, and the satisfaction which *Origines Sacrae* aroused is reflected in Burnet's recommendation of the book as the most suitable kind of reading for ordination candidates. The areas, then, within which authority could be challenged were carefully defined, and the citadel of revelation remained inviolate. This was a compromise with which bolder spirits would not be content; the Latitudinarians consequently

[1] Ibid. I, p. 26, praises Galileo, who 'without a crime outsaw all antiquity, and was not afraid to believe his eyes, in reverence to Aristotle and Ptolemy'.

[2] Ibid. p. 28.

represent a transitional stage between the authoritarian approach so common earlier in the seventeenth century and the sceptical outlook of the generation which followed.

The Latitudinarians lived through one of the most remarkable developments in the intellectual history of mankind. The seventeenth century saw the rise of the modern scientific movement, and in its latter years, and in England, the new understanding of nature was unfolding with bewildering rapidity. The Latitudinarians may not have been familiar with all its details, and certainly most of them did not grasp its ultimate significance, but they were intelligently interested in what was happening, and sympathetic to the claims of the new science. Many of them were more than enlightened spectators. Wilkins played a worthy part in the founding of the Royal Society, and his contemporaries regarded him as a notable scientist in his own right. Ward was equally active in scientific pursuits. Sprat was the historian of the Royal Society, and Glanvill its panegyrist and defender. Because Tillotson had a 'love for the real philosophy of nature', and believed that the 'study of it is the most solid support of religion',[1] he sought and obtained membership in the Royal Society. When Burnet found that a discreet withdrawal from politics left him with greater leisure, he turned to the study of mathematics and chemistry.

Behind this interest lay a firm belief that any separation of religion and science would work to the detriment of both. 'How providentially are you met together', exclaimed Glanvill to the Royal Society, 'in days when people of weak heads on the one hand, and vile affections on the other, have made an unnatural divorce between being wise and good.'[2] He believed that by defining more carefully the respective

[1] T. Birch, *Life of Tillotson*, p. ccxxvii.
[2] Glanvill, *Scepsis Scientifica* (1665), Address to the Royal Society.

provinces of religion and science, the role of each would become clearer, and that conflicts between them would disappear. 'Real philosophy' is useful to religion, and the two will support each other better if 'four heads' are kept in mind. God, he says, is to be praised for His works; His works are to be studied by those who would praise Him for them; the study of nature and God's works is very serviceable to religion; the ministers and professors of religion ought not to discourage but to promote the knowledge of nature and the works of its author.[1]

The seventeenth century was passionately interested in the relations of Church and State. The question had practical importance, no doubt, but it was its religious significance that arrested attention. This is a subject that will require more detailed consideration at a later stage, but for the present it is important to notice how deeply the Latitudinarians were involved in the change which took place in Anglican thought on the subject at the end of the century. At the beginning of the period passive obedience came back with the theory of the divine right of kings. By the end of the century, the Revolution with its attendant developments had practically eliminated the doctrine from English theology. The Latitudinarians had accepted as implicitly as anyone else the identification of loyalty to the Church of England with acceptance of passive obedience, but with the fall of James II they abandoned the theory more quickly and more publicly than any other group of churchmen. This caused a good deal of comment, and from some quarters they were bitterly attacked. Their explanations of why they made the change so rapidly are fragmentary and incomplete, but it is not difficult to detect some of the reasons. As prominent London clergymen they had seen in practical

[1] Glanvill, *Essays...*, IV, pp. 1–2.

experience what unquestioning obedience to a sovereign's will could mean when the king was a fanatical Roman Catholic. Their open-minded attitude to many issues made it easier to re-examine their presuppositions when the logic of events had shown them to be unsound. The very fact that they were more interested in conduct than in theory may have played its part. Whatever the cause, the spectacle of the Latitudinarians as bishops by appointment of William and Mary was the symbol for the end of the century that passive obedience was dead.

Slowly and with great reluctance the seventeenth century recognized that religious differences might find expression in separate religious organizations. Until 1660 it had been agreed by practically all parties that dissent had no real status in the country, and this was also the assumption underlying the Clarendon Code and the repressive measures of the Restoration period. In their attitude to dissenters, the Latitudinarians anticipated the solution put forward in the Act of Toleration. Beyond all others they were willing to consider the possibility of comprehension, and their whole attitude was marked by a reasonable and conciliatory spirit. Stillingfleet's *Irenicum* attempted to prove that many of the issues which divided English religious life could not be settled by an appeal to apostolical authority, and consequently differences need not lead to separation. Stillingfleet modified his attitude as time went on, but his *Irenicum* held an important place among the contributions of the Latitudinarians to current discussion.[1] John Beardmore tells us that Wilkins was best known to his contemporaries 'for his great moderation' to the Nonconformists.[2] Tillotson's

---

[1] Cf. W. H. Hutton, in *D.N.B.*

[2] John Beardmore, *Memorials of John Tillotson*, p. cclxx (Appendix I to Birch's *Life of Tillotson*).

critics bespattered him with abuse because of 'his tender methods of treating with dissenters and his endeavours to unite all Protestants among themselves'.[1] As the period progressed and the threat of.Romanism grew, the folly of Protestant division served as a practical argument to reinforce more theoretical considerations,[2] but their moderation can be traced to their attitude to the kind of issue which divided Anglican and Puritan. Burnet quotes with approval Henry More's remark that 'none of these things [matters of church government and ritual] were so good as to make men good, nor so bad as to make men bad, but might be either good or bad according to the hands into which they fell'.[3] The remark can be duplicated a score of times in Stillingfleet's *Irenicum*. The attitude of the Latitudinarians to Nonconformists could justify itself by an appeal to Christian charity, but it had the added advantage of achieving the results which persecution sought but never secured. The dissenters responded, and many conformed.[4]

The Latitudinarians were liberals in an age of transition. It followed that they were often misunderstood, and (since it was still the seventeenth century) violently abused. They were attacked both for their moderation to dissenters and for the assumed affiliations of their thought. The age had produced great names in abundance, and often the authors were little understood but greatly feared. The Latitudinarians

[1] Birch, *Life of Tillotson*, p. xxi. Cf. Burnet, *A Sermon Preached at the Funeral of...John...Lord Archbishop of Canterbury* (1695), pp. 11, 17.

[2] Burnet, *A Sermon Preached in the Chapel of St James Before His Highness the Prince of Orange*, 23 December 1688 (London, 1689), p. 18.

[3] Burnet, *History of My Own Time*, vol. 1, p. 335.

[4] Burnet, *A Sermon Preached at the Funeral of...John...Lord Archbishop of Canterbury...*, 30 November 1694 (1695), p. 11. In this connexion note also the tribute to the Latitudinarians of a convinced dissenter, *Memorials of the Life of Mr Ambrose Barnes*, p. 200.

were not Hobbists, but on occasion they were accused of being such. Glanvill was an ardent admirer of Descartes, but many of his contemporaries were far from sure that the results of the Cartesian philosophy were desirable. The most common accusation was that the Latitudinarians were disguised Socinians.[1] The bitterness of the attacks can be conveyed only by quotation. In a work entitled *The Charge of Socinianism Against Dr Tillotson* (1695), we are assured that Tillotson's sermons 'are all the genuine effects of Hobbism, which loosens the notions of religion, takes from it all that is spiritual, ridicules whatever is called supernatural; it reduces God to matter and religion to nature. In this school Doctor Tillotson has these many years held the first form, and now diffuses its poison from a high station....His politics are Leviathan, and his religion is latitudinarian, which is none; that is, nothing positive, but against everything that is positive in other religions; whereby to reduce all religion to an uncertainty, and determinable only by civil power....He is owned by the atheistical wits of all England as their true primate and apostle....He leads them not only the length of Socinianism...but to call in question all revelation.'[2] This charge of Socinianism was one which the Latitudinarians were particularly anxious to refute. In order to meet it, Tillotson published in 1693 the sermons on Christology which he had preached in 1679-80. Burnet

---

[1] Cf. *A Letter Out of Suffolk to a Friend in London* (1695), p. 11. Cf. also *Miscellaneous Remarks on the Sermons of Archbishop Tillotson*, by John Jortin, where Tillotson's attitude to the Socinians is contrasted with the following example from 'the masterly and impartial hand of South': 'The Socinians are impious blasphemers, whose infamous pedigree runs back (from wretch to wretch) in a direct line to the devil himself; and who are fitter to be crushed by the civil magistrate, as destructive to government and society, than to be confuted as merely heretics in religion.'

[2] *The Charge of Socinianism Against Dr Tillotson* (1695), p. 13.

repudiated with characteristic vehemence the charge that 'the orthodox Latitudinarians were concealed Socinians; and that they acquiesced in Trinitarian formulas for the sake of lucre or reputation'.[1] At this point the discussion of Latitudinarianism and what it stood for had degenerated into mere recrimination, but the indeterminate character of so much Latitudinarian preaching lent itself both to misunderstanding and abuse.

The doctrinal vagueness which their adversaries twisted to suit the ends of controversy was to a certain extent the inevitable result of preoccupation with other things. The Latitudinarians intentionally avoided certain theological issues because they were satisfied that discussion of such topics led to no good end. There were some subjects whose 'effect has been to teach men to dispute rather than to live'.[2] Endless debate about theological niceties merely obscured the true character of the Christian religion. It was Tillotson's conviction that 'the great design of Christianity was the reforming men's natures, and governing their actions, the restraining their appetites and passions, the softening their tempers, and sweetening their humours, the composing their affections, and raising their minds above the interests and follies of this present world, to the hope and pursuit of endless blessedness. And he considered the whole Christian doctrine as a system of principles all tending to this. He looked on men's contending about lesser matters, or about subtleties relating to those that are greater, as one of the chief practices of the powers of darkness, to defeat the true ends for which the Son of God came into the world, and that they did lead men into much dry and angry work, who while

---

[1] Burnet, *Four Discourses*, quoted in Clarke and Foxcroft, *Life of Gilbert Burnet*, p. 333.

[2] John Beardmore, op. cit. pp. cclxxi–cclxxii.

they were hot in making parties and settling opinions, became so much the slacker in those great duties, which were chiefly designed by the Christian doctrine.'[1] This was the occasion of abuse both in his own day and since. But Tillotson was a 'moral preacher', not because he had no choice, but because he was sincerely convinced that an emphasis on morality was the great need of his contemporaries. It was his avowed purpose to awaken an appreciation of the natural and indispensable character of moral duties. The law of nature no less than the content of revelation placed men under an obligation to do the right. The Christian, of course, was fortunate in having 'the powerful motives and assistance, which our blessed Saviour in His Gospel offers us, to enable and encourage us to discharge our duty', but there is also a 'law in our members' which no human being can neglect. But for some reason the moral appeal of the Latitudinarians lacks both majesty and urgency. Prudential motives are always creeping in,[2] and the specious reasonableness of mere common sense is always present. But though there is nothing exhilarating about the demands of the Latitudinarians, no one familiar with Restoration social history will question the need of their emphasis on moral obligation, nor dismiss with easy disparagement mere 'moral preaching'. Patrick was quite justified in claiming that under certain circumstances 'spiritual' preachers can be positively dangerous. 'They treat of these things [actual duties] in such a manner as not to bring them down to meddle

[1] Burnet, *A Sermon Preached at the Funeral of...John...Lord Archbishop of Canterbury...*, pp. 31–2.
[2] Cf. Tillotson: 'And surely nothing is more likely to prevail with wise and considerate men to become religious, than to be thoroughly convinced, that religion and happiness, our duty and our interest, are but one and the same thing considered under several notions.' Tillotson's *Sermons*, vol. 1. p. 25.

with our lives.'[1] The Restoration period needed nothing so much as some one to 'meddle' with current standards, and the Latitudinarians attempted a necessary, even though a difficult and thankless, task.

It is well to do your duty for its own sake; but if you do, the result is usually some form of good work. The one issues in the other, and it was natural for the Latitudinarians to dwell on the importance of both. They expected concrete results to follow from their preaching; it stressed duty, but the fruits were to be seen in conduct.[2] Bull wrote so persuasively of the importance of good works that he was charged with Socinianism, and it was probably this anti-Calvinistic trend of their preaching that led so often to this particular accusation. The Puritans, if we may believe Patrick, were afraid that 'the insisting so much on good works is legal';[3] the Latitudinarians strenuously maintained the opposite view. What they preached to others, they practised themselves. Patrick and Tenison started the movement for founding charity schools,[4] and Tillotson and Patrick were generous supporters of Thomas Gouge in his philanthropic work among the poor people of Wales.[5] The record of the good works of these men is scattered through the literature of the period. The sober and pedestrian virtues of this school—so uninspiring and so uninspired—make them the easy butt of ridicule, but any judgement of their work must give consideration to its fruits. It was not only in their private concerns that they were zealous in good

[1] S. Patrick, *A Friendly Debate...*, p. 41.
[2] Birch, *Life of Tillotson*, p. cclxxi.
[3] Patrick, op. cit. p. 12.
[4] Patrick, *Autobiography*, p. 128. Cf. Overton, *Life in the English Church, 1660 to 1714*, p. 61.
[5] Patrick, op. cit. p. 214. Cf. Schlatter, *Social Ideas of Religious Leaders, 1660 to 1688*, pp. 128 f.

works. Out of the period dominated by their influence grew the great humanitarian movements which have so profoundly influenced English life.

The Latitudinarians might distrust 'enthusiasm', but their cautious propriety should not obscure the genuinely religious element in their life and work. They were often better than their doctrine. They might not encourage anything that would suggest active proselytizing,[1] but most of them had the strong pastoral devotion which common sense alone can never inspire. Patrick remained in his parish throughout the Plague, even though persuaded that the decision would prove fatal to himself.[2] Burnet's relations with anyone for whom he felt responsible form one of the finest traits in his curiously mixed character. His account of the conversion and death of the Earl of Rochester is almost the only work he wrote in which his insensitiveness and bad taste never obtrude themselves, and it is manifestly the work of a man of genuine religious conviction. His sense of the supreme importance of the pastoral office gives to his book on the subject the simplicity and sincerity which make it still worth reading. Here we see most clearly the spiritual ardour which underlay his Latitudinarianism, and understand something of the missionary zeal which at times showed itself in such unexpected ways. The Latitudinarians grew up in an age in which an intense personal religion was prized and cultivated. They rejected its outward forms, but retained something of its inward reality. But their protest against the abuses of personal religion was clearer than their witness to its abiding value. They transmitted the one but not the

[1] Glanvill, *Essays...*, IV, p. 32. He is not, said Glanvill, greatly concerned to change the minds of others, even though he judges them to be mistaken, 'so long as virtue, the interests of religion, the peace of the world, and their own, are not prejudiced by their errors'.

[2] Patrick, op. cit. p. 55.

other. They were the heirs of Puritanism and the ancestors of the eighteenth century, but what they received from the one they did not pass on to the other. They consequently represent an important stage in the decisive change which was taking place in the spirit of English religious life. If you ignore the Latitudinarians you cannot explain the emergence either of Deism or of eighteenth-century orthodoxy.

Latitudinarianism stood for a temper rather than for a creed. It was primarily an outlook on life and its religious significance. Because of the close relation between the character of that outlook and the prevailing spirit of the age, Latitudinarianism became a profoundly important phenomenon.

The temper of the Latitudinarians was compounded of many elements, but the most obvious was the sovereign assurance that religious belief was eminently reasonable. Irrationality had so recently run riot in English religious life that it seemed necessary 'to make all people feel the reasonableness of the truths, as well as of the precepts of the Christian religion'.[1] Stillingfleet was constantly recurring to this note,[2] and Patrick regarded it as the decisive element in religious discussion.[3] It was the quality in Tillotson which the Deists applauded with such embarrassing cordiality.[4] This emphasis had its value in the seventeenth century, but

---

[1] Burnet, *A Sermon Preached at the Funeral of...John...Lord Archbishop of Canterbury...*, p. 15.

[2] Cf. *Origines Sacrae*, p. 617, as characteristic of many examples.

[3] Patrick, *A Friendly Debate...*, To the Reader. Cf. Glanvill's account of how he converted an atheist: 'I resolved not to exasperate him by hard words, or damning sentences, but calmly and without seeming emotion, discussed the business with him.' *A Whip For the Droll; Fidler to the Atheist* (1668), later included in *Saducismus Triumphantus* (pp. 455 f.).

[4] Cf. Toland's quotation from Tillotson on the title-page of *Christianity Not Mysterious*. Also, Collins, *Discourse of Free Thinking*, p. 171.

it manifestly had its dangers also. In their more serious moments the Latitudinarians were always tempted to adopt a capricious eclecticism. They recognized the good in every school of thought, and tried to appropriate the contribution of each. It was an early gibe at Burnet that in his sermons he blended 'the opposite doctrines of Arminius and Calvin with great eloquence and applause to the no small admiration of the vulgar'.[1] Glanvill proposed to harmonize the best of the thought of Bacon, Descartes, Hobbes, and the Cambridge Platonists, but his attempt to combine specific doctrines from each led in the end to a heterogeneous assortment of ill co-ordinated elements.[2] This, however, was a temptation which beset them only intermittently. The Latitudinarians were not primarily philosophers, but they were always reasonable men. Their reasonableness was constantly declining into what proved little more than enlightened prudence. Their very preference for understatement meant that their appeal to reason often proved merely 'an argument addressed to common sense'.[3] On occasion they could even pitch their sermons in this very modest key,[4] which more than any other factor explains the pedestrian character of their preaching. Because the heroic note has vanished there is no deep sense of urgency in Tillotson, and his sermons now dismay the reader by their uninspired repetition of arguments directed to an unimaginative common sense.[5]

[1] Cunningham, quoted in Clarke and Foxcroft, *Life of Burnet*, p. 84.

[2] Cf. F. Greenslet, *Joseph Glanvill* (New York, 1900), p. 120.

[3] C. H. Smyth, *The Art of Preaching* (London, 1940), p. 156.

[4] Cf. Burnet, *A Sermon Preached in the Chapel of St. James*, 23 December 1688.

[5] Among innumerable examples, perhaps the best is the sermon (*The Wisdom of Being Religious*) which stands first in vol. 1 of the three-volume edition. Cf. also *The Advantages of Religion to Society*, and *The Advantages of Religion to Particular Persons*, Sermons III and IV in the same volume.

Because of the deference they paid to reason, the Latitudinarians tried to eliminate everything that might disturb its orderly exercise. They insisted on the need of a calm dispassionate outlook. 'When the will and the passions have the casting voice, the case of truth is desperate.'[1] Only a temper free from the disturbances of haste or prejudice, of self-interest or violent emotion can expect to further any useful cause. But even a quiet mind can be distracted if asked to deal with too much material, and the Latitudinarians constantly dwelt on the need of simplicity. They advocated a kind of clarity which, by abandoning all abstruse terms, would present truth 'in simple and essential forms'. Glanvill pleaded for a statement of belief which would consist of 'few but simple and essential articles'.[2] Tillotson 'thought the less men's consciences were entangled and the less the communion of the church was clogged with disputable opinions or practices, the world would be the happier, consciences the freer, and the church the quieter'.[3] This attitude in part explains the immense success of the Latitudinarians. They unquestionably wielded a greater influence on the ordinary Londoner than any comparable group of clergy, and they appealed to their hearers because of the directness and simplicity of their approach to religious problems. Questions that had formerly been treated with infinite intricacy and elaboration were either avoided

[1] Glanvill, *Essays*..., I, p. 23.
[2] Glanvill, *Plus Ultra*, p. 139: 'But contenting myself with a firm assent to the few practical fundamentals of the faith, and having fixed that end of the compass, I desire to preserve my liberty as to the rest, holding the other in such posture as may be ready to draw those lines my judgement, informed by the Holy Oracles, the Articles of our Church, the apprehensions of wise antiquity, and my particular reason shall direct me to describe.'
[3] Burnet, *A Sermon Preached at the Funeral of...John...Lord Archbishop of Canterbury...*, p. 31.

altogether or set forth with such simplicity that ordinary men
could understand them with ease. The ascendancy of Tillotson and his friends was doubtless due to a combination of
many factors, but simplicity was certainly not the least
important. But even this, their source of strength, could
prove a weakness. The lines of a picture can be reduced to
such an extent that directness is sacrificed instead of being
sharpened. What the Latitudinarians gained by simplicity
they often lost through vagueness.

Any account of the temper of the Latitudinarians would
be seriously incomplete if it overlooked the charity and
magnanimity which were the most admirable qualities of
their minds. They had seen enough of the havoc wrought by
religious controversy to wish to avoid its bitterness at any
cost, and they represent an honest effort to differ from their
opponents without acrimony. Burnet's incredible tactless-
ness made it difficult for his adversaries to respond, and in
Glanvill the charity which he 'felt toward all diversities of
belief'[1] may have been partly the expression of a naturally
tranquil mind, but with Tillotson it was a quality definitely
cultivated, and maintained even in the face of the gravest
provocation. 'No false imputations', he wrote to Thomas
Firmin, 'should provoke him [i.e. Tillotson] to give ill
language to persons who dissented conscientiously and for
weighty reasons; which he knew well to be the case of the
Socinians, for whose learning and dexterity he should always
have a respect, as well as for their sincerity and exemplari-
ness.'[2] Such an attitude was likely to be misunderstood and
misrepresented by opponents, and it was further subject to
insidious corruption from within. Magnanimity could
become a genial expansiveness and that again complacency.

[1] Glanvill, *Plus Ultra*, p. 140.
[2] *Life of Thomas Firmin* (1698), p. 16.

When Patrick was appointed Bishop of Chichester, he made a revealing entry in his journal. 'I fell', he said, 'into a meditation of the goodness of God, who had brought me into the world, and let me live sixty-three years in much wealth, ease and pleasure...and made me a minister of the Gospel, and placed me in an advantageous position.'[1] We are already on the threshold of the eighteenth century; this communing of a bishop with his prosperous soul is much closer to the genial worldliness of the ecclesiastics of the Enlightenment than it is to the intensity of Laud and his opponents or to the high-minded simplicity of the Cambridge Platonists.

This complacent comment indicates, none the less, the reason why the Latitudinarians are significant. They made no lasting contributions to English religious literature; their works are thin in quality, and, though popular at the time, have proved exceedingly ephemeral. Their sermons, which so profoundly affected the standards and practice of preaching, are dull in their pedestrian propriety and uninspired in their moralism. To the discussion of current religious issues they contributed a certain general approach which was characterized by intellectual candour, ecclesiastical tolerance, lenient orthodoxy, and a love of general principles. But they are important, because they both registered and accentuated an important change in religious thought. The exaltation of the early seventeenth century had been too intense to last, and its breakdown was becoming manifest even before the Restoration ushered in a new day. The danger was that reaction would sweep away the good with the bad—religious conviction with emotional extravagance—and lead to an age bankrupt in thought, corrupt in manners, and impervious to the influence of

[1] Patrick, *Autobiography*, p. 145.

religion. This nearly happened, and, though the results of
the Restoration period seem disastrous enough, they would
have been infinitely worse had it not been for the Latitudinarians. In the reaction against enthusiasm they linked
religion with the rising authority of reason; in the impatience
with restraints they insisted on the obligations of a sober
morality; for the extravagances of the preceding period
they substituted the simple, the lucid, the correct. They
sacrificed Elizabethan splendour, Caroline elaboration, and
the grandeur of the greater Puritans. Instead they set forth
to the age the religion of common sense. They explain how
English religious thought made the transition from Cromwell and Baxter, Hammond and Thorndike, to the Deists on
the one hand and Warburton on the other. In the case of
almost every important theological issue of the time—
authority, Scripture, revelation, miracle—their work explains the developments of the succeeding age. Within their
limited sphere they were effective because of the aim they
pursued. They were anxious to meet the actual needs of their
own day. They proposed to deal with real, not with theoretical, issues. Their ambition was 'to give a statement of
Christianity more satisfying to the present temper of this
age'[1] than anything that had been previously forthcoming.
This involved limitations; within them, they achieved a
striking measure of success.

[1] Stillingfleet, *Origines Sacrae*, Preface to the Reader.

CHAPTER V

THE IMPACT OF THE NEW SCIENCE

It is seldom that mankind inherits a new heaven and a new earth, but in the seventeenth century a new understanding of man, of the nature of his physical life and of the character of his home in space, became gradually available. Over large areas of society the old outlook remained, of course, practically unchanged, and even in circles into which the new knowledge penetrated it was often accepted with reluctance and sometimes violently opposed. Nevertheless, the discoveries of the great sixteenth-century pioneers— Copernicus, Vesalius and Gesner—were available to intelligent men, and Bacon had revealed the significance of the scientific method. His work marked the beginning of the 'new philosophy' in England, even though its results were appropriated with what may seem to us astonishing hesitation. Gradually, however, the authority of Aristotle—the symbol of the scholastic method—was broken, and the discoveries of the later seventeenth century filled in the details of the new world picture whose outlines an earlier period had supplied. By the end of the century, a man like Bentley could assume the validity of the Copernican interpretation of the universe; he could draw largely on the discoveries of Newton; he could quote Harvey on the circulation of the blood and Boyle on 'the weight and spring of the air'; he could produce evidence supplied by the researches of Redi, Malpighi, Swammerdam, and Leeuwenhoek.[1]

[1] Richard Bentley, *Confutation of Atheism, Eight Sermons Preached at the Honourable Robert Boyle's Lecture, in the First Year*, MDCXCII (London, 1693—my references are to the 5th edition, Cambridge, 1724), pp. 253 f., 108, 252, 154f.

Bentley was admittedly a very exceptional man, but he illustrates the extent to which the new science was supplying intelligent people with the materials for a wholly new understanding of the world. It is not surprising that those who watched the unfolding of these wonders thrilled to the prospects that seemed to open before them. 'And perhaps', exclaimed Glanvill, 'no age hath been more happy in liberty of enquiry than this, in which it hath pleased God to excite a very vigorous and active spirit for the advancement of real and useful learning'.[1] Those who shared in the undertaking felt the exhilaration of collaborating with brilliant minds in a task which called forth their full powers and promised incalculable results. 'I am confident', said Sprat, 'there can never be shown so great a number of contemporaries in so narrow a space of the world, that loved truth so zealously; sought it so constantly; and upon whose labours mankind might so freely rely.'[2]

This happy state was largely due to the unhappy times through which England had so recently passed. The age was fortunate in its liberty of scientific search because men had wearied of the turbulence of religious and political dissension. When the nucleus of the future Royal Society began to meet, the primary purpose of its members was to enjoy free intercourse, 'without the wild distractions of that passionate age.' Such gatherings proved a training ground which provided 'the next age' (i.e. the Restoration period) with 'a race of young men...who were invincibly armed against the enchantments of enthusiasm'.[3] The excesses of current controversy quickened the new interest in science,

[1] Glanvill, *Essays...*, III (*Modern Improvements of Useful Knowledge*), p. 1.
[2] Sprat, *History of the Royal Society* (edition of 1702), p. 70.
[3] Ibid. p. 53.

which in turn created an atmosphere fatal to the wranglings of the previous age, 'for', remarked Sprat, 'such spiritual frenzies, which did then bear rule, can never stand long before a clear and deep skill in nature'.[1]

Thus the spirit of contention fostered the pursuit of natural science and then gradually gave way before its steady advances, but there were still other antagonists to overcome. The scholastic method was deeply entrenched both in the educational system and in the minds of the men trained in it. The scientists were not the only ones who protested against the sterile intricacies into which Aristotelianism had hardened.[2] Milton's famous outburst in 'The Reason of Church Government Urged Against Prelacy' expressed the disgust of an enlightened humanist, and Locke's account of his early education reflected the dissatisfaction of a philosopher of the new school.[3] But the revolt against scholasticism was a particular concern of the scientists, because the authority of the existing system cramped and hindered their discoveries at every turn. In the Universities a vast system of authoritative deduction reigned supreme, and it is true, though scarcely credible, that as late as the year 1669 the University of Cambridge presented Cosimo de' Medici with a dissertation condemning the Copernican astronomy.[4] The prevailing system of education laid almost exclusive stress on abstract philosophizing. Pope tells us that when Seth

[1] Ibid. p. 54.

[2] Cf. W. Pope's preference of Horace to Aristotle: 'This I rather believe, because he did not think fit to trouble the world with entelechias, entities, quidities, and such other abstruse, unintelligible metaphysical notions.' *Life of Seth Ward*, p. 94.

[3] Cf. Fox Bourne, *Life of John Locke*, vol. I, pp. 61–2. Cf. Le Clerc: 'The only philosophy then known at Oxford was the peripatetic, perplexed with obscure terms and useless questions.' *Eloge de M. Locke*, in *Bibliothèque Choisie*, t. VI, p. 374.

[4] Cooper, *Annals of the University of Cambridge*, vol. III, p. 536.

Ward discovered certain mathematical works in the library of Sidney Sussex, there was no one in the college who could tell him what they meant.[1] At Oxford, the sterility of the official teaching drove Glanvill to study natural science for himself. Formal logic, he remarks, may be a useful discipline if prevented from becoming 'nice, airy, and addicted too much to general notions', but this, he adds, is precisely what usually happens. Even when science was advancing rapidly and the Royal Society was constantly recording fresh triumphs, Glanvill could complain that 'progress was retarded by the dead hand of Aristotle'.[2] In the centres of higher learning, the 'new philosophy' had to make headway against an entrenched system which

> 'suffered living men to be misled
> By the vain shadows of the dead.'[3]

A decadent scholasticism was an abuse of authority against which the new science protested with special vehemence, but there were other forms of the same evil which it was equally concerned to resist. The weight of the whole classical tradition bore heavily on any new departures in thought, and in one way or another every liberal movement of the later seventeenth century had to assert its right to differ from views hallowed by antiquity. The members of the Royal Society were charged with insolence because they preferred their 'own inventions before those of our ancestors'. 'We approach the ancients', replied Sprat, 'as we behold their tombs, with veneration; but we would not therefore be

[1] Pope, op. cit. pp. 9–10.

[2] Glanvill, *Essays...*, III, p.1. Cf. also *Plus Ultra*, passim. For the retarding effect of Aristotle, cf. also Newton, *Opticks*, Query 31.

[3] A. Cowley, *Verses to the Royal Society*, in *Poetical Works*.

confined to live in them altogether.'[1] The protest became part of the avowed policy of the Royal Society. By resolution its members decided that in their proceedings they would not be guided by the authorities which might be quoted in defence of anything, 'and therefore did not regard the credit of names, but of things'.[2]

But dogmatism assumed many forms, and its most menacing champions were not the defenders of antiquity. Even among educated people the evidence of the new science gained ground very slowly. Early in the Restoration period, the old cosmology was set forth with superb magnificence in *Paradise Lost*, yet Milton was an independent thinker, ready for innovation in many fields. The view of the world which had been fashioned in the early centuries of the Christian era and reduced to perfect logical precision by the great schoolmen was still widely current. 'This strange medley of fact and fable, of truth and falsehood, of good and evil'[3] represented the world view of the vast majority of the contemporaries of Newton. For many of them Copernicus might never have lived, and even fellows of the Royal Society could retain strange fragments from the older thought.[4] It was natural that the findings of the new science should seem to threaten the security of people who had imagined that they inhabited the centre of the universe, and equally natural that they should attack those who disturbed their peace of mind.

[1] Sprat, *History of the Royal Society*, p. 46. Cf. Glanvill, *Essays*..., III, p. 50: The members of the Royal Society, he says, respect the ancients, 'but they do not think that those, however venerable sages, should have an absolute empire over the reasons of mankind'.

[2] Sprat, op. cit. p. 105.

[3] C. E. Raven, *Science, Religion and the Future* (Cambridge, 1943), p. 21.

[4] Note the views of Henry More and Joseph Glanvill on witchcraft and necromancy.

Seen in retrospect, the antagonism of such opponents might seem of small account, but it was no negligible factor at the time. To dissent from orthodoxy could have unpleasant consequences,[1] and the apologists of the Royal Society regarded its critics as deserving at least the civility of a reply. It was consequently of some importance that the new movement was supported by a group of clergymen whose character and position alike commanded respect. Wilkins was a man of sufficient ability to overcome, in the years following the Restoration, the handicap of being Cromwell's son-in-law, and became bishop of Chester. In Burnet's well-known words, he was one of those who, in the declining days of the Protectorate, 'studied to propagate better thoughts, to take men off from being in parties, or from narrow notions, from superstitious conceits and a fierceness about opinions. He was also a great observer of natural, and a promoter of experimental philosophy, which was then a new thing and much looked after'.[2] Wilkins' scientific ability may have been good though not brilliant, but he had the invaluable gift of recognizing the original work of others, and assimilating its results into his own thought. His *Treatise on Natural Religion* was important as an illustration of the kind of apologetic which commended itself to an able man aware of what was happening in the realm of science. This was a field which theologians of the older school ignored, and though there is no marked originality in Wilkins' work, it is an example of the cordial way in which the 'new philosophy' and the old religion could agree together. Seth Ward, like Wilkins, was a member of the group which met at Wadham College before the Restoration,

[1] Even in 1710, Whiston lost his chair at Cambridge because of his heterodoxy.

[2] Burnet, *History of My Own Time*, vol. 1, pp. 332–3.

and, like him, supported the Royal Society with his influence when he was raised to the episcopal bench. The relative prestige of bishops and scientists has altered since the end of the seventeenth century, and it is easy to forget how considerable a help the interest of these bishops was.[1]

The clerics who defended most effectively the aims and efforts of the Royal Society were Joseph Glanvill and Thomas Sprat. The first need, according to Glanvill, was to remove misconceptions due to faulty information. Many of the attacks on the Royal Society sprang from prejudice;[2] and many simply from ignorance.[3] His opponents, he said, did not know what they were talking about. 'They consider not that the design is laid as low as the profound depths of nature, and reacheth as high as the uppermost storey of the universe, that it extends to all the varieties of the great world, and aims at the benefit of universal mankind.'[4] The critics, he added, are mistaken when they assume that the Royal Society is a body whose purpose it is to devise new theories and notions. Scientists, beyond all others, are opposed to speculative doctrines; 'their first and chief employment is to report how things are *de facto*...their aims are to free philosophy from the vain images and compositions of fancy, by making it palpable and bringing it down to the plain objects of the senses'.[5] While some opponents objected because the Royal Society had already done too much, others taunted it with

[1] Cf. Sprat, op. cit. p. 132: 'Of our churchmen, the greatest and most reverend, by their care and passion and endeavours in advancing this institution, have taken off the unjust scandal from natural knowledge, that it is an enemy to divinity. By the perpetual patronage and assistance they have afforded the Royal Society, they have confuted the false opinions of those men who believe that philosophers must needs be irreligious.'

[2] Glanvill, *Essays*..., III, p. 50.   [3] Ibid. p. 53.

[4] Glanvill, *Plus Ultra*, p. 88.

[5] Glanvill, *Essays*..., III, pp. 36–7.

achieving nothing. 'What has it done?' they asked, and Glanvill boldly retorted that it had accomplished more than 'all the philosophers of the notional way since Aristotle opened his shop in Greece'.[1]

This ancient controversy may seem to have little immediate relevance to changes in religious thought. Actually it had the closest possible relation. The parties on both sides were clerics, and they took the matter with the utmost seriousness because they recognized that ultimately these issues affected the character of their religious beliefs. Science was introducing new methods, but those previously in favour had been pressed into the service of religion. They had encouraged the arrogance of dogmatism; by undermining this spirit, science had delivered men's minds from 'bold and peremptory conclusions, which are some of the greatest hindrances to intellectual improvements in the world'.[2] By recognizing the difficulties even in its own discipline, it had encouraged the humble and teachable disposition which can learn the ways of truth. The definition of scientific method was at once an acknowledgement of the limited field which science cultivated and a challenge to the arbitrary attitudes of the traditionalist. The 'Free Philosophers' were called sceptics, because they were not willing to pore over the writings and opinions of other people; they sought truth in 'the great book of nature', and in their quest proceeded warily, without too great an eagerness 'to establish maxims and positive doctrines'.[3]

Glanvill finally turned directly to the underlying issue of the bearing of the new science on religion. Christianity, he said, is not and cannot be prejudiced by the activities of the Royal Society. Ill-informed men, quick to jump to hasty

[1] Glanvill, *Essays*..., III, p. 38.   [2] Ibid. I, p. 1.
[3] Ibid. II, p. 44.

conclusions, may think otherwise, but Glanvill has no doubt
that they are wrong. Some may think that the naturalist is
the secret ally of the atheist; their misconception is only
serious because it is not restricted to the vulgar, but influences
even those who are responsible for the instruction of the
people. Actually the study of nature is useful in 'most of the
affairs wherein religion is concerned'. It cultivates an outlook fatal to all the principal enemies of belief; it overthrows
atheism, sadducism, superstition, enthusiasm, and the
humour of disputing. Even the charge that science under-
mines the authority of Scripture is disproved. So far from
encouraging men to ignore the Bible, the knowledge of God
in His works disposes the mind to love Him in His word.

What, then, should be the attitude of Christian leaders to
the Royal Society and its endeavours? Some will lack the
time and others the disposition to pursue such studies
themselves, 'yet they ought to think candidly and wish well
to the endeavours of those that have; 'tis a sin and a folly
either in the one or the other' (i.e. in layman or cleric) 'to
censure or discourage those worthy undertakings'. Hence
men of right understanding can only be gravely disturbed
when those supposed to be religious leaders abuse natural
scientists—'the irreligion of which injurious carriage
nothing can excuse but their ignorance'.[1]

In Sprat's *History of the Royal Society*, the new movement
had an apologia which contemporaries hailed as a model of
what such a work should be. Many of his arguments are the
same as Glanvill's, though the indebtedness was obviously
on Glanvill's side. There is the same attack on dogmatism,
the same protest against authority, the same complaint of the
antipathy of obscurantists. He dwells on the incompatibility
of science and superstition; he shows how the progress of

[1] Ibid. IV, p. 31.

the new philosophy has ended the tyranny of sterile controversies. He points out the various forces which in the past have hindered the advance of science, and emphasizes the baleful influence of religious controversy. 'For whatever hurt or good comes by such holy speculative wars...yet certainly by this means the knowledge of nature has been very much retarded.'[1] Over against the fury of these empty struggles, he places the cautious concern of the Royal Society with indisputable matters of fact. They recognize the need of ceaseless care to ensure the utmost accuracy, and for that reason they will not leave facts to be determined by the individual judgement—'nor', he adds, will they commit them 'to devout and religious men alone; by all these we have been already deluded'.[2] In investigating phenomena they 'have been cautious to shun the overweening dogmatizing on causes on the one hand; and not to fall into speculative scepticism on the other'.[3]

In describing the spirit of the new science, Sprat is in close accord with Glanvill, but he gives a much fuller account of the subject-matter which the Royal Society has taken as its province. It deals, he says, with God, Man and Nature, but lest this very inclusive statement should breed misunderstanding, he immediately explains the great limitations scientists accept in connexion with the first of these. 'They meddle', he says, 'no otherwise with divine things, than only as the power, and wisdom, and goodness of the Creator is displayed in the admirable order and workmanship of the creatures.'[4] This statement is important. In effect Sprat declares that they propose to deal only with natural phenomena; he immediately makes clear that they will investigate them with the strictest attention to evidence and the most

[1] Sprat, op. cit. pp. 25 f.   [2] Ibid. p. 73.
[3] Ibid. pp. 101–2.   [4] Ibid. p. 82.

rigorous exclusion of *a priori* arguments,[1] but he also assumes that the evidence will declare to them the character of God. The disciplines of natural science have become in effect an alternative approach to the ultimate questions of theology.

Since this is the aim and spirit of science, Sprat finds it natural that 'the greatest and most reverend' of 'our churchmen' should have given the Royal Society their commendation and support.[2] And well they might, for the Church of England stands only to gain from the endeavours of the Society. With others it might be different; those who put their trust in 'implicit faith and enthusiasm' might fear the findings of science, but 'our church...can never be prejudiced by the light of reason, nor by the improvements of knowledge, nor by the advancement of the works of men's hands....From whence', he concludes triumphantly, 'may be concluded that we cannot make war against reason, without undermining our own strength.'[3]

Sprat has already proved in some detail that experimental science does not challenge the accepted forms of Christian theology. It will not destroy the doctrine of the Godhead, nor discourage the worship of God; it contains nothing that would encourage its devotees to challenge the doctrine of salvation or the teaching of the primitive church. 'It may be suggested', he says, 'that the sensible knowledge of things may in time abolish most of these, by insinuating into men's minds that they cannot stand before the impartiality of philosophical investigations. But this surmise has no manner of foundation.'[4]

It might seem that Sprat has eliminated any antagonism between religion and science, and left us with an identity of interest and a partnership of activity. But he himself at once

[1] Ibid. pp. 83–99.   [2] Ibid. p. 132.
[3] Ibid. p. 370.   [4] Ibid. pp. 348–55.

declares that though the two are not hostile to nor in any way incompatible with each other, they must nevertheless be kept rigorously apart. Christianity should not be made dependent on any school of philosophy; 'religion ought not to be the subject of disputations; it should not stand in need of any devices of reason'. The substance of religion, like law, is simply promulgated, and in the last resort its deepest doctrines can only be accepted by a 'plain believing'. 'Nor ought philosophers to regret this divorce; seeing they have almost destroyed themselves by keeping Christianity so long under their guard; by fetching religion out of the church and carrying it captive into the schools, nay have made it suffer banishment from its proper place'—and in the process have very much corrupted the substance of their own knowledge.[1]

This question of the relation of the 'new philosophy' to religion was one to which the scientists of the day were constantly recurring. Boyle agreed with Sprat. The two were in no way opposed to each other; every effort should be made to remove the appearance of antagonism, but in the last resort each fared better if they kept apart. Newton, on the contrary, wished to see the relationship kept close and intimate.[2] To these men and their contribution we must presently turn, but before doing so it is important to notice the way in which the rise of the new science had brought

[1] Sprat, op. cit. pp. 355–6.
[2] Note the very illuminating comment of Professor G. N. Clark, that Newton's seemingly unrelated activities were connected by a desire to find in each area a single principle which would co-ordinate a mass of confused and complicated material. The law of gravitation did this with striking success in the world of physics; and his researches into chemistry on the one hand and into Biblical prophecy and apocalyptic on the other had the same purpose but not the same result. In other words, Newton's purpose and method led him inevitably from the field of science to that of religion. Clark, *Science and Social Welfare in the Age of Newton*, p. 84.

with it new problems for religion. Those who attacked the Royal Society did so not only in what they assumed to be the interests of Christianity but in defence of the 'philosophy' with which their faith was traditionally allied. Aristotelian scholasticism, as we have seen, was the foundation of the theology, philosophy and science taught at the Universities; theology might become crabbed, and science might be starved, but there need be no incompatibility between them when they both deduced their systems from the same presuppositions. To men accustomed to this outlook, the new science with its patient waiting upon fact and its repudiation of all presuppositions, seemed positively atheistical. When to this was added the impact of a new cosmology, it is scarcely surprising that fearful souls cried out that the ark was being overthrown. It was difficult to accept Glanvill's assurance that the true sceptic, so far from being a disbeliever, was one who neither derogates from faith nor despairs of science.[1]

The interpreters of the new discipline played an invaluable part in defending its aims and explaining its achievements, but the important work was done by the practising scientists themselves. Their discoveries supplied the material which Sprat and Glanvill expounded, and opened the new vistas which involved so fundamental a revision of current conceptions of the universe. This entailed far-reaching modifications in the interpretation of the world, but the character of the men whose work compelled the changes made it relatively easy for contemporaries to accept them. The leading scientists of the period were for the most part earnest Christians, and they continually related their discoveries to a religious interpretation of the world. The earnestness of Boyle's devotional life impressed his contemporaries as

[1] Glanvill, *Essays...*, III, p. 43.

deeply as the brilliance of his scientific achievements.[1] Ray's religious sincerity was attested as convincingly by his life as by his works. For Newton, Christianity was of basic and primary importance; so far from being a conventional interest or an incidental appendage to his scientific work, it was one of the dominant concerns of his life.

It was natural that these men should maintain the most intimate relation between their scientific discoveries and their religious beliefs. In spite of Boyle's contention that theoretically they might be kept apart, he actually believed that his experimental science had a direct bearing on his Christian faith. 'It appeared to those who conversed most with him in his enquiries into nature, that his main design in that, on which as he had his own eye most constantly, so he took care to put others often in mind of it, was to raise in himself and others, vaster thoughts of the greatness and glory, and of the wisdom and goodness of God.'[2] In his will, the final article relating to the Royal Society wishes its members 'also a happy success in their laudable attempts to discover the true nature of the works of God, and praying, that they and all other searchers into physical truths may cordially refer their attainments to the glory of the great author of nature and to the comfort of mankind'.[3] In his first letter to Bentley, Newton declared that 'when I wrote my treatise about our system, I had an eye upon such

[1] Cf. Burnet, *Discourse on the late Hon. Mr Boyle*: 'I might here challenge the whole tribe of Libertines to come and view the usefulness, as well as the excellence of the Christian religion, in a life that was entirely dedicated to it, and see what they can object.' Boyle proved, adds Burnet, 'to how vast a sublimity the Christian religion can raise a mind, that does both thoroughly believe it, and is entirely governed by it'.

[2] Burnet, op. cit. p. 10. Cf. also, E. A. Burtt, *The Metaphysical Foundations of Modern Physical Science*, p. 188.

[3] Quoted in Richard Boulton's *Life of the Hon. Robert Boyle* (1725), p. 22.

principles as might work with considering men, for the belief of a Deity'.[1]   John Ray regarded 'the objects of his study, the order of the universe, the life of plants and animals, the structure and functioning of nature, as the manifestation of the mind of God'. The joy and wonder which accompanied his work were 'essentially religious' in character, and his discoveries bore for him 'a profound religious and indeed Christian significance'.[2]

Men so deeply persuaded of the importance of religion could not limit their attention to remarks scattered incidentally throughout their scientific-works. Both Boyle and Newton wrote extensively on theological matters. In Newton's case, his works on Biblical subjects were inspired by an intellectual rather than a devotional interest, and as a result were directly related to the remainder of his work.[3] Their importance, however, is now strictly limited. They disclose a considerable amount of erudition; they show Newton as an ingenious critic of texts; and at certain significant points they indicate the direction in which his mind was moving. They suggest that Newton was an Arian in his theological sympathies, and this is confirmed by his unpublished writings.[4] In this respect he reflected a trend noticeable among certain of his contemporaries; if, they said, they could eliminate from Christianity the doctrine of the Trinity, it would be easier for them to reconcile theology and

[1] Newton, *Opera*, vol. IV, p. 429.

[2] C. E. Raven, *John Ray, Naturalist* (Cambridge, 1942), p. 455.

[3] G. N. Clark, *Science and Social Welfare in the Age of Newton*, p. 83.

[4] Cf. L. T. More, *Isaac Newton*, p. 640. Cf. also H. McLachlan, *The Religious Opinions of Milton, Locke and Newton* (Manchester, 1941), p. 172. The latter work, whose intention is evidently limited to a desire to prove that Milton, Locke and Newton were Unitarians, restricts itself in the case of Newton to his Biblical writings, and ignores the important implications of the religious comments contained in the *Principia, Opticks*, etc.

science. Newton's work on 'Two Notable Corruptions of Scripture' attacked the authenticity of two texts often quoted in defence of this article of belief, but his reluctance to publish this and other works[1] of clearly Unitarian character show that he had no desire to be a leader in any matter so certain to issue in bitter controversy.

Boyle's religious works are more extensive in their scope and less controversial in their implications. Some of them are devotional in character;[2] some are Scriptural,[3] and some set forth his views of the relation of reason[4] and science[5] on the one hand and religion on the other. They are the expression of a devout and humble mind, and for our purposes most of them are only important as explaining the immense veneration with which contemporary Christians regarded Boyle.

The leaders of English science were sincere believers, and they were convinced that their faith was fortified by their discoveries. Scattered throughout their works are abundant indications of the line of reasoning they pursued. Certain fundamental facts point, they said, to the existence of God. His works in particular bear constant witness to His wisdom and creative power. Human reason and intelligence are impossible to explain if there be no creative Reason behind them. 'I make great doubt', said Boyle, 'whether there be not some phenomena in nature which the atomists cannot satisfactorily explain by any figuration, motion or connection

---

[1] Cf. *Queries Regarding the Word Homoousios; Paradoxical Questions Concerning the Morals and Actions of Athanasius and His Followers* (published by Brewster, vol. II, pp. 342 f.).

[2] E.g. *Occasional Meditations; Of the Veneration Due to God.*

[3] E.g. *Of the Style of Scripture.*

[4] E.g. *The Reconcilableness of Reason and Religion.*

[5] Cf. *The Christian Virtuoso; The Excellence of Theology,* setting forth the pre-eminence of divinity over science.

of material particles whatsoever; for some faculties and operations of the reasonable soul in man are of so peculiar and transcendent a kind, that as I have not yet seen them solidly explicated by corporeal principles, so I expect not to see them in haste made out by such.'[1]

Even greater stress was laid on the significance of order and beauty in the universe at large. This, indeed, was the argument to which the scientists most frequently revert. The regularity of nature's functioning was unintelligible save in terms of a creative purpose to which phenomena respond. Such beauty as surrounds us was manifestly meant to correspond to the design of some wise Providence which gave both the gift and the power to receive it. They were continually encountering examples of adaptation. Newton found them in the movements of the heavenly bodies, Ray in the life of plants and animals, but to both alike they pointed to the creative power of God. 'That the consideration of the vastness, beauty and regular motions of the heavenly bodies; the excellent structure of animals and plants; besides a multitude of other phenomena of nature and the subserving of most of these to men; may justly induce him as a rational creature to conclude that this vast, beautiful, orderly, and (in a word) many ways admirable system of things, that we call the world, was framed by an author supremely powerful, wise and good, can scarce be denied by an intelligent and unprejudiced considerer.'[2] Newton, with his greater mastery of style, presented essentially the same argument. 'The main business of natural philosophy', he said, 'is to argue from phenomena without feigning hypostases, and to deduce causes from effects, till we come to the very first cause, which certainly is not mechanical; and not only to

---

[1] Boyle, *Works*, vol. II, pp. 47f.
[2] Ibid. vol. v, pp. 515f.

unfold the mechanism of the world, but chiefly to resolve these and such like questions. What is there in places almost empty of matter, and from whence is it that sun and planets gravitate toward one another without dense matter between them? Whence is it that nature does nothing in vain; and whence arises all that order and beauty which we see in the world? To what end are comets, and whence is it that planets move all one and the same way in orbs concentric, while comets move all manner of ways, in orbs very eccentric? and what hinders the fixed stars from falling upon one another? How came the bodies of animals to be contrived with so much art, and for what ends were their several parts? Was the eye contrived without skill in optics, or the ear without knowledge of sounds? How do the motions of the body follow from the will, and whence is the instinct in animals? Is not the sensory of animals that place to which sensitive substance is present, and into which the sensible species of things are carried through the nerves and brain, that there they may be perceived by their immediate presence to that substance? And these things being rightly despatched, does it not appear from phenomena that there is a being incorporeal, living, intelligent, omnipresent, who in infinite space, as it were in his sensory, sees the things themselves intimately, and thoroughly perceives them; and comprehends them wholly by their immediate presence to himself?'[2]

The fact of God and the reality of His creative power are the great religious affirmations which the scientists deduced from their discoveries. This was perhaps natural; the evidence of the new philosophy had been used for their own purpose by men whom Boyle attacked as 'atheists and prophaners'. The contemporary assault on religion had come

[1] Newton, *Opticks*, pp. 344 f.

from those who saw in natural law a substitute for a creative and sustaining power. It consequently seemed a circumstance of the utmost importance that scientists wielding the authority of Boyle and Newton declared that their researches gave no ground of confidence to the atheist. Even gravity— so soon to acquire an almost magical appeal—was not regarded by Newton as possessed inherently by matter. It was, he said, dependent upon the power of God, but in any case, whether it was essential to bodies or not, a divine creation was implied.[1]

The issue at stake, then, was the reality of God; having established that a wise Creator was responsible for fashioning the earth, Boyle and Newton interpreted His character in terms which traditional theology had made familiar. But it was with neither the nature of God nor the manner of His working that subsequent developments were chiefly concerned. The continuing functions which Boyle and Newton assigned to God were considerably less dramatic than the creative activity which framed the universe. Boyle insisted that God had not abandoned the world, and Newton, by his emphasis on the power and dominion of God,[2] made it necessary to find some adequate activity for God to discharge.[3] Boyle claimed that God, having set the universe in motion, constantly kept it from disintegrating. Newton assigned to God two specific functions: He prevented the fixed stars from collapsing in the middle of space, and He kept the mechanism of the world in perfect working order.

[1] Cf. E. A. Burtt, *The Metaphysical Foundations of Modern Physical Science*, p. 287.

[2] 'The supreme God is a Being eternal, infinite, absolutely perfect; but a being, however perfect, without dominion cannot be said to be Lord God....' *Principia*, II, 310.

[3] This in spite of the occasional suggestion that the reign of law can now control the world.

It was this latter suggestion, as Professor Burtt has shown, that finally brought Newtonian metaphysics into disrepute. There was a touch of the absurd in seriously assigning to God, as one of His major tasks, the responsibility of keeping His universe in good repair. It was demonstrated, step by step, that the exceptional tasks reserved by Newton as the sphere of divine operation were actually not irregular, but the province of fixed law. The ultimate consequences of the Newtonian system lie, however, far beyond the boundaries of our period, and it is only necessary to indicate the points which proved historically significant.

In the early eighteenth century, complacency was the persistent temptation of educated Englishmen. 'All the dearest ambitions of men and of Britons had been realized; the constitution had been established and "freedom" secured; Homer and Vergil had been equalled if not outdone, and the law which preserves the stars from wrong had been made manifest, and the true workings of the mind had been revealed. All these things had been done not only by Englishmen but by Christians.'[1] But 'the law which preserves the stars from wrong' had not been set forth in terms intelligible to the ordinary reader.[2] If the Newtonian conception of the universe became within a generation a part of the outlook of educated men, it was not because they had read the *Principia*. The findings of the new physics had to be interpreted for the benefit of the ordinary person; as regards the religious significance of Newton's discoveries, one of the earliest as well as one of the most important contributions was Richard Bentley's *Confutation of Atheism*.

---

[1] B. Willey, *The Seventeenth Century Background*, p. 264.
[2] When Bentley began his study of Newton, Craig sent him a most formidable and discouraging list of books as prolegomena to the *Principia*. Cf. Jebb, *Bentley*, p. 26.

In his will, Boyle had provided for the institution of an annual series of eight sermons, 'for proving the Christian religion against notorious infidels', and Richard Bentley, a young scholar whose fame was rapidly increasing, was the first lecturer appointed by the trustees. Bentley's attack on the atheists was twofold—negatively he demonstrated the indefensible position of those 'engaged in that labyrinth of nonsense and folly';[1] positively he proved the necessity of a belief in God. His whole method is significant. He made no appeal to Scripture; its authority was not admitted by his opponents and he did not even postulate that it must be included as part of the relevant material. 'But however there are other books extant which they must needs allow of as proper evidence: even the mighty volumes of visible nature, and the everlasting tables of right reason, wherein if they do not wilfully shut their eyes they may read their own folly written by the finger of God in a much plainer and more terrible sentence, than Belshazzar's was by the hand upon the wall.'[2] The emphasis on reason is revealing, and in claiming that religion imposes 'nothing repugnant to man's faculties or incredible to his reason',[3] Bentley was testifying, at the end of our period, to a belief which had steadily gained ground throughout a generation.

Bentley's detailed refutation of atheism[4] is now chiefly interesting as a scintillating display of controversial skill. It is in stating his own case that he expounded, in so illuminating a way, the bearing of the new science on religious thought. His main points were those which Boyle and Newton had already advanced. The proof of God's existence

[1] Bentley, *Confutation of Atheism*, p. 4.
[2] Ibid. pp. 2–3.   [3] Ibid. p. 16.
[4] Atheism, it should be noted, is regarded as the legacy of Hobbes. Ibid. p. 3.

was drawn, in the first place, from the nature of man's reason and intelligence;[1] in the second, from the evidence of order, beauty and purpose in the world.[2] Of the two arguments, Bentley manifestly regarded the second as the more important. Certainly he dealt with it with much more verve and at far greater length. He examined first the evidence furnished by the human organism, and proved 'that the organical structure of human bodies, whereby they are fitted to live and move and be vitally informed by the soul is unquestionably the workmanship of a most wise and powerful and beneficent maker'.[3] With infinite ingenuity he varied the argument from design. 'Nay, even the very nails of our fingers are an infallible token of design and contrivance....It is manifest therefore that there was a contrivance and foresight of the usefulness of nails antecedent to their formation.'[4]

In the last three sermons (VI, VII, VIII), Bentley turned to the evidence supplied by 'the origin and frame of the world'. His indebtedness to Newton was frankly acknowledged. In order to prove 'with the greater clarity and conviction' that atoms could never have fashioned themselves 'into this present frame of things', he proposed to give a brief account of 'the most principal and systematical phenomena that occur in the world now that it is formed'.[5] He began with gravitation, 'lately demonstrated and put beyond controversy by that very excellent and divine theorist, Mr Isaac Newton, to whose most admirable sagacity and industry we shall frequently be obliged in this and the following discourse.'[6] His next sentence made clear

[1] Sermon II.   [2] Sermons III–VIII.
[3] Bentley, op. cit. p. 91. Of particular interest is his detailed attack, reinforced by the recent discoveries of Redi, Malpighi, etc, on the suggestion that life could spontaneously emerge out of inert matter.
[4] Ibid. p. 184.   [5] Ibid. p. 251.   [6] Ibid. p. 253.

the rôle Bentley had accepted for himself. 'I will not entertain this auditory', he said, 'with an account of the demonstration; but, referring the curious to the book itself for full
satisfaction, I shall now proceed and build upon it as a truth
solidly established, that all bodies...'.[1] Theological learning
was already beginning to take the findings of the new science
for granted; its next task was to draw from them the proper
deductions.

Throughout the remainder of this remarkable work,
Bentley was drawing out, with infinite ingenuity and a
bewildering wealth of material, the religious significance of
Newtonian physics. It is not necessary to follow the argument in detail; in spite of its intricacies, the main purpose is
clear enough. Bentley was proving to his contemporaries
that the latest discoveries of science, even when minutely
examined, gave no confidence to the enemies of religion.
On the contrary, they confirmed the central affirmations of
belief—that God exists, and that He created the universe and
all the living things our world contains.

The end of the seventeenth century was an age of transition. The men who made the great discoveries in science
might be earnest Christians, but the belief of many of their
contemporaries was unsettled none the less. The faith which
Boyle restated was seventeenth-century orthodoxy, shorn
only of its antiquated cosmology, but he was alarmed at the
signs of revolt against that faith. He founded his lecturership
to confute atheists, and Sprat noted that the age was marked
by all the signs of religious decline.[2] In such an age, what was
the effect of science on religious thought?

[1] Ibid. p. 253.
[2] Sprat, *History of the Royal Society*, p. 376: 'The generality of
Christendom is well nigh arrived at that fatal condition which did
immediately precede the destruction of the religion of the ancient world:

In the first place, it accentuated the tendency to magnify the rôle of reason in religion. The trend in this direction was perhaps the most striking single feature of later seventeenth-century thought, and it was undoubtedly reinforced by the rise of natural science. It required no great prescience on Sprat's part to recognize that any triumphs won in his life-time would not go to 'enthusiasm'. It was equally obvious to him that science was strengthening the emphasis on reason. This, he hoped, would lead to a restatement of religion to which his generation would respond.[1] The natural counter-part to the increasing rationalism was an attack on authority. This, in turn, subtly influenced the character of religious thought. The traditional forms were maintained, but there was less emphasis on dogma.[2] Some beliefs (though not always the ones we might expect) were called in question; others were reinterpreted in a broader and more flexible sense. The rigid, detailed systems of theology so popular earlier in the century were passing rapidly into disrepute.

The scientists did not challenge the prevailing statements of belief; indeed, for the most part they were scrupulously loyal to them. Miracles, though certain ultimately to be challenged in an age obsessed with natural law, were still treated with deference and care.[3] Scripture, likewise,

when the face of religion in their public assemblies was quite different from that apprehension men had of it in private. In public they observed its rules with much solemnity, but in private regarded it not at all.'

[1] Sprat, op. cit. p. 375.

[2] Cf. G. N. Clark, *The Seventeenth Century*, p. 318. Note also Sprat's comment: 'In a gross and sensual age, the deepest mysteries of our religion may be proper, to purify the stupidity of men's spirits; but there must be an application of quite different and more sensible prescriptions, in a subtle, refined, and enthusiastical time.' Op. cit. p. 377.

[3] Boyle carefully left room for special providences, but it is notable that he stressed the importance of the regular rather than of the unusual. It became increasingly customary, however, to extend the rule of law to its utmost limits, and then allow, for courtesy's sake, exceptions to

retained its virtually unchallenged authority.[1] Yet, in the case of both these subjects, the scientists introduced slight modifications, which, though apparently leaving the substance of belief unaltered, opened the door to a demand for serious changes. The results only became apparent later—in the Deistic controversy, for instance—but the ferment was already at work.

In ways they scarcely understood, the seventeenth-century scientists had helped to change the general outlook in philosophy and religion.[2] They had shaken the old system of education and modified the whole conception of the universe. But what the results of these things would be they did not see. They had at their disposal material which might reasonably have led to important changes, but actually did not. The true explanation of fossils was gaining ground, but it was only used in religious debate to demonstrate the reliability of the story of the Flood. The old beliefs in in-

cover Scriptural miracles (cf. Bentley's *Confutation*, p. 150). But God had performed these spectacular actions only 'in dark and ignorant ages', and there were weighty reasons why no 'prodigies' should astonish the intelligent period in which the Royal Society had birth. Newton, it should be noted, believed that if miracles were better understood, many of them would prove to be examples of the working of laws concerning which we are now ignorant (cf. Portsmouth Papers, quoted by L. T. More, *Isaac Newton*, p. 623).

[1] Boyle believed that the study of the Bible was both more important and more rewarding than the study of nature. Newton gave at least as much time to pondering the problems of Biblical interpretation as to examining the structure of the physical world (cf. More, op. cit. p. 637; also J. W. N. Sullivan's comment, that if Newton neglected the subjects where his genius lay, it was because he regarded them as relatively less important, *Isaac Newton*, p. 13). But Newton and Sprat both stated decisively that while the prestige of Scripture stood firm, this gave no special authority to private interpretations of the Bible; we do not value it less because we refuse to accept the tyranny of other people's views about it.

[2] Cf. L. Hodgson, *The Doctrine of the Trinity* (New York, 1944), pp. 123–4.

stantaneous acts of creation and in the accepted chronology of the world were undisturbed. The representatives of the new outlook claimed that it was a perversion of Scripture to use it to establish matters (such as astronomy) with which it was not primarily concerned, but they still quoted the folk-lore of Genesis as a literal and authoritative account of the early history of human life upon the earth.[1]

In one respect, science introduced a change of profound importance in accepted methods of thought, and this had significant results in theology. The 'new philosophy' refused to argue from presuppositions, however plausible or venerable they might be. This had been the unchallenged practice of the previous age; it explained the poverty of the earlier science, which 'had never been able to do any great good toward the enlargement of knowledge, because it relied on general terms'.[2] The new science declared that there can be no profitable search for truth which does not begin with evidence and remain scrupulously loyal to it. 'The philosophy that must signify either for light or use must not be the work of the mind turned in upon itself, and conversing only with its own ideas; but it must be raised from the observations and applications of sense, and take its account from things as they are in the sensible world.'[3] In no area had discussion become so remote and abstract as in theology. This had already brought it into disrepute; now, under the combined influence of Locke[4] and Newton, the old method was hopelessly discredited. But it did not follow that theology began to treat in any fruitful way the material provided by religious experience. The approach might seem obvious, but the proprieties of the eighteenth century were

---

[1] Bentley, op. cit. p. 93.   [2] Sprat, op. cit. p. 16.
[3] Glanvill, *Essays*..., III, p. 23.
[4] Cf. N. Kemp Smith, *John Locke*, p. 17.

already beginning to paralyse the religious imagination. It is one of the tragedies of English theology that a new method replaced the old at a time when the insight necessary for its constructive use was lacking.

Two further changes, significant though somewhat indirect, remain to be noted. The first is the way in which the scientist found in his work a sense of what can only be described as religious vocation. Science summoned its followers to combat ignorance and superstition—as true a crusade, said Sprat, as any war upon the Turks.[1] In this task they felt a community of interest and purpose which transcended all customary barriers—'of country, of interest, or profession of religion'—and in which each helped the other as he was able. In natural science and its pursuits, many minds were discovering a new means of expressing a zeal which had hitherto found an outlet through more conventional religious channels.

This spirit, however, extended far beyond the circle of the great discoverers. The new science taught ordinary people the joys of observing nature. It established as a national characteristic an awareness of and devotion to the study of the manifold forms of life. This was a complete break with the past; hitherto men had been apt to regard nature with fear and apprehension. The change might not in any immediate or obvious way affect the churches, but its religious consequences were of the utmost importance. As the seventeenth century closed, Englishmen were beginning to realize that 'the treasures of nature are inexhaustible',[2] and the discovery contributed an element of permanent and incalculable value to English life.

[1] Sprat, op. cit. p. 57.
[2] John Ray, *The Wisdom of God, Manifested in the Works of Creation*, p. 126.

CHAPTER VI

THE RELIGIOUS SIGNIFICANCE OF JOHN LOCKE

THE importance of some thinkers is even greater than the intrinsic value of what they have to say. Locke epitomized the outlook of his own age, and anticipated the thought of the succeeding period. To emphasize the astonishing scope of Locke's influence in no way suggests a disposition to depreciate the inherent value of his philosophy, but part of the importance of his work lies in the immense prestige which it acquired; indeed, for over a hundred years, his *Essay Concerning Human Underst*·*rding* determined the course of European thought.[1] The range of Locke's influence was vastly wider than the circle usually affected by the writings of philosophers. He created a new mentality among intelligent people; he offered a satisfying interpretation of the workings of the human mind, and provided a framework within which the ordinary person's thinking could be done. While Newton was establishing the prevalent conception of the physical universe, Locke was fashioning that picture of the mental world which became a commonplace in the eighteenth century. This was partly due to the comparative ease with which the average reader could follow the argument of the *Essay*, but it was also the result of the indirect but all-pervasive influence which Locke exerted.

[1] Cf. A. S. Pringle-Pattison, preface to Locke's *Essay* (Oxford, 1924), p. xiv. Professor N. Kemp Smith claims that on the appearance of Locke's *Essay*, he 'became the dominant philosophical influence throughout Europe', and retained that position throughout virtually the whole of the eighteenth century; cf. *John Locke* (Manchester, 1933), p. 8; also pp. 12 and 13.

As Locke's authority increased, the bearing of his work on religious thought became steadily more apparent. Locke, of course, had sometimes dealt with specifically religious subjects, but it was not this fact which determined the extent of his influence on theology. His incidental comments on religion were often more important than his explicitly theological work, and the spirit in which he approached Christianity was more significant than what he actually said about it. Locke summed up an attitude to religious issues which was steadily gaining ground as the seventeenth century ended, and his immense influence made it almost universal in the early years of the eighteenth century.

But even in his philosophical work religion occupied an important place. The inevitable conclusion toward which the *Essay* steadily moves is the certainty of God's existence. We are intuitively aware that we ourselves exist; if we concede that fact—and no reasonable man, said Locke, can deny it—we reach by demonstration the assurance that there is a God. In this lies the distinctive quality of religious conviction. 'But though this be the most obvious truth that reason discovers, and though its evidence be (if I mistake not) equal to mathematical certainty; yet it requires thought and attention; and the mind must apply itself to a regular deduction of it from some part of our intuitive knowledge, or else we shall be as uncertain and ignorant of this as of other propositions which are in themselves capable of clear demonstration.'[1] Locke thus disposed at a single stroke of the belief in innate ideas. Throughout the seventeenth century, many of the foremost religious writers had clung to the conviction that God had imprinted on the mind of man certain indelible truths, and that of these ideas the assurance of His own existence was at once the clearest and the

[1] Locke, *Essay Concerning Human Understanding*, IV, 10, 1.

most important. It was by quite a different approach that Locke arrived at a belief in God. Man starts with himself— he 'knows that he himself is'—but he also knows that 'nothing can produce a being, therefore something eternal'.[1] Thereafter it was relatively simple for Locke to show that such an eternal being must be most powerful, most knowing, existing from eternity—'and therefore God'. 'Thus from the consideration of ourselves, and what we infallibly find in our own constitutions, our reason leads us to the knowledge of this certain and evident truth, that *there is an eternal, most powerful, and most knowing Being*, which whether any one will please to call *God*, it matters not. The thing is evident; and from this idea duly considered, will easily be deduced all those other attributes which we ought to ascribe to this eternal Being.'[2]

Locke was uncompromising in asserting the inescapable character of belief in God. 'It is plain to me', he said, 'we have a more certain knowledge of the existence of a God, than of anything our senses have not immediately discovered to us. Nay, I presume I may say that we more certainly know that there is a God, than that there is anything else without us.'[3] This was reassuring doctrine for the closing years of the seventeenth century, and the character of Locke's argument admirably illustrates the trend of thought in this period. The significance of Locke's proof of the existence of God does not lie in the fact that he exalted the part reason plays in the search for truth. The emphasis on reason had been growing steadily stronger ever since the Restoration, and was continued—fortified, of course, by Locke—throughout most of the subsequent century. Locke supplied a detailed and

[1] Locke, *Essay*..., IV, 10, 3.
[2] Ibid. IV, 10, 6.
[3] Ibid. IV, 10, 1.

(as it seemed) a scientific account of what many people had felt must be the true origin of our idea of God. He did more than affirm the importance of reason in religion; he explained how it worked, and made it seem both necessary and inevitable. He laid bare the workings of the mind, with the result that those who followed him could confidently affirm as fact what had previously been put forward as hypothesis. It is difficult for us now to recapture any adequate awareness of the tremendous effect Locke's argument produced. The dark mysteries of the human mind had seemingly been explored and its secret places laid open to the scrutiny of men. The cool dispassionate ease of Locke's work seemed to symbolize the completeness of this victory. If we overlook this fact, we can hardly hope to understand the confident assurance of the early eighteenth century. Intelligent men were not perplexed by insoluble difficulties or overwhelmed by mysteries beyond their grasp. The secrets of the heavens had been disclosed by Newton, those of the human mind by Locke. In both regions, the principle which resolved chaos into order was the same. The evidence of reason ran through all things. Its unifying power could no longer be treated as an intuition. It had been conclusively proved, and the demonstration had had an immediate bearing on theology. Locke reaffirmed the rôle of reason in religion, but at the same time he lifted it to a new plane of confident authority. He appropriated a widely diffused but ill-defined conviction, and gave it clear and persuasive form. The results rapidly became apparent. The tone of the Deistic controversy already shows the effect of Locke's work, but this is only one example among many. Everywhere the authority of reason went unquestioned. However much antagonists might differ, they agreed in this—that their arguments would stand or fall as they were able to abide the test of reason. Rationalism became 'a habit of thought ruling all minds',[1] and as time went on it exercised a more and more constricting influence on religious thought. The area which men were willing to explore steadily diminished. 'The title of Locke's treatise, *The Reasonableness of Christianity*, may be said to have been the solitary thesis of Christian theology in England for the greater part of a century.'[2]

From this it naturally followed that Locke's authority confirmed another tendency already clearly manifest in English religious thought. All the intellectual forces of the period combined to discredit reliance on authority, and one by one the more progressive theologians of the Restoration era had emphasized the need for greater independence of thought. In Locke the revolt against tradition found its most effective spokesman. Untold mischief, he claimed, had resulted from a dull acquiescence in formulations uncritically transmitted from one generation to the next. 'So much as we ourselves consider and comprehend of truth and reason, so much we possess of real and true knowledge.'

It is clear, in fact, that Locke's doctrine of God was related closely and at many points to the main currents of thought in his age. At times he confirmed and amplified arguments which had been commonly accepted, but he was quite prepared to dissent from positions which were invested with considerable prestige. Descartes had recently restated the ontological argument for the existence of God. The effect on contemporary opinion had been tremendous, but Locke refrained from using it, and ultimately repudiated it altogether. He referred to it in the *Essay*, but declined to discuss

[1] Mark Pattison, *Essays*, vol. II, p. 45. As Pattison pointed out, rationalism as applied to this period bears no suggestion that the truths of religion were denied. It rather suggests a certain spirit in which these truths were approached.

[2] Ibid. p. 46.

it in detail. It might or might not establish what it claimed to prove, but Locke thought it was questionable wisdom to insist so largely on one argument as to ignore all others.[1] Subsequently, however, he explicitly rejected the ontological argument,[2] and Professor Gibson has pointed out that in a paper dated 1696 (and published by Lord King), Locke claimed that it could not carry conviction, because it involved an inference from idea to real existence.[3] 'Real existence', said Locke, 'can be proved only by real existence; and, therefore, the real existence of a God can only be proved by the real existence of other things.'

But the fact that Locke differed from Descartes at this point is perhaps chiefly important because it indicates why Locke acquired so vast an influence. By his own confession, he was deeply indebted to Descartes, but his innate independence of mind, strengthened possibly by his scientific studies, enabled him to use Descartes' material with considerable freedom. He was able to borrow or reject with discrimination. He adopted Descartes' 'doctrine of clear and distinct ideas and his rationalist approach to all problems', but these, especially when supplemented by a proper recognition of the part played by experience, were precisely the concepts most likely to appeal to popular understanding.[4]

At the end of the seventeenth century, the prestige of mathematics stood high. The law of gravitation supplied the norm by which all phases of the search for truth were judged. Newton had shown that the vast complexity of the universe was governed to its remotest confines by one uniform mathematical order, and no area of thought could escape the

[1] Locke, *Essay*..., IV, 10, 7.
[2] Locke, *First Letter to Stillingfleet. Works*, vol. IV, pp. 53–6.
[3] J. Gibson, *Locke's Theory of Knowledge*..., (Cambridge, 1917), p. 169.
[4] Cf. N. Kemp Smith, op. cit. p. 15.

influence of such a discovery. Against this background, Locke's contribution to religious thought finds its proper place. He insisted that the material of thought is provided by the five senses, and that thought itself is a process conducted in a spirit of detachment which refuses to be deflected by enthusiasm. If you begin with 'self-evident facts and self-evident propositions, and proceed by mathematically correct deductions', is there any reason why your search for truth should yield in the religious sphere results less dependable than in the realm of physical science? Locke thought not. It is 'as clear as demonstration can make it', he said, 'that there must be an eternal Being.'[1] His claim that the evidence for the existence of God is 'equal to mathematical certainty'[2] is significant; this, Locke believed, was the most cogent argument you could advance to prove your point. But in the process, Locke lost as much as he gained. He offered the kind of God that mathematical procedures can establish. Campbell Fraser pointed out that the expression Locke habitually used—'a God'—is significant. The notably impersonal character of his 'eternal Being' is partly the result of the method by which he proved that God exists. Locke's God is the final term in a demonstration, and has the quality which such an approach might be expected to produce. He is proved by an appeal to a restricted kind of evidence. The processes of logical demonstration outweigh the disclosures of man's total experience. The argument left out of account many aspects of life which religion ignores to its serious impoverishment. This is the great weakness of Locke's treatment of the central concept of belief, and he transmitted it, with all the weight of his authority behind it, to the eighteenth century.

The seventeenth century ends, consequently, with a

[1] Locke, *Essay*..., IV, 10, 13.   [2] Ibid. IV, 10, 1.

reaffirmation of the being of God, but its character epito-
mizes the change which had taken place in English religious
thought. With cool, dispassionate clarity, God was set forth
as a necessary postulate, wholly reasonable and satisfying
to the mind, and upheld by evidence conforming to the
standards of the intellectual discipline which then commanded unquestioning assent. The Puritans of the Interregnum had believed in God with no less assurance than
Locke himself, but the intellectual framework of their faith
was completely different. The evidence supplied by religious
experience held a place of paramount importance, and the
prominence of the 'pilgrim motif'[1] brought God and His
purposes into the closest possible relation to the moral
problems of mankind. The intensity of the Puritans' preoccupation with God would have made Locke's mathematical approach seem ridiculously irrelevant. Their God might
be grim; at times He might even seem capricious, but there
was no escape from the paramount demands with which He
confronted His believers. The Puritans believed in God not
so much because they had proved that He was plausible as
because they felt that His sovereign purposes had laid hold
upon their life and thought. By the end of the century, men
were prepared to accept with assurance the reality of God,
but only after a dispassionate assessment of the evidence.
They declared themselves in favour of an 'eternal Being',
but He lacked the majesty and splendour of the God the
Puritans had worshipped. 'All passion spent' might stand
as the epitaph of seventeenth-century theology, and Locke,
more than any other man, was responsible for giving
religious thought the self-possessed assurance which it
carried into the Age of Reason.

[1] Cf. W. Haller, *The Rise of Puritanism* (New York, 1938), pp. 148 f.,
190.

Locke was eager to prove the existence of God and to establish the primary place of reason in religion. But if you exalted reason, you had to come to terms with revelation. This was clearly shown by the character of religious thought in the generation following the Restoration. The extravagant terms in which some of the sectaries had defined revelation had made it thoroughly suspect. To counteract the claims of those who 'believe without foundation that their impulses come from God',[1] reason had been consistently pressed into service. The reality of revelation was not questioned, but even when its abuses had been checked, there remained the difficult question of the relation between what God discloses and what man discovers. Locke dealt with this question more explicitly than most of his predecessors, and the influence of his treatment of the subject is clearly seen in later thought.

Locke's contribution lay in his attempt to define with greater care than had hitherto been done the interdependence of these two crucial terms. '*Reason*', he said, 'is natural *revelation*, whereby the eternal Father of light, and Fountain of all knowledge, communicates to mankind that portion of truth which he has laid within the reach of their natural faculties. *Revelation* is natural *reason* enlarged by a new set of discoveries communicated by God immediately, which reason vouches the truth of, by the testimony and proofs it gives that they come from God. So that he that takes away reason to make way for revelation puts out the light of both; and does much-what the same as if he would persuade a man to put out his eyes, the better to receive the remote light of an invisible star by a telescope.'[2] Locke, then, explicitly

---

[1] The phrase is Leibniz's (quoted by Pringle-Pattison, op. cit. p. 360, n. 1). Compare Butler's treatment of enthusiasm, *The Analogy of Religion*, II, vii, 13.   [2] Locke, *Essay*..., IV, 19, 4.

stated that Christianity was a religion of both reason and revelation; the importance of his contribution is his clear definition of the way in which revelation is received by man. Though he conceded that 'the bare testimony of revelation is the highest certainty',[1] he claimed that we can only judge whether a truth has really been disclosed by God if we exercise our reason. The material with which revelation deals must be 'our simple ideas', and for these 'we must wholly depend on our reason'.[2] Moreover, 'revelation cannot be admitted against the clear evidence of reason', and therefore no proposition can be received for divine revelation if it be contradictory to our clear intuitive knowledge'.[3] But there are some matters on which we have no 'clear and distinct knowledge'; here our unaided faculties cannot bring us to the truth. Only revelation can help us, and whatever is disclosed to us in these regions is 'the proper matter of faith'.[4] But here the delicate equipoise of Locke's distinctive position becomes apparent. Where God has been pleased to disclose the truth, such revelation 'must carry it against the probable conjectures of reason', but 'it still belongs to reason to judge the truth of its being a revelation, and of the signification of the words wherein it is delivered'.[5] As Locke stated it in an alternative form, 'whatever God hath revealed is certainly true; no doubt can be made of it...but whether it be a divine revelation or no, reason must judge'.[6]

This is the only way, Locke said, in which the extravagances of credulity can be curtailed; without a definition of this kind, reason will wholly forfeit its foothold in religion. But the even balance which Locke so adroitly maintained was easily disturbed. He himself set forth his argument as

---

[1] Ibid. IV, 16, 14.   [2] Ibid. IV, 18, 3.
[3] Ibid. IV, 18, 5.   [4] Ibid. IV, 18, 7.
[5] Ibid. IV, 18, 8.   [6] Ibid. IV, 18, 10.

a corrective to the irrationality of 'enthusiasm', but those who followed him used it to challenge affirmations which Locke was not in the least disposed to question. Moreover, the intellectual atmosphere of the period tended to fix men's attention on one half of his argument in such a way as to obscure the other. The position which Locke had stated was briefly this—God's existence can be proved by reason; this truth is supplemented by revelation; but revelation itself is subject to the scrutiny of reason. Given the mental outlook of the age, it was natural that the part played by reason should gradually eclipse the place given to revelation. In the Deists we see this process already at work; to pursue the matter further would carry us into the history of eighteenth-century thought.

Locke himself, however, was partly responsible for obscuring the rôle which he assigned to revelation. In the *Essay* he was dealing with religion in general terms, but in *The Reasonableness of Christianity* he expounded in detail his conception of what revelation actually involved. The title of this work is in itself sufficient to suggest that those who magnified the rational element in Locke's attitude to religion received ample encouragement from Locke himself. The appeal throughout is to the understanding of sensible men.[1] Locke cites his authorities—his quotations from Scripture are exhaustively detailed—but his use of them admirably illustrates his approach to religious questions. He went to the Bible, he tells us, because the prevailing 'systems of divinity' seemed unsatisfying and inconsistent,[2] and he

---

[1] Cf. Oman's comment: 'God is there [in *The Reasonableness of Christianity*] shown to have acted in a sensible, business-like manner, and Christ to be the incarnation of Divine commonsense.' *The Problem of Faith and Freedom*, p. 105.

[2] Locke, *The Reasonableness of Christianity*, Preface. (All references are to the 1st edition, 1695.)

looked for a statement of belief which would be free from all intricacy and confusion. In other words, he was approaching the whole question of revealed religion in the spirit which the increasing rationalism of the later seventeenth century dictated. He wanted a form of belief which would be clear, direct, and simple.

The emphasis on simplicity is important. It is characteristic of Locke's treatment both of small details and of large principles. Scripture, he said, is not a collection of abstruse writings; it says exactly what on the surface it appears to say, and is 'therefore generally to be understood in the plain, direct meaning of the words and phrases'.[1] When the sacred writers speak of death, they mean death— nothing more or less.[2] This according to Locke is perfectly natural; they were writing 'for the instruction of the illiterate bulk of mankind'. But the simplicity is as much a matter of substance as of form. When Locke 'betook himself' to 'the sole reading of the Scriptures...for the understanding of the Christian religion',[3] he was amazed to find how plain and intelligible the 'mysteries' of the faith actually were. The things a man had to believe were few and simple. All that was necessary for salvation was to have faith in Jesus as the Messiah. Belief in one God was a necessary condition of such faith, and amendment of life was its natural consequence, but Locke's exposition of Christianity consists of little more than a demonstration that one simple statement expresses the entire substance of the faith. 'Salvation or perdition', he said, 'depends upon believing or rejecting this one proposition.'[4]

This radical simplification represents Locke's most characteristic contribution to seventeenth-century religious

---

[1] Ibid. p. 2. [2] Ibid. pp. 4–5.
[3] Ibid. Preface. [4] Ibid. p. 43.

thought. At certains points—for example in his emphasis on reason—he amplified what others had said, but his drastic modification of the structure of traditional Christian theology was his own. Locke had certain marked affinities with the Latitudinarians,[1] but, for all their doctrinal vagueness, there is nothing in their writings to match his complete and detailed overthrow of the accepted systems of theology. Even more striking is the contrast between Locke's position and certain representative Socinian statements of belief. At many points the doctrinal agreement is close, but Socinianism, in spite of its divergence from orthodoxy, retained the accustomed theological forms. Its system differed from Calvinism in content but it was no less complicated in structure.[2] If Locke's treatise on the reasonableness of Christianity had been less encumbered with detailed exegesis, its striking plea for simplicity might have been even more effective than it was, but its influence was manifestly great. The prestige of all the familiar theological systems was waning. With the passage of time they had hardened into inflexible rigidity, and an age awakening to the claims of reason was ready to see them modified or even overthrown. Men did not pause to ask why traditional theology had arisen; they did not see that originally it drew its impulse from the need of dealing adequately with some of the profoundest issues of man's spiritual life. The plea for simplicity was necessary, but its results are seen in the thin and superficial plausibility of eighteenth-century theology.

The effect of Locke's ruthless revision can best be studied at one particular point. The doctrine of justification by faith

---

[1] Cf. Fox Bourne, *Life of Locke*, vol. II, pp. 77, 153-4, for the influence of the Latitudinarians on Locke.

[2] Cf. R. S. Franks, *History of the Doctrine of the Work of Christ*, vol. II, p. 159.

had held a distinctive place in Protestant theology for more than a century and a half. Locke did not entirely ignore it, but he unquestionably changed its meaning. God, said Locke, had 'found out a way to justify some';[1] those who obeyed the law of faith received the appropriate reward—they escaped death, which is the penalty of sin. Now the law of faith demands that everyone should believe what God requires him to accept,[2] and this is summed up in the simple statement to which Locke constantly recurred—Jesus is Messiah. But there is no clear indication why this belief should decisively affect the relation of the believer to God. The heart of the Reformation had been the claim that the humble acceptance of what Jesus Christ had done places a man on a new footing with God. For Locke, the benefits which Christ confers on the believer can be quite simply stated, and they point to a religious experience wholly different from the intensities of Pauline faith as interpreted by St Augustine and Martin Luther. We are indebted to Christ for a clearer perception of the reality of God, a surer grasp of our duties, deliverance from useless ceremonial, encouragement to live a good life, and an assurance that the Holy Ghost will help us.[3] At only one point did Locke in any way refer to the traditional reformed doctrine of the work of Christ. 'We know little', said Locke, 'of this visible, and nothing at all of the state of that intellectual world, wherein are infinite numbers and degrees of spirits out of the reach of our ken or guess; and therefore know not what transactions there were between God and our Saviour, in reference to His kingdom. We know not what need there was to set up a head and a chieftain in opposition to "the prince of this world, the prince of the power of the air," etc., of which there are

---

[1] Locke, *The Reasonableness of Christianity*, p. 15.
[2] Ibid. pp. 24–5.   [3] Ibid. pp. 260f.

more than obscure intimations in the Scriptures.'[1] But this brief reference is left wholly undeveloped. Locke's own version of justification stems from his belief that the reward of faith is deliverance from death; where we fall short of what is required of us, faith makes good the deficiencies of our obedience, and the substance of this faith is (as we have seen) the simplest possible affirmation. Those who lived before the advent of Christ are justified because they looked for his coming; those who have lived since, because they have received him as Messiah; and those who have never heard of him, can trust to the mercy of God, provided they have accepted the 'light that lighteneth every man that cometh into the world'.[2] It is not necessary to emphasize how fundamentally this differs from seventeenth-century orthodoxy.

The simplification of doctrine could go on further and still retain the designation Christian. From Locke's drastic modification of theology there followed two important consequences: morality assumed a new importance and authority a new guise.

To give added substance to his exposition of Christianity Locke laid earnest stress on the necessity of right conduct. The bare statement of belief in Jesus as Messiah was not, he conceded, the entire message of the Apostles; 'what they taught...contained a great deal more, but that concerned practice and not belief'.[3] But manifestly our best efforts fall far short of what is required of us, and so amendment of life must stand in the forefront of the Christian message. 'Repentance is as absolute a condition of the covenant of grace as faith, and as necessary to be performed as that.'[4] But

[1] Locke, *The Reasonableness of Christianity*, p. 255.
[2] Ibid. pp. 243 f.   [3] Ibid. p. 92.
[4] Ibid. p. 194; cf. also p. 199: 'These two, faith and repentance; i.e. believing Jesus to be the Messiah and a good life; are the indispensable conditions of the new covenant.' Note also p. 228.

repentance, if genuine, would result in a serious effort to express in daily life the sober integrity which the later seventeenth century esteemed so highly. This preoccupation with morality[1] was related to a parallel trend in the Latitudinarians; what Locke was stating in his books, Tillotson was saying in his sermons, but no one else set forth the claims of the good life so simply and so acceptably as Locke.

Locke, however, had no illusions about the unaided appeal of morality. Those who are disinterested enough to follow righteousness for its own sake are relatively few in number, and Christianity is not a cult for specialists but a 'religion suited to vulgar capacities'.[2] There must therefore be inducements strong enough to persuade men to be good, and Locke found them in the rewards which he believed are attached to right conduct. He did not hesitate to urge people to be good on the grounds that they would find it profitable. 'The philosophers, indeed, showed the beauty of virtue; they set her off so as to draw men's eyes and approbation to her; but leaving her unendowed, very few were willing to espouse her. The generality could not refuse her their high esteem and commendation; but still turned their backs on her and forsook her, as a match not fit for their turn. But now there being put into the scales on her side "an exceeding and immortal weight of glory", interest is come about to her, and virtue is now visibly the most enriching purchase, and by much the best bargain.'[3] This may now seem ethically weak and spiritually bad, but it is in keeping with Locke's whole treatment of Christianity. In the ministry of Jesus he detected consistent evidence of a calculating prudence, which delicately adjusted means to ends. It must be remembered,

---

[1] Locke, *Essay...*, IV, 3, 18; IV, 12, 11.
[2] Locke, *The Reasonableness of Christianity*, p. 302.
[3] Ibid. pp. 287–8.

also, that Locke lived in an age which accepted the idea of rewards without too critical a scrutiny, and the appeal to self-interest was 'the favourite passion'[1] of the period.

If persuasion is needed to make men good, authority is equally necessary. Locke did not set much store by moral insight, since he thought that ordinary people would lack it. He expected that 'the day-labourers and tradesmen, the spinsters and dairy maids' would be able to follow only the simplest kind of reasoning, and as a result it would be necessary to tell them what to do and what to believe. 'The greatest part', he said, 'cannot know, and therefore they must believe.'[2] Consequently, authority occupies a curiously inconsistent place in Locke's simplified Christianity. Having swept away the complicated superstructure of theology, he still found his residue above the capacity of average people. In spite of the simplicity and reasonableness of what he expounded, Locke conceded that most people would have to accept the truth because they were told to receive it.

Locke believed that he had consistently established his case by appeal to the clear witness of the Scriptures. In his attitude to the Bible, he both reflected the past and anticipated the future. He had grown up in a Puritan atmosphere, and he retained the characteristic Puritan reverence for the inspired word of God. He accepted the Bible as absolutely infallible. 'It has God for its author, salvation for its end, and truth without any mixture of error for its matter.' Yet Locke, unlike many Puritans, recognized that the authority of Scripture could not be equated with his own interpretation of its words. In this respect he represented an interesting transitional position. What the Bible says is decisive in any

[1] The phrase is Butler's—cf. *The Analogy*, I, iv. 4; I, v. 38; *Sermons*, I, 6; XI, 8; II, 15.
[2] Locke, *The Reasonableness of Christianity*, p. 285.

discussion, but we have to determine its precise meaning with care. Hence our use of the text must be discriminating as well as reverent. Here Locke introduced an exegetical principle of great importance. Like most controversialists of the period, he appealed to one part of the Bible as more authoritative than others, but he gave an illuminating reason for his choice. In the Gospels, he said, we have the key to the Divine purpose, and he dismissed the Epistles of the New Testament as of secondary value. The letters of St Paul are 'occasional' literature, written to meet a specific need at a particular time and place. As a result, they are only fragmentary statements of the truth. 'I do not deny, but the great doctrines of the Christian faith are dropt here and there, and scattered up and down in most of them. But 'tis not in the Epistles we are to learn what are the fundamental articles of the faith, where they are promiscuously, and without distinction, mixed up with other truths which were...only occasional. We shall find and discern those great and necessary points best in the preaching of our Saviour and the Apostles, to those who were yet strangers, and ignorant of the faith, to bring them in and convert them.'[1]

Underlying this distinction between the relative value of different parts of the Bible is a clear principle: it is 'the truth which is to be received and believed, and not scattered sentences in Scripture-language, accommodated to our notions and prejudices.'[2] So Locke outlined what he regarded as the proper method of Bible study, and it is sufficiently important to be stated in his own words. 'We must look into the drift of the discourse, observe the coherence and connection of the parts, and see how it is consistent with itself, and other parts of Scripture, if we will conceive it right. We must not cull out, as best suits our system, here and there

[1] Ibid. p. 295.   [2] Ibid. p. 291.

a period or a verse; as if they were all distinct and independent aphorisms.'[1] Locke was directly attacking the abuse of 'proof texts', but incidentally he anticipated a most important development in Biblical study. He affirmed that the Bible possesses unity, within which there is room for wide variety. By consciously setting various strata of the Bible at different levels and dealing with them as their inherent nature demanded, Locke approximated to 'the principle of the modern science of Biblical theology'.[2] Locke was apt to use his discovery in a haphazard and tendentious way, but that does not obscure the importance of what he did. As the seventeenth century was closing, he outlined an approach to the Bible which has become the basic presupposition of all recent historical criticism. At this point he parted company with his contemporaries, and anticipated the attitude of modern students of the Bible.

The sixteenth century had stated the Protestant doctrine of the Church, and had settled many of its practical implications. But in England certain issues remained to be decided, and in the period which followed the Restoration two of them in particular demanded attention—the relation of Church and State, and the status of religious minorities.

After the experiments of the Interregnum, most Englishmen were content to return to the Established Church as they had known it before the Civil War. Subsequent events proved, however, that a national church had definite disadvantages. When its titular head was a king like Charles II, the Church might find itself seriously embarrassed and even compromised, while James II's attempt to restore Romanism convinced his subjects that further safeguards were urgently needed. Locke was not content to consider merely the

[1] Locke, *The Reasonableness of Christianity*, p. 292.
[2] R. S. Franks, op. cit. vol. II, p. 164.

practical problems of an Established Church. In an early essay on the Roman commonwealth,[1] he discussed in detail the implications of a 'religious institution'. He set forth in characteristic terms the difficulties which arise when an established form of religion is committed to an elaborate doctrinal scheme. 'If schisms and heresies were traced up to their original causes, it would be found that they have sprung chiefly from the multiplying articles of faith, and narrowing the bottom of religion by clogging it with creeds, and catechisms and endless niceties about the essences, properties and attributes of God.'[2] This is an early but characteristic form of Locke's plea for a simplified religion, but from it he drew certain inferences regarding the authority a ruler may rightfully exercise. Since all men agree as to the 'common principles of religion', a lawgiver can legitimately require his subjects to accept them. If there is to be uniformity, however, he must not venture beyond an effort to enforce a belief in God and an acknowledgement of our duty 'to be innocent, good, and just'. This implies, of course, a large measure of toleration, but it also suggests certain principles which ought to govern the relation of Church and State. The civil authorities have a legitimate but limited measure of control; they must not exceed it, nor must they allow others to infringe their rights. Locke was emphatic that the power of the priesthood must be curbed. 'Priestcraft and tyranny', he said, 'go hand in hand.' Persecutions, he added, 'are generally made to gratify the pride, the ambition, or the interest of the clergy', and he noted with dismay the situation which prevailed throughout most of Europe in his own day. Locke's argument presupposes, then, that a government will be entitled to demand

---

[1] *Reflections Upon the Roman Commonwealth*; cf. Fox Bourne, op. cit. vol. I, pp. 149 f.   [2] Ibid. p. 149.

conformity to a simple form of religious belief, but will not undertake to force its subjects to accept any particular doctrinal system. It is the responsibility of the citizen to 'do his utmost to live up to the ideal of the Christian life as set forth in the Bible'; it is the duty of the State to make that possible. For an attempt to give practical expression to these views, it is necessary to look beyond England to the New World. The thought of American liberals like Madison and Jefferson bears clear traces of the influence of Locke; so does the constitution they helped to frame.[1]

Whenever Locke touched on the relation of Church and State he raised the question of religious toleration. Probably no other issue facing his contemporaries possessed for him a comparable importance. Toleration followed naturally both from his conception of the nature of knowledge and from his view of the true character of the Christian faith. Detailed consideration of this subject must be postponed until a later chapter, but any discussion of the significance of Locke would be sadly incomplete if it did not include at least a passing reference to the profound importance of his advocacy of liberty of conscience.

Locke spoke to a generation ready to receive precisely what he was prepared to say. The prestige of reason was already high, but he gave it a new status because he defined with a new precision its essential nature. He showed that religion, so often deflected from its proper course by irresponsible 'enthusiasm', was eminently reasonable and simple. To an age whose virtues were sober and pedestrian he preached the claims of a morality which was earnest even though it might appear prosaic. His utilitarianism could go

[1] Note Article VI of the Constitution of 1787, and the First Amendment, 1791. Cf. H. P. van Dusen in *Church and State in the Modern World* (New York, 1937), pp. 37–9.

to astonishing lengths,[1] but he rejected materialism as a creed incapable of explaining the mysteries of life. He understood Newtonian science and interpreted it to a period increasingly conscious of its importance. The general tone of his writings, said Professor Alexander, 'is that of equable common-sense, without emphasis, without enthusiasm, restrained in its judgment, careful of measure, never dull but reflecting evenly from a candid surface, modest when it is most original, because concerned with the faithful presentment of things, rather lambent than fiery, an inspired pedestrianism'.[2] To such a writer the end of the seventeenth century was ready to respond. But the praise of common sense is not the final word regarding Locke. With impressive consistency and selflessness he gave himself to the pursuit of truth, and this explains the peculiar dignity of his works. 'He was always, in the greatest and in the smallest affairs of human life, as well as in speculative opinions, disposed to follow reason, whosoever it were that suggested it; he being ever a faithful servant, I had almost said a slave, to truth; never abandoning her for anything else, and following her for her own sake purely.'[3]

[1] Cf. his attack on poetry in *Thoughts Concerning Education*: 'Methinks the parents should labour to have it [the poetic vein] stifled or suppressed as much as maybe; and I know not what reason a father can have to wish his son a poet, who does not desire to have him bid defiance to all other callings and business...for it is very seldom seen that anyone discovers mines of gold or silver in Parnassus. It is a pleasant air, but a barren soil; and there are very few instances of those who have added to their patrimony by anything they have reaped from thence.' The meagre royalties which Milton received for *Paradise Lost* would doubtless have seemed to Locke a conclusive reason why the poem should never have been written.

[2] S. Alexander, *Locke*, p. 23.

[3] Lady Masham to Jean Le Clerc, quoted by Fox Bourne as a motto, *Life of Locke*.

CHAPTER VII

JOHN TOLAND AND THE RISE OF DEISM

THE folly of James II made the Revolution of 1688 a religious event of the first importance. The threat of Romanism had been raised; it was met, and the Protestant faith held the field—apparently unchallenged. Even in the realm of theology the Revolution had significant results. It created conditions which made possible a critical examination of the form of belief which had so recently triumphed, and thereby it opened a new phase in the discussion of religious problems.

The controversy with Romanism, which had occupied so much time and attention, had worked itself out, and could largely be ignored for a long time to come. Toleration for Protestant dissenters virtually ended another debate which had raged intermittently for nearly a generation. The Protestant faith, though to all appearance firmly established, was not immune from criticism. It had defeated its foes, and now its own adherents were free in a new way to examine the presuppositions of their belief. 'The time was ripe', remarks Professor Sorley, 'for the discussion of the content and basis of Protestant theology.'[1] Moreover, the Revolution had given toleration the respectability which belongs to success. The idea was supported by the rapidly increasing authority of Locke; some might object and many might be dubious,[2] but the granting of toleration meant that the bounds of

[1] W. R. Sorley, *History of English Philosophy* (Cambridge, 1920), p. 145.

[2] Cf. *The Letters of Humphrey Prideaux...to John Ellis...1674–1722* (Camden Society, 1875), p. 154; note also Toland, *Christianity Not Mysterious*, p. 113.

permissible discussion had been vastly enlarged. At the moment when men were ready to examine the tenets of Protestantism, they found themselves free to do so. One result was the great Trinitarian controversy; another was the rise of Deism.

Deism was not, strictly speaking, a new phenomenon. Lord Herbert of Cherbury had advanced many of the ideas which became characteristic of the school, and early in the eighteenth century his connexion with the movement was explicitly recognized.[1] His five fundamental religious truths[2] served as the foundation of Charles Blount's religion of reason, and so passed directly into the antecedents of Deism. Blount defended the merits of natural religion, and even emphasized the advantages of the various heathen faiths.[3] His translation of the *Life of Apollonius of Tyana* (1680) gave him a chance to suggest by means of sneers and innuendoes that the miracles of Christ were really very much the same as the impostures of Apollonius. But the implied attack on Christ's person was actually much less significant than the indications scattered throughout his writings, that religion was only an expression of the baseness and credulity of man.

In himself, Blount was not a person of much importance, but he is worth noting because he put in writing thoughts which many of his contemporaries were content to leave as spoken words. Blount expressed what was in many minds— otherwise Charles Leslie would never have attacked him as

[1] Cf. Halyburton, *Natural Religion Insufficient* (1714).

[2] Lord Herbert's five fundamental truths were: (1) that God exists; (2) that it is a duty to worship Him; (3) that the practice of virtue is the true mode of doing Him honour; (4) that man is under the obligation to repent of his sins; (5) that there will be rewards and punishments after death.

[3] Blount, *Anima Mundi* (1679), passim.

he did. His *Short and Easy Method With the Deists* is important because, in spite of its brevity and ease, it was necessary at all. The kind of argument Leslie used is most effective when there is no need to state it. 'To defend the undeniable is a grave admission that denial has touched us.'[1]

Blount opened the attack on revelation, but the dangerous fact was that many Englishmen were living 'as if God were dead'.[2] This was a much more serious threat to religion than any amount of theoretical infidelity. The members of the court might go to chapel at Whitehall or St James', but the tenor of their lives defied the substance of everything they heard when they were there. To the sympathy of this element in society anyone attacking traditionalism in religion could confidently appeal. In addition there were many who had no share in the excesses of high society but who sat equally light to the claims of religion. The gentleman of fashion was defined by Shaftesbury as a person 'to whom a natural good genius or the force of a good education has given a sense of what is naturally graceful and becoming'. The wits of the coffee houses were too much addicted to banter to consider seriously the essentials—let alone the intricacies—of religion.[3] Their presence encouraged a new kind of discussion and determined the manner in which it should be conducted.

As the century ended, public opinion was more and more directed and controlled by the men of wit and fashion. The tyranny of the coffee house was increasing, and of necessity the manner of religious debate changed. The weighty armour which controversialists had formerly carried

[1] John Oman, *The Problem of Faith and Freedom*, p. 95.
[2] Ibid. p. 91.
[3] Cf. *The Letters of Humphrey Prideaux*...(letter written in 1693), p. 162.

might still be useful in some quarters, but the refinements of patristic learning were lost on the men who were now the arbiters of taste. They considered themselves competent to judge of any matter worthy of an intelligent man's attention, but they expected that it would be presented in such a way that any intelligent man could understand it. The same canons which now ruled in the pulpit held good in the press. Those who discussed religion in books and pamphlets had to be as simple and direct as Tillotson had been in his sermons. The infinite elaboration which had once been customary was regarded now as a conspiracy to forestall the exercise of reason and so to leave men's minds enchained in superstition. This, as we shall see, had important consequences in determining the character of the deistic controversy.

By the end of the century, public opinion was ready to consider seriously the problems which the Deists raised. Lord Herbert of Cherbury had indicated the approach to religion which the Deists developed. Thomas Hobbes and the Cambridge Platonists had in various ways helped to focus men's attention on the demands of rational theology. Controversy could now be carried on with a freedom hitherto scarcely possible, and men were ready to discuss in simple and intelligible terms the significance of the Protestant faith. Blount had shown the measure of sympathy which views like those of Deism could command, but he was too isolated and too erratic to be more than the forerunner of the school.

In 1696 John Toland published anonymously his *Christianity Not Mysterious*. With the appearance of this little book the deistic controversy began in earnest. Toland was not a great writer, and in many ways his work was slight enough, but the charged state of the intellectual atmosphere made it profoundly important. It created an astonishing degree of consternation, and the civil power was summoned to deal with so dangerous a book.[1]

Behind Toland's book contemporaries sensed the rapidly increasing authority of John Locke. Toland, indeed, did not mention Locke by name, and never appealed directly to his writings, but the connexion was too obvious to be missed. Locke, of course, was not responsible for the inferences which the Deists drew from his work; indeed, he explicitly and emphatically repudiated them, but the fact remains that Locke had already indicated the issues with which controversialists were to be concerned for many a day to come. His writings had this effect at least, that they firmly and irrevocably placed all discussion in the court of reason,[2] and *Christianity Not Mysterious* was important because it professed to apply precisely those principles which Locke had outlined. In the first section of his book, Toland discussed the character of reason, and his dependence on Locke is too obvious for anyone to miss. The point from which his whole argument proceeds is the view that knowledge consists in the agreement of ideas. When discussing the four means of knowledge available to us, he gives pride of place to the experience of the senses and the experience of the mind; the first corresponds exactly to Locke's sensation, the second to Locke's reflexion. In many places the very words he uses are the words of Locke. When he contrasts the 'plain, convincing instructions of Christ' with 'the intricate, ineffective declamations of the scribe'[3] he might easily be quoting from *The Reasonableness of Christianity*. His appeal

[1] *Christianity Not Mysterious* was presented as a nuisance by the grand jury of Middlesex, and was ordered to be burnt by the parliament of Ireland. Robert South loudly applauded the action of the Irish legislators.

[2] Cf. Mark Pattison, *Essays*, vol. II, p. 45.

[3] Toland, *Christianity Not Mysterious*, p. xxi.

to 'the simplicity of truth'[1] is worthy of Locke himself. More important than verbal echoes is the similarity which links his conceptions to those of Locke. In dealing with revelation he is as closely indebted to Locke as when he is discussing the character of reason.

At the same time, it is quite possible to exaggerate the significance of this dependence. Toland was manifestly inspired by Locke, but he was not subservient to him. He was more aggressive in applying his principles, and he carried the discussion much further than Locke. Whereas Locke was content to show that Christianity is reasonable, Toland proved that nothing contrary to reason and nothing above it can be a part of Christian doctrine. Even the phrasing of his title[2] indicates the kind of inference he drew from Locke's views. 'Reasonable' now means 'not mysterious'; anything that 'can be properly called a mystery' is excluded. It is possible, moreover, to exaggerate the degree to which the Deists as a whole were the disciples of Locke. They used his phrases and certain of his conceptions, they took advantage of his authority to gain a hearing for their views, but they did not seriously attempt to develop his philosophical position.[3] The Deists were not primarily philosophers at all, and, in so far as they were, their fundamental assumptions were apparently closer to those of Spinoza than to those of

[1] Ibid. p. 54.

[2] *Christianity Not Mysterious, or a Treatise Shewing That There is Nothing in the Gospel Contrary to Reason, nor Above it; and that no Christian Doctrine can be properly called a Mystery.*

Cf. F. R. Tennant, *Miracle* (Cambridge, 1925), p. 7. As Dr Tennant points out, the Deists were not philosophical Deists at all. Indeed, the view of the relation of God to the world maintained by philosophical Deism was one which the English Deists emphatically repudiated, and which, in common with their more orthodox contemporaries, they denounced as atheism. Cf. Bentley's definition of Deism, *Confutation of Atheism*, p. 7.

Locke. Consequently, though the debt they owed to Locke is extensive, it is comparatively superficial. They appealed to him because he had done more than anyone else to establish the current 'climate of opinion'. He had exalted reason, and it was to reason that they appealed, but they were not interested in nor concerned with Locke's basic presuppositions.

In the preface to *Christianity Not Mysterious*, Toland clearly indicated the method he proposed to follow. 'I prove first', he said, 'that the true religion must necessarily be reasonable and intelligible. Next I show that these requisite conditions are found in Christianity. But seeing a man of good parts and knowledge may easily frame a clear and coherent system, I demonstrate, thirdly that the Christian religion was not formed after such a manner, but was divinely revealed from Heaven.'[1] In this brief statement, Toland defined both his position and the way in which he intended to unfold it. The second and third parts of his scheme he deferred to subsequent works, but, though these were never written, it is easy enough to supply, from what he actually completed, the unfinished parts. Probably the second of his three projected works was never written because Toland realized that the first had made it superfluous. Even the contents of the third can be conjectured without difficulty. But more important than Toland's specific intentions or his failure to achieve them is the manner of approach which marks his work. It is here that he makes a genuine contribution and registers an important change. His method is that which, with slight variations, all the Deists adopted. It is true that many of his immediate successors would have allowed no place for the third part of Toland's scheme, but in all essential respects his method is theirs, and this

[1] Toland, op. cit. Preface, p. xxvii.

represents a decisive break with the traditions of theological controversy. Much of the literature of seventeenth-century debate is now almost unreadable. The solemn parade of authorities, the meticulous care with which every sentence, almost every clause, of an adversary's work is refuted, reflects a temper wholly different from that of the modern age. In Toland, however, both the method and the outlook are such as 'distinguish modernity from nearer antiquity'.[1] You may agree with him or not, but at least you can read him with relative ease.

The outline and argument of *Christianity Not Mysterious* are comparatively simple. Here, again, a comparison with one of Andrewes' sermons shows how far religious discussion had moved since the beginning of the century. It was Toland's aim to show that Christianity conforms in all respects to the canons of reason. In the first section of the book he defined reason, and in the second he proved that the doctrines of the Gospel are not contrary to it. Finally, he carried the discussion a stage further by demonstrating that there is nothing mysterious, or above reason, in Christianity.

Reason is manifestly the crucial term in the discussion, and Toland, as we have seen, approached it in much the same way as Locke. He equated it with demonstration, and described it as 'that faculty of the soul which discovers the certitude of anything dubious or obscure, by comparing it with something evidently known'.[2] Reason is 'the only foundation of all certitude'; 'nothing revealed, whether as to its manner or existence, is more exempt from its disquisitions, than the ordinary phenomena of Nature'.[3] The material with which reason deals comes to us from ex-

---

[1] F. R. Tennant, *Miracle*, p. 96.
[2] Toland, op. cit. p. 12.   [3] Ibid. p. 6.

perience or authority, and under the latter Toland carefully reserved a place for 'divine authority or divine revelation'.[1] But even so he allowed no invasion of the domain of reason. In His wisdom God has made all things, even the truths He discloses, answerable to reason. He 'who had enabled us to perceive things and form judgments of them, has also endued us with the power of suspending our judgments about whatever is uncertain, and of never assenting but to clear perceptions'. He has provided 'that we should discern and embrace the truth, by taking it out of our power to dissent from an evident proposition'.[2] Since, then, God has made it possible for us 'to bow before the light and majesty of evidence',[3] all our false notions are due to 'our own anticipation and inattention'. If we destroy ourselves, the fault is wholly ours. There remains, of course, the disconcerting fact that people seem to choose the wrong rather than the right and to prefer falsehood to truth. But this was no problem to Toland. The explanation was that 'the evident propositions' have not been made evident; if others do not see the cogency of our argument, it is because, through the use of ill-digested material, we have failed to make its nature clear.[4]

In connexion with Toland's use of reason, three comments will suffice. It was manifestly effective, because it determined one of the salient features of the deistic controversy. It was successful because it appealed to the prevailing standard of judgement, and took advantage of the immense prestige Locke had recently conferred on reason. In the second place, Toland's use of the term is open to the criticism which applies to all the chief deistic writers. They regarded the human reason as a static and infallible faculty,

[1] Toland, op. cit. pp. 14f.   [2] Ibid. p. 20.
[3] Ibid. p. 21.   [4] Ibid. pp. 21–2.

possessed by the human mind from the very first.[1] Finally, the importance of Toland's position is due to the results of his insistence on reason as the sole instrument for acquiring and judging truth. This had far-reaching consequences in the theology of the eighteenth century.

Granted the authority of reason, it was a matter of no slight importance to determine the nature and authority of revelation. To Toland its rôle was perfectly clear; to him it was no more than a 'means of information'.[2] He conceded that it possesses a high degree of authority, since 'it is the manifestation of truth by truth itself, to whom it is impossible to lie'.[3] But it is both dangerous and useless if once allowed to escape into the realm of the irrational. It has often been advanced as though it had 'a right of silencing or extinguishing reason'.[4] Actually anything a person believes must be within the bounds of reason and possibility; 'I say possibility,' added Toland, 'for omnipotence itself can do no more'.[5] If we do not recognize the authority of reason, even divine revelation could not save us from 'the impostures and traditions of men'.[6] Anything, therefore, that is revealed, whether by God or men, must be both intelligible and possible, and he regarded divine revelation as notably distinguishable by its greater certainty. Men might deceive us; God will not. 'We are then to expect the same degree of perspicuity from God as from men, though more of certitude from the first than from the last.'[7] But even God could not communicate with men 'if what he said did not agree with their common notions'.[8]

[1] Cf. F. R. Tennant, *Philosophical Theology*, vol. II (Cambridge, 1930), p. 224.
[2] Toland, op. cit. p. 38.   [3] Ibid. p. 14.
[4] Ibid. p. 37.   [5] Ibid. p. 39.
[6] Ibid. p. 41.   [7] Ibid. p. 43.
[8] Ibid. p. 133.

So, while Toland maintained revelation as a useful term in the religious vocabulary, he gave it a meaning quite different from that assigned to it by most of his contemporaries. Unlike the later Deists, he neither denied nor disparaged revelation, but he subtly altered its significance, and his position, if pressed to its logical conclusion, would have rendered revelation largely superfluous. At times, indeed, he himself suggested as much. He was not willing to decide the delicate question of precedence between these two disputed terms; 'in a word, I see no need of comparison in this case, for reason is not less from God than revelation; 'tis the candle, the guide, the judge he has lodged within every man that cometh into the world'.[1] It was only a short step to assign to reason, as some of his successors did, all the functions of revelation.

It was Toland's principal purpose, if we may judge by the disposition of his material, to prove that nothing mysterious had any rightful place in Christianity. He appealed to the New Testament to show that the word is properly used only of things which were once obscure or hidden, but from which 'the veil is actually taken away'.[2] 'Doctrines so revealed cannot now be properly called mysteries.'[3] It is true that our knowledge is limited at many points; we know no more of bodies than is useful or necessary, but we can claim to 'comprehend anything when its chief properties and their several uses are known to us'.[4] Many Christian doctrines, even those that seem abstruse, we can explain as 'familiarly' as we do natural things. Neither God nor eternity is a mystery. By 'God' we understand His attributes and properties, which we know; if we are ignorant of His essence, we are no wiser as regards any of His creatures. So Toland

[1] Toland, op. cit. p. 146. [2] Ibid. p. 73.
[3] Ibid. p. 74. [4] Ibid. p. 77.

returned to the confident affirmation that in the Christian Scriptures the word 'mystery' is used 'not from any present inconceivableness or obscurity, but with respect to what they were before this revelation'.[1]

Around 'reason', 'revelation', and 'mystery' Toland arranged practically all he had to say. Much of it was neither very original nor very profound, but nearly all his principal points represented a departure from what had been generally characteristic of seventeenth-century theology. Moreover, at many incidental points his position is significant in view of subsequent developments.

Deism ultimately became a strong attack on orthodox Christianity, but Toland wrote as a professed believer in the Protestant faith and as a loyal member of the Church of England. He was anxious, of course, to free it from superstitious accretions, but throughout he took its essential validity for granted. In this Toland represented an interesting development. As the seventeenth century ended, the impetus to theological debate came from within the Church, but not from among the professed theologians.[2] Locke is a notable instance of the layman's interest in religious discussion, and so, in spite of his diffidence in publishing, is Newton. Eventually the lay contributions to theology became bitter and destructive, but to the end of the seventeenth century the motive was an earnest desire to cleanse Christianity and restore it to its primitive simplicity. In this respect Toland was wholly characteristic of his times. He was not disguising bad principles beneath fair professions. 'I write with all the sincerity and simplicity imaginable', he said in the preface to his work,[3] and he

---

[1] Ibid. p. 91.
[2] Cf. W. R. Sorley, op. cit. p. 145.
[3] Toland, op. cit. p. x.

claimed the freedom and assurance of those who defend or illustrate the truth.[1] At the end he returned to the same theme—'I have undertaken to shew others what I'm fully convinced of myself.'[2]

Toland wrote as a member of the Christian community, but he never disguised his contempt of the constituted leaders of the Church. He was not yet a critic from without, but he anticipated the new day in the sharpness and severity of his attacks on theologians and ecclesiastics. This was a very different note from that struck by Izaak Walton or John Evelyn. Here we have theology by a layman who frankly repudiated the guidance of the leaders of the Church. He accused those who normally wrote theology of a bigoted attachment to the externals of the faith.[3] They treated mere sounds 'as if they were the essence of true religion, but these empty words have been invented by some leading men to make plain things obscure, and not seldom to cover their own ignorance'. Even Scripture was wrested from its true meaning to support their 'scholastic jargon'.[4] The whole character of theological learning cried out for reform. 'But the common method of teaching and supporting this mystery of iniquity is still more intolerable. How many voluminous systems, infinitely more difficult than the Scriptures, must be read with great attention by him that would be master of the present theology? What prodigious number of barbarous words (mysterious no doubt), what tedious and immethodical directions, what ridiculous and discrepant interpretations must you patiently learn and observe, before you can begin to understand a professor of that faculty?'[5] The obscurantism of 'the numerous partisans of error' would have been

[1] Toland, op. cit. p. i.   [2] Ibid. p. 174.
[3] Ibid. p. vi.   [4] Ibid. pp. xi–xii.
[5] Ibid. p. xxiv.

serious enough in itself, but the motive behind it, Toland hinted, was love of gain.[1] The leaders would not see the light lest the truth might prove too costly in its demands.

The authorities of the past commanded no more respect from Toland than those of the present. To 'the plain paths of reason' he contrasted the 'impenetrable labyrinths of the Fathers'.[2] Even when he proved that the Fathers were on his side, he dismissed them with a contemptuous reference to their negligible weight in any modern discussion. This depreciation of authority, though by no means original, is important in more respects than one. It is only necessary to read the theology of the seventeenth century to realize the weight which a quotation from the classics of the Fathers carried. The kind of protest which Toland voiced was necessary if discussion was ever to emerge from the undergrowth of pedantry and learning. Toland was not the first to object, nor was he alone. Tillotson's sermons indicate the new way in which the discussion of religion was intended to persuade rather than overawe the hearer.[3] The authority of those addressed had displaced the authority of those to whom appeal was made. The cult of reason was definitely reacting on the value attached to the opinions of the past. In many ways this was wholly salutary; it helped to lift the heavy hand of a tradition which was often largely lifeless. At the end of the century the Deists recapitulated one of the most significant developments of their age. All the progressive movements of the previous generation had insisted that religious thought must be freed from an authoritative scholasticism; the Deists amplified and emphasized the arguments which others had set forth. This explains also

---

[1] Ibid. p. vii.   [2] Ibid. p. xxiii.
[3] Cf. Leslie Stephen, *English Literature and Society in the Eighteenth Century*, p. 50.

their adoption of the method of doubt in their search for intellectual certainty; it was their substitute for 'the arrogance of groundless opinion'. But for our purposes the protest against authority is also important as an illustration of one of the marked limitations of the Deists. They belonged to an age which had seen historical interest revive but which had as yet acquired no historical outlook. They were naïvely unconscious of any progress in the past, and as a result they could neither understand the character of other ages nor appreciate their records. They judged the writings of other days by the standards of their own time, or else compared them with a wholly mythical picture of a vanished golden age. Toland was incapable of appreciating the Fathers whom he denounced because he was unable to visualize the times in which they lived.

One by one Toland demolished the concepts to which his opponents usually appealed. He would give no special deference to authorities, either living or dead, and revelation became the appeal of God to man's reason. In the same drastic way he dealt with another term which had been much beloved by seventeenth-century writers. Faith was utterly dethroned from the high position assigned it by Puritan and Anglican alike. As the eighteenth century dawned it had become nothing more 'than a firm persuasion built upon substantial reasons'.[1] In Abraham's willingness to offer up Isaac we are confronted with an example of 'very strict reasoning from experience, from the possibility of the thing, and from the power, justice, and immutability of him that promised it'. This is a long step from the mentality of the middle years of the seventeenth century.

Miracle, like revelation, eventually became one of the storm centres of the deistic controversy. Toland did not

[1] Toland, op. cit. p. 138.

represent the developed position of his school, but in important respects he anticipated its conclusions. He first introduced the subject while proving the unalterably rational character of Christianity. Its essentially intelligible nature was proved by 'the miracles, method and style of the New Testament'.[1] If the appeal of Christ had not been to men's understanding, His miracles would have served no useful purpose; they act, indeed, as safeguards against any demand that we should believe 'revealed nonsense'.[2] At the same time, Toland admitted that miracles are often the final refuge of the advocates of mystery. Though a miracle is 'some action exceeding all human power and which the laws of nature cannot perform by the ordinary powers', he maintained rigorously that anything 'contrary to reason cannot be a miracle'.[3] It is clear where this will ultimately lead. When he demanded that a miracle 'must be something in itself intelligible and possible'[4] he was opening the way for the suggestion that miracles, as usually defined, were neither the one nor the other. This inference was promptly drawn, and the characteristic of most of the deistic writers is the supercilious attitude they adopted whenever miracles were mentioned. They did not deny on *a priori* grounds the possibility of miracles; they even admitted that for the vulgar they might serve a useful apologetic purpose. But when religion consisted in the performance of duties, miracles were utterly superfluous. This attitude, of course, was never adopted by the average English writer on religion, but in part it reflected, and in part it created, a different approach to the whole question. Miracle, as Toland quite justly pointed out, had been the last court of appeal for many seventeenth-century writers. In the eighteenth century it

[1] Ibid. p. 46. [2] Ibid. p. 49.
[3] Ibid. p. 150. [4] Ibid. p. 152.

remained, with prophecy, a favourite defence of the validity
of revelation, but the deistic protest had had its effect.
Miracle was treated in a more guarded and cautious fashion,
and its place in a rational system of belief was constantly
emphasized.

Parallel to the depreciation of miracles was the repudiation
of superstition. The possibility of miracle in an ordered
world was carefully limited to occasions when there was
'some weighty design becoming the divine wisdom and
majesty'. This was the surest safeguard against superstitious
tales, stories of the activities of witches, and accounts of the
miracles performed by the devil. There were multitudes of
such stories current in all parts of the English countryside,
and they were seen as an infallible measure of the backward
—even barbarous—condition of the people. Here again
Toland reflected a change which was making steady headway at the end of the seventeenth century. Only a few years
before, a fellow of the Royal Society like Glanvill could
assiduously gather tales of tapping devils in the belief that
he was undergirding the cause of true religion. Henry More,
a distinguished philosopher and a Cambridge don, regarded
a belief in witches and evil spirits as a defence against the
advance of atheism. Yet throughout the period the fear of
witchcraft was steadily declining. The number of prosecu-
tions fell off, and by the end of the century trials for witchcraft had virtually ceased.[1] In this respect Toland spoke for
the new day. It was a task worthy of an apostle, he said, 'to
convince the mind, to dispel ignorance, to eradicate superstition, to propagate truth and reformation of manners'.[2]

No study of changes of thought would be complete if

[1] W. Notestein, *History of Witchcraft in England from 1558 to 1718*
(1911), pp. 282f.
[2] Toland, op. cit. p. 55.

it ignored the attitude men adopted toward the Christian Scriptures. Throughout the seventeenth century the authority of the Bible had been paramount. The Deists never went so far as to question the special place it occupied in all religious discussion, but already the attitude was changing. The old veneration had disappeared. Toland assumed the divinity of the New Testament,[1] and appealed to it constantly, but he insisted that its authority, like that of all revelation, must be tested by reason. The proof of the divinity of Scripture depended on reason, for 'if the clear light of the one be anyway contradicted, how shall we be convinced of the infallibility of the other?'[2] Toland realized that this was a marked departure from accepted standards. It was common enough in the seventeenth century to make Scripture and reason appear contradictory, but the belief of those who did so, said Toland, was 'at the mercy of every gust of doctrine.... To believe the divinity of Scripture or the sense of any passage thereof, without rational proofs and an evident consistency, is a blameable credulity and a temerarious opinion, ordinarily maintained out of a gainful prospect.'[3] This explains Toland's consistent appeal to the original meaning of the New Testament. His lack of historical perspective meant that he actually appealed, not to the intent of the first-century writers, but to the reason of his own day. But though the method might not achieve its desired results, the change of attitude is too important to ignore.

Christianity Not Mysterious appeared in 1696. A hundred years later Edmund Burke could dismiss the Deists as a school of writers wholly ignored and largely forgotten. For a short time they profoundly affected English religious

[1] Ibid. p. xxvi.   [2] Ibid. p. 31.
[3] Ibid. p. 36.

thought, and then disappeared into obscurity. From Toland's book—the first important contribution to the main controversy—it is easy to detect some of the reasons why their influence was so ephemeral. There are faults of taste and good feeling so gross as to force themselves inescapably upon the reader's notice. The egotistical note is too prominent—as in the self-conscious posturing as a lone champion of light against obscurantist hordes, or in the touch of bravado with which Toland classes himself with St Paul as one who does not 'value this cheap and ridiculous nickname of heretic'.[1] As Sir Leslie Stephen pointed out, Toland often introduced new arguments without recognizing the conclusions to which ultimately they tended;[2] he lacked the insight or the courage to press his points to their logical conclusion. He hinted, of course, that there were penalties for those too free in their speculations about truth, but he also claimed to be above considerations of mere prudence. It is only fair to remember, however, that if he failed to see where the discussion would eventually lead, he could claim in this the company of many men, before this time and after, who were both abler and wiser than himself. Mark Pattison pointed out a more serious defect when he insisted on the religious shortcomings of the Deists. They were the advocates, he said, of a thin creed, an intellectualism devoid of all true religious fervour. They stood aloof from any missionary venture, they brought forth no practical fruits.[3] This is a severe indictment, but sometimes you feel that when Toland proves his point it is only because he has ignored the true character of religious experience.[4] Though

[1] Toland, op. cit. p. 174.
[2] Leslie Stephen, *English Thought in the Eighteenth Century* (1876), vol. II, p. 110.
[3] Mark Pattison, *Essays*, vol. II, pp. 84f.
[4] Cf. John Oman, *The Problem of Faith and Freedom*, p. 108.

he wrote about the Christian religion, he maintained, as did the Deists generally, a consistent silence regarding its Founder. He was apparently unconscious of the omission, and unaware of its possibly damaging results. The serious aspects of man's plight wholly escaped him, and his treatment of sin was little short of trivial. If a drunkard says 'I cannot give over drinking', he really means, remarked Toland, 'I will not'. To overcome our human frailties we need only acknowledge them, and amendment of life is simple enough to those who are not self-deceived.[1] This is indeed to 'heal the hurt of my people slightly'.

When to these defects we add the obsolete presuppositions the Deists accepted and the crude learning they displayed, it is not surprising that they have been neglected by posterity. The neglect, says Dr Tennant, is undeserved. For all their shortcomings, these men, he claims, represent 'the beginning of modernity in English theology'.[2] They advocated a natural theology which may be open to criticism at many points, but they realized that if revelation were wholly divorced from an underlying natural religion it would run the risk of degenerating into superstition. For all the defects of their conception of reason, they saw that in the pursuit of truth it is a guide we cannot ignore, for even God is powerless to speak to us if we forsake its leading. Their positive contributions to religious thought were comparatively few, and their writings soon forgotten, but they helped to create a new outlook which had important consequences in the eighteenth century, and whose effects, for good and ill, are not exhausted even yet.

[1] Toland, op. cit. pp. 59, 62.
[2] Tennant, *Miracle*, p. 96.

CHAPTER VIII

THE CHURCH AND THE CIVIL POWER

WHEN the Restoration brought back old forms of government in Church and State, most Englishmen unquestionably hoped that in the future any serious changes would be superfluous. They believed that the new day demanded an effort to confirm and strengthen the institutions which had so recently been shaken, and they looked forward to a period which might be constructive in aim but would certainly be conservative in temper. But in one sphere after another the expectations of thoughtful men proved false. The changes which took place might not be dramatic or spectacular—even the political revolution which ended the period was singularly orderly in character—but they were often far-reaching in their effects, and in large part the fascination of Restoration history lies in the struggle between the old forms men desired to keep and the new forms they were forced to accept.

In no region did change seem more unlikely than in the realm of political theory. The recent civil turmoil reinforced the general desire for stability; men wanted a theory of sovereignty which would fortify the re-established form of government. But in the seventeenth century political thought was still largely influenced by theology. The arguments which theorists used were related at every point to religious issues; they were enforced by appeals to Scripture; if challenged, it was in the name of a more satisfactory understanding of the Bible.

This general tendency was accentuated by the nature of

the theory which found special favour in the generation
following the Restoration. The belief that kings ruled by
divine right was an ancient theory; the events of the first half
of the seventeenth century had given it a new importance;
with the return of Charles II it came back with vastly
enhanced authority. For nearly thirty years it was the view
expounded by both political theorists and theologians. With
the fall of James II it was overthrown, completely and for
ever. Few changes in religious thought were more decisive
in character.

The antecedents of the theory of divine right reach back
into the Middle Ages. When first developed, the theory was
necessary as a defence against the encroachments of an
aggressive papacy, and it played a notable part in the struggle
to establish the independence of national sovereignties. 'The
doctrine was an essential element in the struggle against the
political claims of the papacy',[1] and it further proved its
usefulness in helping to make possible the English Reformation. It was only natural, therefore, that the leaders of the
Elizabethan Church should be at pains to elaborate the
theory and indicate its logical consequences. The obvious
deduction to be drawn from the divine right of kings was
the subject's duty of giving unquestioning and unlimited
obedience. This was, of course, more than simply a natural
inference suggested by reason; it was a defence against what
seemed the dangerously democratic tendencies which were
already gaining ground, and which could also quote Scripture for their purpose. The necessity of non-resistance to
constituted authority early became a fixed element in the
teaching of the English Reformers. A rebel, it appeared,
'was worse than the worst prince, and rebellion worse than

[1] J. N. Figgis, *The Divine Right of Kings* (Cambridge, 1914; 2nd ed.),
p. 15.

the worst government of the worst prince'.[1] This was an emphasis which King James I both welcomed and amplified. In a series of works—*Basilikon Doron*, *The True Law of Free Monarchies*, *The Duty of a King in His Royal Office*—he embroidered with wearisome iteration his favourite theme of the divine character of monarchy. 'The state of monarchy', he declared, 'is the supremest thing upon earth, for Kings are not only God's lieutenants upon earth, and sit upon God's throne, but even by God himself they are called Gods....God hath power to create or destroy, make or unmake at his pleasure, to give life or send death, to judge all, and to be judged nor accomptable to none: to raise low things, and to make high things low at his pleasure, and to God are both soul and body due. And the like power have Kings.'[2] This was manifestly doctrine which kings might well delight to expound, but it was also a claim which clerics were ready to echo. The divine right of kings had proved effective as a defence against the pretensions of Papists and Puritans alike, and Monarchy and Church made common cause against both.[3] In the canons of 1604 and 1640 the origins of society are established in God, and those who resist authority are declared to receive to themselves damnation.

[1] From the homily on Obedience, *Second Book of Homilies*, issued by the Queen's authority in 1563.

[2] *The Duty of a King in His Royal Office*. This work is a revision of the second part of *Basilikon Doron*, and appeared in 1642. [Quoted by L. M. Hawkins, *Allegiance in Church and State* (London, 1928), p. 4.]

[3] Note the way in which this twofold antipathy remained a constant factor in the discussion of the divine right of kings. Cf. Filmer, *Patriarcha* (edition of 1884), p. 11: 'This tenet [that man is naturally endowed with freedom] was first hatched in the schools, and hath been fostered by all succeeding Papists for good divinity. The divines, also, of the Reformed Churches have entertained it....It contradicts the doctrine and history of the Holy Scriptures, the constant practice of all ancient monarchies, and the very principles of the law of nature.'

But the doctrine, though embellished by churchmen and elaborated with delight by kings, was not widely held among the people. The story of the struggle between Charles I and his parliaments makes it perfectly clear that many even of the royalists would not accept the theological arguments with which bishops might defend the royal supremacy. Strafford, as firmly convinced as anyone that the king's authority must be strengthened, founded his case on considerations of a much less theoretical nature. The opponents of the king, meanwhile, apppealed to precedent and law in a way which really evaded the crucial question of the ultimate source of sovereignty. The struggle between king and parliament might for the present leave the theoretical problem unsolved, but in the end it decided the issue in its own way. At the beginning of the conflict many royalists might dissent from the theories of absolute sovereignty advanced by the king and his immediate advisers. The overthrow of the royal cause, however, brought about an increasingly close identification between the support of monarchy and the acceptance of the doctrine of divine right. The results of challenging the king's authority appeared so serious that the claims of passive obedience acquired a wholly new insistence. More and more the opponents of Cromwell found themselves committed to the doctrine of non-resistance to hereditary and legitimate rulers, and this in turn was only a logical inference from that conception of royal rights which throughout the Interregnum steadily gained ground among those who opposed Cromwell's 'tyranny'.

The fear of anarchy and the desire to curb social unrest became complementary manifestations of a single deep-seated concern. The dread of civil turmoil was perhaps the most conspicuous legacy which the Civil War bequeathed to English life, but it is important to remember that at every turn religious motives supported political apprehensions.[1] When the Restoration finally brought back the old forms of government, leaders both in Church and State were in complete agreement as to the theological basis on which their views of monarchy should rest. Before the wars, the clergy had been prepared to support a view of kingship which many even of the king's supporters viewed with grave distrust; now they all stood on common ground. In a day when men dreaded chaos beyond all else, the divine right of kings had an immediate practical bearing on political issues.

The theory had played an important part in bringing back King Charles II to his father's throne, and its results quickly became apparent in the legislation of the new reign. The prevailing interpretation of monarchy in large part explains the fear of and antipathy to the Nonconformists: these were the men who had conceived rebellion in their hearts and had

---

[1] For an expression of the views of the great majority of the clergy at a time when the struggle between king and parliament was manifestly moving toward a crisis, cf. Cardwell, *Synodalia*, vol. 1, p. 389: 'The most high and sacred order of kings is of Divine Right, being the ordinance of God Himself, founded in the prime laws of nature, and clearly established by express texts both of the Old and New Testaments. A supreme power is given to this most excellent order by God Himself in Scripture, which is, that kings should rule and command in their several dominions all persons of what rank or estate soever, whether ecclesiastical or civil....For any person or persons to set up, maintain or avow in any their said realms or territories respectively, under any pretence whatsoever, any independent coactive power, either papal or popular, (whether directly or indirectly,) is to undermine their great royal office, and cunningly to overthrow that most sacred ordinance which God Himself hath established; and so is treasonable against God as well as against the king. For subjects to bear arms against their kings, offensive or defensive, upon any pretence whatsoever, is at least to resist the powers which are ordained of God; and though they do not invade, but only resist, yet S. Paul tells them plainly they shall receive to themselves damnation.'

been guilty of the hideous crime of regicide.[1] It explains the determination to force on those who in all other respects were loyal citizens an explicit repudiation of the Covenant and of the right, under any circumstances whatsoever, to resist authority. It culminated in the Clarendon Code, and inspired the declaration which the Act of Uniformity required of all schoolmasters: 'I A.B. do declare that it is not lawful upon any pretence whatsoever to take arms against the King, and that I do abhor that traitorous position of taking arms by his authority against his person or against those that are commissioned by him.'[2]

In the first flush of triumph, churchmen were not content that their views should find expression in the laws of the land. With wearisome monotony they embellished their favourite theme in books, pamphlets and sermons. Even though their view had gained complete ascendancy, they considered it their duty to confirm their people in unquestioning acceptance of the fullness of the king's authority and the limitless extent of the subject's obedience. The revised Prayer Book, with its commemoration of the death of the late king and of the restoration of his son, provided added pretexts for preaching passive obedience, and each year on 30 January and 29 May 'the pulpits rang with the revived tenets of divine indefeasible hereditary right, of passive obedience, and of the sinfulness of rebellion'.[3] Such themes were almost mandatory on the State holy days, but they were

[1] Note Seth Ward's conviction that the late rebellion had been the occasion for God to show miraculously His great mercy in the restoration of the legitimate ruler: '...but the Lord liveth, which hath delivered us from the tyranny and bloody rage of the wild fanatical enthusiasts'. *Against Resistance of Lawful Powers* (1661), pp. 37–8.

[2] The Act of Uniformity, 14 Car. II, c. 4.

[3] Norman Sykes, *Church and State in England in the Eighteenth Century* (Cambridge, 1934), p. 23.

common enough at other times as well. Robert South, perhaps the most popular preacher of the early years of the Restoration period, returned repeatedly to this congenial subject. 'The Church of England', he claimed, 'glories in nothing more than that she is the truest friend to kings, and to kingly government, of any other church in the world; that they were the same hands that took the crown from the King's head and the mitre from the Bishops'.[1] The subject lent itself admirably both to South's fervent loyalty and to his bitter hatred of 'fanaticks', but it was soberly set forth by men with far less brilliant and incisive powers of speech. Even the Latitudinarians accepted in its fullness the prevailing view. In the famous incident of Lord William Russell's trial and execution, Burnet and Tillotson laboured hard to persuade the condemned man to acknowledge the sinfulness of resistance, and Tillotson set forth his views with the greatest clarity. There were, he said, three reasons for the position that the Church adopted. 'First that the Christian religion doth plainly forbid the resistance of authority; secondly, that though our religion be established by law (which his lordship argued as a difference between their case and that of the primitive Christians), yet in the same law which established our religion, it is declared *that it is not lawful upon any pretence whatsoever to take up arms* etc. Besides that, there is a particular law declaring the power of the militia to be solely in the king. And this ties the hands of subjects, though the law of nature and the general rules of Scripture had left us at liberty, which he believed they did not, because the government and peace of human society could not well subsist upon these terms; thirdly, his

[1] R. South, *A Sermon Preached at Lambeth Chapel upon the Consecration of the Lord Bishop of Rochester, Nov. 25, 1666. Sermons* (3rd ed. 1704), vol. I, p. 221.

lordship's opinion was contrary to the declared doctrine of all Protestant churches.'[1] Stillingfleet categorically declared 'that our church doth not only teach them [passive obedience and non-resistance] as her own doctrines; but which is far more effectual, as the doctrines of Christ and his Apostles and of the primitive church'.[2] It is no wonder that after the Revolution Charles Leslie was able to twit Stillingfleet on his inconsistency.

The writings of even the most popular preachers might have only a limited circulation, but the same doctrine was set forth in the most widely read of all contemporary manuals of devotion. Parallel to our duty to parents, says the author of *The Whole Duty of Man*, is our obligation to 'the supreme magistrate', whom we must regard as 'one upon whom God hath stamped much of his own power and authority, and therefore paying him all honour and esteem, never daring, upon any pretence whatsoever, to "speak evil of the ruler of our people" (Acts xxiii. 5)'.[3] 'We owe such an obedience to the supreme power', he adds, 'that whoever is authorized by him we are to submit to.... And 'tis observable that those precepts were given at a time when those powers were heathens, and cruel persecutors of Christianity; to shew us that no pretence of the wickedness of our rulers can free us of this duty. And obedience we must pay, either active or passive; the active in the case of all lawful commands; that is, whenever the magistrate commands something which is not contrary to some command of

[1] T. Birch, *Life of Tillotson* (London, 1820), p. lxxiv; also cf. p. lxxxiii. Note also Burnet, *History of My Own Time* (ed. by O. Airy), vol. II, pp. 377f.; Clarke and Foxcroft, *Life of Burnet*, pp. 268f.

[2] E. Stillingfleet, *Vindication of Answer to the King's Papers*, p. 389.

[3] (Allestree), *The Whole Duty of Man* (London, ed. of 1735), Sunday xiv, p. 288.

God, we are then bound to act according to that command of the magistrate, to do the things he requires: But when he enjoins anything contrary to what God hath commanded, we are not then to pay him this active obedience; we may, nay, we must refuse thus to act....But even this is a season for the passive obedience; we must patiently suffer what he inflicts on us for such refusal, and not to secure ourselves rise up against him....Here is very small encouragement to any to rise up against the lawful magistrate; for though they should so far prosper here, as to secure themselves from him by this means, yet there is a King of kings, from whom no power can shelter them; and this damnation in the close will prove a sad prize of their victories.'[1]

This doctrine, preached by individuals of all schools of thought, was supported by the Universities with all the collective authority they possessed. In 1681 the University of Cambridge presented an address to King Charles II, and took the opportunity to set forth in uncompromising terms the doctrines of divine right and passive obedience. 'We will still believe and maintain', they declared, 'that our kings derive not their title from the people but from God; that to Him only they are accountable; that it belongs not to subjects either to create or to censure, but to honour and obey their sovereign, who comes to be so by a fundamental hereditary right of succession, which no religion, no law, no fault or forfeiture can alter or diminish.'[2] Two years later, when the Exclusion Bill and the discovery of the Rye House Plot had stirred public feeling to its depths, the University of Oxford published its 'judgment and decree...against certain pernicious books and damnable doctrines, destructive to

[1] *The Whole Duty of Man*, pp. 290–1.
[2] Address of the University of Cambridge to King Charles II, printed in the *History of Passive Obedience*, p. 108.

the sacred persons of princes'.[1] After giving an imposing
list of 'points deemed destructive of civil order',[2] the members of convocation affirmed that 'we decree, judge, and
declare all and every of these propositions to be false,
seditious and impious; and most of them to be also heretical
and blasphemous, infamous to Christian religion and
destructive of all government in church and state'.[3] Members
of the University were forbidden to read works setting forth
such doctrines, and the books themselves were ordered
publicly to be burnt. Furthermore, all teachers were urged
to impress upon the minds of the young 'that most necessary
doctrine which in a manner is the badge and character of the
Church of England, of submitting to every ordinance for
the Lord's sake...teaching that this submission is to be
clear, absolute, and without exception of any state or order
of men'.[4]

It is manifest that a doctrine so generally accepted must
have commended itself on grounds more solid than its appeal
to resurgent patriotism. Actually, the considerations which
originally gave force to the doctrine of divine right still made
it useful in Restoration England. At first it had been forged
to defend the supreme political power against what seemed
the excessive claims of extreme clericalists.[5] The threat had
originally come from Rome; subsequently the Calvinists had
advanced claims which, however different in form, were

[1] The Judgment and Decree of the University of Oxford, passed in their
Convocation, July 31, 1683, Against Certain pernicious books and Damnable
Doctrines, Destructive to the Sacred Persons of Princes...(Oxford, 1683).

[2] Note particularly the insistence laid on the ninth point, about the
obligation of Christians to accept passive obedience. Ibid. p. 4.

[3] Ibid. p. 7.

[4] Ibid. p. 8.

[5] It is one of the conspicuous merits of Figgis' The Divine Right of
Kings that he makes perfectly clear the motives which made the doctrine
of divine right so popular a theory.

essentially similar in their purpose and effect. Against both these foes the leaders of Restoration England felt that there was need of constant vigilance, and the weapon which had once proved so serviceable was again furbished for the fight. The antipathy to Nonconformists was compounded of many elements, but hatred of their political opinions was probably stronger than any other single factor. The religious claims of dissenters might be dismissed as preposterous, but what made them so dangerous were the consequences which had followed in the realm of politics. It was as rebels—actual rebels in the past, potential rebels in the present—that the churchmen of the Restoration feared and hated the Nonconformists. Even after the Revolution, 'Jack Presbyter' was a figure whom loyal churchmen felt it necessary to watch carefully and resist wherever possible.

The fear of Roman interference was even more intense. Opposition to papal claims was a settled tradition in English public life, and much of the anti-Roman literature of the Restoration aimed to uncover the interference which the Pope would practise if he had a chance. The sermons extolling the king's inalienable rights and demanding of the subject unqualified obedience returned again and again to an exposure of the sinister designs of Rome. *The Papal Tyranny as it was Exercised over England for Some Ages*[1] is only one of many works which supplied the historical background; *The Jesuits' Policy to Suppress Monarchy*[2] might draw its examples from the past but even the title illustrated the nature of the fear awakened among Englishmen by the most effective of the emissaries of the Pope. The Jesuits were dreaded far more on political than on religious grounds. It

[1] The author was Peter du Moulin, and the work appeared in 1674.
[2] *The Jesuits' Policy to Suppress Monarchy Historically Displayed* (London, 1669).

was not their dogma nor even the moral basis of their
methods which alarmed the English mind. They were regarded as the shameless exponents of the lawfulness of
resisting princes; they acquiesced in, and even advocated,
tyrannicide, and they justified their policy by appealing to
the sovereign power of the Pope. Throughout the Restoration period the fear of Popery was steadily increasing, and
the apprehension to which even the ephemeral literature of
the divine right of kings bears testimony found monumental
expression in the work of one of the greatest English scholars
of the time. Barrow's carefully reasoned *Treatise of the Pope's
Supremacy* is unintelligible except against the background of
contemporary fears. In the Preface to the Reader, Barrow
confidently claims 'that whosoever shall carefully peruse
this treatise shall find that this point of the Pope's supremacy...is not only an indefensible but an impudent cause
as ever was undertaken by learned pens'. He then proceeds
to prove, with the inexhaustible patience which seventeenth-
century learning could command, that it was indeed true
that Romanism claimed 'that the civil principality is subject
to the sacerdotal'.[1] Having established this fact, he could
assert without fear of contradiction that 'among modern
controversies there is scarce any of greater consequence than
that about universal supremacy'.[2] Point by point Barrow
then dealt with the papal claims, until, having presumably
wearied the patience of all except the hardiest readers, he
returned to the relation between Church and State. The
Pope, as he pointed out, 'doth pretend to be above all
princes...but in the primitive times this was not held'.[3]
Scripture, history and the evidence of common sense unite

---

[1] Barrow, *Treatise of the Pope's Supremacy. Works* (London, 1861),
vol. III, p. 4, col. 1.

[2] Ibid. p. 20, col. 1.   [3] Ibid. p. 188, col. 1.

against such arrogant claims. 'No power', Barrow added, 'can have a higher source, or firmer ground, than that of civil government hath; for "all such power is from heaven".'[1] The full measure of Roman arrogance is proved by placing side by side the requirement of obedience and the practice sanctioned by the Pope. 'God by indispensable law hath obliged us to retain our obedience to the king, even pagan; charging us, under pain of damnation to be subject to him and not to resist him. But the pope is ready upon occasion to discharge subjects from that obligation, to absolve them from their solemn oaths of allegiance, to encourage insurrection against him, to prohibit obedience.'[2] As usual, Barrow substantiated his charge with copious quotations from Roman Catholic literature, and then closed the argument with an appeal to Holy Scripture and common sense. Few writers could bring to bear on any subject the massive learning with which Barrow attacked the papal claims, but there is nothing original in his central position. He upheld the rights of the king, and insisted on the duty of absolute obedience, and he believed that Romanism was the most dangerous obstacle to both. In this he was in complete agreement with almost all his Anglican contemporaries.[3]

The first signs of a major cleavage in the Church of England appear in the discussion of the origins of sovereignty. In the first instance, men had been content to quote the words of Scripture, draw from them the inference that God had invested kingship with an inalienable sovereignty, and then fortify their claims with further quotations from the Bible. The method had certain manifest defects; it

[1] Barrow, op. cit. p. 189, col. 2.

[2] Ibid. p. 197, col. 1.

[3] Cf. *The True Protestant Subject, or the Nature and Rights of Sovereignty Discussed and Stated* (1680), p. 3.

condemned those who used it to an intolerably tedious style of composition; it invited opponents to use the same method for their ends, and so proved inconclusive. But it made it possible to state an uncompromising position with great assurance, and buttressed the conviction that 'a king (properly so called) is a supremacy of power, independent from all earthly authority'.[1] Even though the king may have bound himself to observe 'certain rules of administration', it is impossible to infer from this that the people's consent plays any part in establishing the monarch's right to rule. Subjects are not obliged to obey because they are parties to a compact; 'they stand indispensably bound by the command of God, which exacts from them honours and obedience, even to evil kings, and expressly prohibits all manner of forcible resistance against the supreme magistrate, upon any pretence whatsoever. Thus to live and thus to do is safe, commendable, and consonant to the principles of our Christian faith.'[2]

We have the same view of the origin of sovereignty in the most influential work on the subject published during the Restoration period, but the method of proof has been changed in an important respect. Filmer's *Patriarcha* was at once the ablest and the most popular defence of the extreme royalist claims, but its significance lies in the fact that its altered approach invited a more effective kind of reply.

[1] *The True Protestant Subject...*, p. 25.
[2] Ibid. p. 27. Note the author's comment that the plea with which an 'ignorant and unsteady sort of people' support the opposite view 'has so much of unregeneracy in it, and so little of reason, that there's no great danger of any sober Christian's being seduced with it'. Note also the claim advanced in *The Case Stated Touching the Sovereign's Prerogative and the People's Liberty...* (1660), p. 4: 'In the first place it behoves the subject to take notice that the king's authority is *Jure Divino*, he is set over us by God Himself, he hath not his reign or crown by our favour; for says God, "by me kings reign", it is plainly not by us.'

Filmer recognized that his case would be stronger if it rested on an appeal to the order of nature rather than on a catena of texts. The order of nature, of course, has been established by God, and the only reliable account of its origins is in the book of Genesis. So Filmer seized upon the fact of patriarchal authority. On Adam the fullness of sovereignty had been bestowed; from him it was lineally transmitted to his eldest son. Filmer reinforced his argument by citing the Old Testament patriarchs, and then drew the necessary inferences regarding the abiding character of hereditary kingly rule. Whatever the form of government, its authority 'is the only right and natural authority of a supreme father. There is, and always shall be continued till the end of the world, a natural right of a supreme father over every multitude'.[1] 'If we compare the natural rights of a father with those of a king, we find them all one, without any difference at all but only in the latitude or extent of them: as the father over one family, so the king, as father over many families, extends his care to preserve, feed, clothe, instruct and defend the whole commonwealth.'[2] Others had sensed that the metaphor of fatherhood was suggestive; Filmer was the first to seize on it as the principle which could illuminate the essential nature of kingship.

The popularity of his work[3] proves that Filmer had given

---

[1] Filmer, *Patriarcha* (edition of 1884), p. 20. Note Locke's contention that 'this subjection of children being the fountain of all regal authority' is the crucial point in Filmer's work. 'This position', he adds, is 'the foundation of all their doctrine who would have monarchy to be *jure divino*.' Locke, *Two Treatises of Government* (London, 1884), pp. 111–12.

[2] Filmer, op. cit. p. 21.

[3] As to the popularity of *Patriarcha*, note Locke's frank admissions: '...a treatise that made such a noise at its coming abroad...the applause that followed it...a man who is the great champion of absolute power, and the idol of those who worship it.' *Two Treatises of Government*, pp. 77–8.

clear expression to what had vaguely been in many minds, but he had prepared his own undoing. His appeal was to 'the very principles of the law of nature',[1] but it was possible for his opponents to assert that he had misconstrued those principles. Filmer had claimed that 'there want not those who believe that the first invention of laws was to bridle and moderate the overgreat power of kings; but the truth is, the original of laws was for the keeping of the multitude in order'.[2] This kind of categorical statement proves nothing, and it invited opponents to retort by reaffirming their own view. This is exactly what happened. Throughout the period the view was slowly gaining ground that sovereignty resides, in part at least, in the people. If that is so, then kingship must rest on some sort of contractual basis, and law must be the means whereby even kings can be controlled. During most of the period, this was not a popular or influential view; but it clearly carried some weight, or the defenders of divine right would not have attacked it so often and with such vigour.[3] A growing section of the Whig party discovered that this view could both justify their political aims and commend itself to the new intellectual temper which was emerging. Moreover, the defenders of divine right had greatly simplified the task of their opponents. Filmer, as we have seen, had shifted the appeal from the words of Scripture to the law of nature; in so doing he had paved the way for a new kind of attack. As John Locke cogently proved, Filmer had not established any real identity

[1] Filmer, op. cit. p. 11.
[2] Ibid. p. 50.
[3] As an example, note the comment of the author of *The True Protestant Subject* (1680), p. 23: 'There are another sort of these creatures that will needs have the supreme authority to be originally in the people, to whom they make the prince to stand obliged for it, as being their proper gift. But this assertion is notoriously untrue.'

between the law of nature and his interpretation of the story of Adam. Step by step, Locke demonstrated that even if Adam possessed the kind of sovereignty that Filmer stipulated, there was nothing to prove that he could or did transmit it in any such manner as the theory of divine right presupposed.[1] It was consequently possible to appeal to the law of nature for totally new ends, and Locke initiated a movement in political thought which finally found full expression in the works of Jean-Jacques Rousseau.

However great the theoretical interest of the debate may have been, political considerations rapidly lifted it to a different plane and made it a matter of immediate practical concern. The attempt to pass the Exclusion Bill brought the whole issue into the forefront of men's thinking; it accentuated existing differences, and prepared for the sudden overthrow of a theory which to all appearances had established an impregnable position. The minds of Englishmen had been deeply disturbed by the conversion of the Duke of York to Romanism, and the course of events did nothing to allay the apprehensions of those who regarded with horror the prospect of a popish ruler on the throne. The apologists of divine right found their belief in passive obedience increasingly difficult to commend to others; to urge their contemporaries to accept suffering, with prayers and tears but without repining, was to offer hard doctrine. Many were not ready to accept it. In the activities of the Whigs they found a political lead; in works like Johnson's *Julian the Apostate* they received a vigorous statement of an alternative position. Those who uncritically supported the heir apparent were, according to Johnson, adjusting 'the doctrine of passive obedience for the use of a popish successor'; they would end by making their countrymen 'an easier prey to

[1] Locke, *Two Treatises of Government*, chs. III–IX.

the bloody Papists'.[1] The purpose of his appeal to the past was both to emphasize the nature of the impending danger and to justify resistance to it. Pope Gregory had pointed out 'that Julian stole a persecution upon the Christians under a shadow of gentleness, for he always disclaimed his being a persecutor. And we for aught I know, may be exposed to the bloodiest persecution that ever was, under the meek pretences of passive obedience.'[2] The argument is both bold and simple. The danger is real and imminent; Popery is no imaginary threat; once it becomes a reality, there will be only two alternatives before the Protestants of England: they can apostatize or be wiped out.[3] Faced with this prospect, the attitude of those who urge passive obedience is absurd.[4] Their appeal to Scripture will not abide scrutiny,[5] and their claim that history supports them can be disproved by citing the Christian attitude to Julian the Apostate.[6] The Fathers of the early Church had no such belief in the law of inheritance as their present-day successors imagine; if that be so, the obligation of passive obedience is left suspended in mid-air. The fatal consequences of non-resistance are evident to the simplest intelligence,[7] and its principles run counter to indefeasible human rights—the right of a man 'to live and resist murder (even his own) upon all occasions'.[8] Present throughout the book, and giving incisiveness to Johnson's

[1] (Samuel Johnson), *Julian the Apostate, being a short account of his Life, the Sense of the Primitive Christians about his Succession, and Their Behaviour Towards Him* (London, 1682), p. 89.

[2] Ibid. p. 88.   [3] Ibid. pp. 78–9.

[4] Ibid. Preface to the Reader, pp. iv–v.

[5] Ibid. Preface to the Reader, p. viii.

[6] Ibid. passim, especially pp. 93 f.

[7] Cf. ibid. p. viii: '. . . the doctrine of passive obedience, which when it is taught without any regard to laws, and is prescribed both without law and against law, is not evangelical but Mahumetane, and the very Turkish doctrine of the bow-string.'   [8] Ibid. p. 92.

fiercest attacks, is a deep hatred of Popery[1] and an intense belief that it is indistinguishable from sheer paganism.[2]

The discontent reflected in *Julian* appeared in much more striking form in the Rye House Plot and its sequel. The literature inspired by the executions of Lord Russell and Algernon Sydney gave further expression to the rising dissatisfaction with current political theories, but did nothing to enhance the reputation of the alternative view. Many people had found *Julian* a shocking work,[3] and apparently its subversive doctrines had promptly inspired rebellion. Consequently, when George Hickes replied to Johnson in *Jovian*, he carried public sympathy with him. The appeal to history, as he showed, can furnish more than one verdict. The law of hereditary succession is the 'fundamental law of monarchy',[4] and any attempt to interfere with its operation is 'opposition to the will of God'. With uncompromising vigour, Hickes set forth the most absolute view of the unlimited powers of kings,[5] and drew thence the most rigorous inferences as to the duty of passive obedience.[6] Behind the express injunctions of the Gospel, Hickes found the authority of 'the common laws of sovereignty'; these require 'passive obedience, which is but another name for non-resistance; these laws are in eternal force against the

[1] Cf. p. 91. In speaking of papal claims, Johnson asks 'where is it said in the word of the Lord...that the world is only made for banditti?'

[2] Ibid. pp. 99f. The polytheism, idolatry, and cruelty of both are affirmed and abundantly illustrated.

[3] Cf. the reference in (Bartholomew Shower), *An Antidote Against Poison* (1683), p. 5, to 'that venomous book, *Julian*'.

[4] Hickes, *Jovian* (1683), Preface.

[5] Ibid. p. 212: 'He hath none to share with him in the sovereignty, but all authority and power is derived from him like light from the sun;...he hath no sharers or co-partners with him in the sovereignty; none coordinate with him in government; no equal nor superior, but only God, to whom alone he is subject.'

[6] Ibid. ch. x, pp. 199f.

subject in defence of the sovereign, be he good or evil, just or unjust, Christian or pagan; be he what he will, no subject or number of subjects can lift up his hand against his sovereign, and be guiltless by these laws'.[1] But lest this should seem a counsel of despair when faced with the rising threat of persecution, Hickes insisted that Englishmen were in no real danger at all.[2] The first defence is 'the watchful providence of God'; the second and third are the conscience and honour of the prince himself. No king of England would be willing to suffer in the eyes of his contemporaries and at the bar of history by taking any steps that would brand him as a persecutor. Further there is the protection afforded by the laws of the realm. A popish successor could not oppress his subjects even if he wished because the laws would frustrate his endeavours. 'Wherefore a popish prince, though he were never so blood-thirsty and had never so little regard to humanity and his coronation oath, would be infinitely puzzled to persecute his Protestant subjects.'[3] Hickes was manifestly weakening his theoretical argument by these appeals to contingent circumstances, but his fatal concession was his claim that to anyone acquainted with the future James II, the whole discussion could only seem entirely irrelevant. Those who pointed to dangers ahead were unprincipled agitators, and their arguments bore 'no relation to the expectations those entertain who really know the Duke of York'.[4]

As soon as the Duke of York became the King of England, he promptly proved how unwarranted had been the confidence of men like Hickes. His initial declaration might be reassuring to nervous Anglicans, but his deeds soon belied his words. His conduct during his brief reign precipitated

[1] Ibid. p. 203.
[2] Ibid. ch. XII, pp. 263 f.
[3] Ibid. p. 273.
[4] Ibid. p. 203.

the crisis which ended in his downfall and in the overthrow
of the theory which had served as the buttress of his throne.
The supporters of absolute royal supremacy had laboured
hard to prove that neither heresy nor apostasy could in-
validate a king's claim to the subject's loyalty.[1] To argue
from harsh and oppressive methods of government was
beside the point.[2] Hickes had categorically stated that 'in
all sovereign governments subjects must be slaves as to this
particular: they must trust their lives and liberties with their
sovereigns'.[3] To James this was the true voice of the Church
of England, and he assumed that loyal Anglicans would be
bound to acquiesce in whatever he might choose to do. This
is proved by his attitude to Bishop Ken;[4] it speaks clearly in
the vehemence with which he brushed aside the opposition
of the Fellows of Magdalen;[5] it explains his anger when
confronted with the resistance of the seven bishops.[6] The full
implications of the increasing opposition to James were not

[1] Cf. *The True Protestant Subject...*, p. 39, where the author proves to
his own satisfaction that 'civil authority may fall upon those who are
wholly unworthy of it, and neither incapacity nor irreligion annihilates
a prince's right to the crown'. Cf. also the claim of *The Case Stated
Touching the Sovereign's Prerogative and the People's Liberty*, p. 4: 'It is the
plain witness of Scripture that were he never so wicked, he is not to be
dealt with according to his deservings.'

[2] Cf. Seth Ward, *Against Resistance of Lawful Powers*, pp. 29–30.

[3] Hickes, *Jovian*, p. 242. Note also *The Case Stated...*, p. 5: 'Princes
are like the bond of wedlock, once make them the fathers of our country,
and we take them for better, for worse; we may persuade them, we cannot compel them without breach of divine precepts; once let them be
the Lord's anointed, and it is sacrilege to touch them, I mean unfit-
tingly.' Note also the tenor of the sermon (on I Tim. ii. 1) preached by
Bishop Turner at the coronation of James II, 23 April 1685.

[4] Plumptre, *Life of Ken* (2nd ed. 1890), vol. I, pp. 286f.

[5] Anthony à Wood, *Life*, vol. III, pp. 361–3; Bramston, *Autobiography*, p. 285; *The Hatton Correspondence* (Camden Society, 1878),
vol. II, pp. 73f.

[6] Plumptre, op. cit. vol. I, p. 307: 'This is a standard of rebellion...
I am king; I will be obeyed. Is this your Church of England loyalty?'

immediately apparent. Even those who felt that they could no longer acquiesce in the royal policy did not see what the ultimate end would be, and James certainly failed to recognize the delicate equipoise of the doctrine of passive obedience. Hickes himself had conceded that subjects might use all *lawful* means to reclaim their sovereign from misguided ways, but when some refuse co-operation others are sure actively to resist. At all events, every contemporary observer records enough to make it plain that anyone except a headstrong fool would have realized that there were limits to the constraint which passive obedience could lay upon the impatience of an awakened people. Actually James II had been warned; some years before, Bishop Morley had assured him that in an emergency he could not count on the acquiescence which passive obedience seemed to promise.[1] The debate rapidly passed out of the region in which theories could control events. James lost his throne, and developments in the new reign soon forced the clergy to reconsider the doctrine which they had for so long accepted as the 'distinguishing badge of the Church of England'.

With new rulers on the throne, the question of appropriate oaths at once arose. Certain concessions were made to Tory scruples in the matter, but it was immediately apparent that those who had upheld the divine right of kings were faced with a most difficult decision.[2] The great majority salved their consciences as best they could, took the required oaths, and tacitly abandoned the political theories they had held. Many were not convinced that William's claim to the

[1] Morley, from his death-bed, sent word to James, through Lord Dartmouth, that 'if ever he depended on the doctrine of non-resistance he would find himself deceived. The clergy might not think proper to contradict that doctrine in terms, but he was very sure they would in practice.' Cf. Plumptre, op. cit. vol. I, p. 298.

[2] Cf. *The Hatton Correspondence*, vol. II, p. 99.

throne was actually valid, but they acquiesced in his *de facto* possession of it. Bramston, after much searching of heart, concluded that whatever might be said of those who invited him William had been justified in coming to seize the throne of England; James II might have a right to his subjects' allegiance if he ever returned to claim it, but meanwhile sound government was necessary, and obedience to those actually in power was the only condition on which it could be had.[1] Bohun found comfort in conceding that William had the rights belonging to a conqueror; in addition he had certain claims of his own, and even stronger ones through his wife.[2] Such concessions were often the result of much anxious thought. In a letter dated 15 May 1689, William Nicolson reveals clearly enough the embarrassment felt by many Englishmen. 'We have now a Prince and Princess seated on the throne, in whom we are ready enough to acknowledge all the accomplishments we can wish for in our governors, provided their present possession of the crown were unquestionable; and therefore, methinks we should rather greedily catch at any appearance of proof that may justify their pretensions than dwell on such arguments as seemingly overturn them'.[3] Throughout the early months of the new reign, anxious clergymen were searching for some formula that would satisfy their consciences and allow them to pursue their vocation, and well-wishers were lavish with advice. Some of it, like the blundering efforts of Burnet to satisfy the mind of Ken,[4] did more harm than good, but most of the clergy found a measure of reassurance by dwelling on the

[1] Bramston, *Autobiography* (Camden Society, 1845), p. 355.

[2] Ed. Bohun, *Non-Resistance or Passive Obedience noway Concerned in the Controversies now Depending.*

[3] Nicolson, *Epistolatory Correspondence*, vol. I, pp. 7–8.

[4] Cf. Clarke and Foxcroft, *Life of Burnet*, p. 301. Also Plumptre, op. cit. vol. II, pp. 46f.

demands of the existing situation and ignoring questions of abstract theory.

The inconspicuous clergyman could now be grateful for his obscurity, but certain leaders of the Church had been such prominent advocates of passive obedience that some defence of their dramatic change was obviously necessary. Burnet's *Pastoral Letter* was an emphatic but infelicitous justification of taking the new oaths,[1] and it chiefly appealed to two considerations: James II, having fatally weakened his position at every possible point, had forfeited his rights by 'abdication', while William, both by conquest and possession, was now entitled to the loyalty of Englishmen.[2] A more serious statement of the case for acquiescence was Stillingfleet's *Discourse Concerning the Unreasonableness of a New Separation*.[3] Schism, he claimed, could not be justified 'when the difference is only upon the account of a case of conscience, wherein wise and good men may easily differ', and those who had been so quick to denounce the scruples of Nonconformists should be reluctant to force a division when they found themselves dissatisfied.[4] He regarded the question of the oaths as the crux of the whole matter; if those who object to them have any case at all, 'it must either be from the continuing obligation of the former oaths, or from the nature of the present oaths'.[5] It was consequently necessary to

---

[1] Note that Burnet's *Pastoral Letter* on the new oaths aroused such bitter feeling that it was ordered to be burnt by Parliament. Cf. Lathbury, *A History of the Non-Jurors*, pp. 72–3.

[2] Note Reresby's account of Burnet's vehement way of asserting William's rights to the throne, *The Memoirs of Sir John Reresby*, p. 431.

[3] *A Discourse Concerning the Unreasonableness of a New Separation, on Account of the Oaths, with an Answer to the History of Passive Obedience, so far as relates to them* (London, 1689).

[4] Ibid. p. 1. Cf. p. 3: 'Is separation from our Church become a duty with those who so lately looked on it as so great a fault in others?'

[5] Ibid. p. 3.

examine the nature of oaths in general, and Stillingfleet proved—at least to his own satisfaction—that political oaths are essentially different from those that bind individuals to one another. All obligation in society is conditioned by 'the common good' of the nation as a whole, and magistrates, who often impose oaths for their own security, have no right to use them as an obstacle to public welfare. 'Therefore... how strict soever the expressions may be, if the keeping of the oath be really and truly inconsistent with the welfare of a people, in subverting the fundamental laws which support it, I do not see how such an oath continues to oblige. For there is no relation of mankind to one another, but there is some good antecedent, which is the just measure of that obligation they stand in to each other.'[1] This position is then developed at length, and finally applied to the case of 'the present oaths'. Stillingfleet claimed that he was not asserting the lawfulness of resistance; the central issue, he believed, was clear and simple: 'whether the law of our nation doth not bind us to allegiance to a king and queen in actual possession of the throne, by consent of the three estates of the realm'.[2] He dismissed the theoretical arguments of his opponents as either irrelevant or opposed to the fundamental position he had already established. Those who were ill at ease about their oaths to James II, must realize that 'the interests of the common good' outweigh the claims of any individual, and both the evidence of English history and the clear witness of Scripture confirm the point.[3] To give way to recrimination only confuses the

[1] Stillingfleet, op. cit. p. 5.

[2] Ibid. p. 9. One of the strongest statements of this particular argument occurs in *The Case of Allegiance in our Present Circumstances Consider'd, In a Letter from a Minister in the City to a Minister in the Country* (London, 1689), pp. 22–4.

[3] Stillingfleet, op. cit. pp. 13 f. and 34 f.

issue: 'as to the dreadful charge of perjury and apostasy, which some, of much greater heat than judgment have made use of against those who hold it lawful to take the oaths, if what I have said be true, it is little less than ridiculous.'[1]

Stillingfleet's defection might create concern, but it was Sherlock who aroused the most bitter resentment among the defenders of the old position. Circumstances made his apostasy particularly hard to accept,[2] and it was only natural for Sherlock to try to defend his actions. With unusual distinctness, his work[3] reflects the disturbed conditions of the time. All the familiar arguments of the conformists are there, but so is an illuminating confession of the difficulties of seeing what is the right course, and an ardent defence of his sincerity throughout. 'I prayed heartily to God, that if I were in a mistake, he would let me see it; that I might not forfeit the exercise of my ministry; and I thank God I have received that satisfaction I desired.'[4] The more scurrilous among his foes were quick to suggest that the desired satisfaction was more substantial than mere peace of mind,[5] but Sherlock also had a word for those who were so eager to defame their brethren. In 'an age of great profaneness

---

[1] Ibid. p. 41.

[2] After consistently denying the lawfulness of the oaths, Sherlock suddenly conformed, and was at once promoted to the Deanery of St Paul's. Such 'apostasy' invited abuse, and one of the commonest charges was that his wife had coerced him into conforming.

[3] Sherlock, *The Case of the Allegiance Due to Sovereign Powers* (1691).

[4] Ibid. Preface, p. iii.

[5] Note, however, the charitable allowances made by some of the Non-Jurors: 'Some there were who could not be brought to transfer their allegiance from him [i.e. from King James II] to another, by invocation of God's name: but who now, upon second thoughts, considering the desperate state of his affairs, were willing to be convinced, that both their interest and duty might be made to go together, and that a right of *providential possession* ought no longer to be disputed by them.' Kettlewell's *Life*, p. 112.

and infidelity', anything that discredited the clergy and brought their sincerity into disrepute was harmful to religion. The enemies of the Church had been making the most of the acquiescent attitude of Anglicans; those who felt obliged to take the oaths must defend their position (as he was doing); those whom conscience compelled to dissent should exercise forbearance.

Events had conspired to overthrow the theory of divine indefeasible hereditary right; with it fell the doctrine of passive obedience. Practical men, living in the present and facing the future, acknowledged the fact, and changed the political theories they held. But some were content to live in the past, and the Non-Jurors have all the forlorn attractiveness of men committed to lost causes. The smallness of their numbers proves that their favourite doctrine had outlived its power to command assent, but it is significant that they could force the only High Church schism in the history of the Church of England. They included some of the most saintly and many of the most learned churchmen of their time, but the world they lived in had passed away. The doctrine they defended had been fashioned to meet a need that no longer existed, and though men might yield them the respect usually conceded to misguided sanctity, they could only influence their own day in minor ways. To the very end they upheld the rightness of their cause.[1] Some,

[1] Cf. *A Defence of the Profession which the Right Reverend Father in God, John, late Lord Bishop of Chichester, made upon his death-bed: Concerning Passive Obedience and the new Oaths* (1690), pp. 7–8: '... And whereas that religion of the Church of England taught me the doctrine of non-resistance and passive obedience, which I have accordingly inculcated upon others, and which I took to be the distinguishing character of the Church of England, I adhere no less firmly and steadfastly to that, and in consequence of it, have incurred a suspension from the exercise of my office and expected a deprivation. I find in so doing much inward satisfaction....'

like Sancroft, maintained their distinctive witness without loss of charity; 'notwithstanding he and they [the conformists] might go different ways with respect to public affairs, he trusted yet that heaven-gates would be wide enough to receive both him and them'.[1] Many, however, lapsed into bitterness, and Granville's letters from Saint-Germain breathe a spirit that for years infected English life.[2] The leaven of non-juring rancour undermined the morale of the loyalist Tories and brought the whole party into disrepute.[3] The recurrent cry that the Church was in danger gained added force from the witness of the Non-Jurors, and aggravated the unrest of English public life. From time to time they robbed the Church of the services of high-minded and conscientious men like William Law, but gradually they lost both in influence and in numbers. Like the Jacobites, they dwelt, with nostalgic ineffectiveness, on a situation which had passed away. In an age increasingly governed by prudence and common sense, they witnessed to convictions which some might still respect but which very few were willing to accept. Meanwhile, the Church of England stood on the threshold of the eighteenth century. Instead of the high-flown fervours of divine right and passive obedience, bishops now commended both by precept and example that complacent Erastianism which reached its full development in Walpole's England.

[1] Kettlewell, *Life*, p. 159.
[2] Cf. the illuminating series of letters given in *The Remains of Dennis Granville* (Surtees Society, 1860, 1865). His letter of 19 March 1687/8 gives one of the most extreme statements of the doctrine of passive obedience (vol. II, p. 228); a series of letters to the bishop, clergy, etc. of Durham (vol. I, pp. 97–117) contrasts his fidelity to Church of England principles with their apostasy, and reflects the *naïveté* and lack of realism of the extreme Non-Juror. Note also his bitter letter to Beveridge, July 1692 (vol. II, pp. 235 f.).
[3] Cf. Feiling, op. cit. p. 294.

Seldom has a doctrine suffered such sudden and complete eclipse. Up till the very eve of the Revolution the vast majority of Anglicans accepted divine right and passive obedience as mandatory teachings of the Church. Some might try to modify the rigours of one or the other theory; a very few might call both in question, but together they represented the political theory most commonly held throughout the Restoration period. Then, under the impact of events, they disappeared at once and for ever. They might linger on, a forlorn survival, in small groups and unimportant circles, but essentially the overthrow of divine right supplies the most striking example of a dramatic change that can be found anywhere in the history of English thought. What explains a reversal so complete?

The theory is intelligible only in the light of the purposes it was designed to serve. The practical ends could now be secured in other ways; since the theory itself had grown obsolete, only the pressure of events was necessary to discredit it for ever.

We have already seen that the divine right of kings was a bulwark against the intrusion of extreme forms of clericalism. The original threat to the autonomy of national sovereignty had come from Rome, but in time the new Calvinism from Geneva advanced political claims which were essentially of the same nature. Against both of these, the theory of divine right supplied a useful weapon of defence, and since both were still a threat in 1660, the doctrine retained its ancient appeal. But in the course of the next thirty years conditions changed. Events proved that the aggressions of Rome could be met without appealing to the theory of divine right. Actually, the reign of James II had shown that in a crisis the theory—with its concomitant emphasis on passive obedience—could abet rather than control the advances of Romanism. It appeared that Popery and the claims of divine right were no longer counter-balancing forces, and in their momentary union they were repudiated together. With regard to Puritanism, an opposite development produced a similar result. With the passing of a generation, the political threat from Nonconformity seemed much less serious than it had on the morrow of the great rebellion. Granville might frantically appeal to the danger from Puritanism and point to symptoms which recalled 1642,[1] but no one paid much attention to his warnings. The political forces of Puritanism could be contained in other ways; indeed, once the dissenters had proved that they had a share in the equipoise of the nascent party system, it was even safe to grant them toleration. In fact the dangers of clerical interference were over; in so far as they still existed they could now be met in ways more satisfactory than an appeal to the divine right of kings.

In other important respects the theory had discharged its special functions and could safely be forgotten. Throughout the seventeenth century it had borne consistent witness to the need of continuity in the national life. An age appalled at the results of political disorder was glad to welcome any influence which would strengthen the law-abiding habits of the people. So the divine right of kings gave a rationale to the move to restore the monarchy; it also curbed the turbulent forces which might have threatened the new régime. This explains the fervent denunciations of resistance which the theory inspired; it also illuminates the delicate weighing of the threat of persecution against the danger of disturbing the succession which formed so marked a feature of the

[1] *The Remains of Dennis Granville* (Surtees Society), vol. 1, pp. 33 f.

Exclusion Bill debates.[1] But the Revolution proved conclusively that law and order were now strongly established
in English public life. Political rebellion could only succeed
when given the overwhelming support of the most influential
elements in the community; once it had that sanction, it
could take place with a regulated propriety which has few
parallels in history. Even the 'myths' of the Revolution—
such as the fiction of the abdication of King James—served
to emphasize continuity and order. A major political adjustment could now be made, not with the help of passive
obedience but against its protests. As a stabilizing force in
the community it had manifestly outlived its usefulness. .

The theoretical foundations of the doctrine had also
crumbled. The mode of thinking on which it rested had
largely been superseded. It belonged to an age when
theology and political theory were intimately—indeed in-
separably—interwoven. That day had passed. In de-
molishing Filmer's arguments, Locke might still appeal to
the authority of religious truth, but the fact remains that
between them they had altered the general character of the
discussion. The law of nature began to supersede the words
of Scripture; in the first instance the natural law might be
established by the will of God,[2] but it was an easy step for
the next generation to proclaim its autonomy. Already the
burden of proof has shifted to those who would control
political forms by an appeal to Biblical statements. The

[1] Cf. *Journals of the House of Lords*, vol. XIII, pp. 684f.; A. Grey,
Debates of the House of Commons (1667–94), vol. VIII, pp. 21f.; Foxcroft,
Life of Halifax, vol. I, pp. 233 f.

[2] Cf. *A Brief History of the Succession of the Crown of England* (1688/9)
(Harleian Miscellany, 1744, vol. I, pp. 448f.): 'That government is of
nature, and derived from God, is manifest. Nothing is more natural in
man, than the desire of society, and without government society would
be intolerable.'

inferences to be drawn from natural law must be accepted unless unequivocal Scripture proof can be produced to the contrary,[1] and in time even this proviso was abandoned.

A new spirit was making itself felt in the discussion of political theory; with this spirit the claims of divine right were incompatible. A city minister, writing in 1689 to enlighten a country colleague about the facts of the new day, denounced the servile attitude which had infected English political thought. Certain principles, he remarked, had been 'too earnestly obtruded and too easily entertained amongst us', but if they 'rather enslave than oblige our consciences, and are as inconsistent with truth as they are with the present revolution, we must take the honest courage to break off those bands, and assert our liberty'.[2] Foremost among these constricting views he mentioned the theory 'that a monarchial form of government and the appropriation of it to a particular person or family is *jure divino*'. No one, he said, denies the existence of a permissive right, but there is no evidence to support the kind of theory which has till lately been so confidently advanced. The prevalent conception of monarchy was, it is clear, undergoing a serious change. It was still confidently affirmed that political order was of divine establishment, but the forms under which it was organized might vary widely and should be left to the constitutional requirements of each time and place.[3] In some countries, monarchy might suit the people's needs; in others, a republic might be more appropriate. Even granting that England was accustomed to the rule of kings, it did not

---

[1] *A Brief History of the Succession*...(Harleian Miscellany, vol. 1, p. 460).
[2] *The Case of Allegiance in our Present Circumstances Consider'd, In a Letter from a Minister in the City to a Minister in the Country* (1689), pp. 3f.   [3] Ibid. pp. 6–7.

follow that their power is 'absolute and unlimited'. Only the folly or ill will of sycophants would accept a theory so completely at variance with the facts of English history. If, remarked the author of *The Case of Allegiance*, there were any validity in the claims of divine right, absolute monarchy might be able to establish a case; as it is, any careful student can recognize that 'the mixed form of government' which prevails in England has arisen out of English conditions and the circumstances of English history. At no time have the people conceded absolute power to their kings; a system of balanced rights has always been the mark of English political life. Whether this represents a correct reading of history or not is beside the point; the important fact is that royal absolutism is challenged in the name of parliament and the people. The constitutionalism of 'a minister in the City' is a far cry from the almost servile prostration of Granville before the king's majesty, but Granville belonged to the past; the new conception of monarchy had all the forces of the future on its side; and it was frankly and explicitly hostile to the theory of divine right.

It was inevitable that the old views should be called in question. The new reliance on reason—so pronounced a feature of later seventeenth-century thought—made men's minds sensitive to the extravagant character of the theories which had been so widely held. A sober and moderate appeal to history and to common sense is the mark of most of the pamphlets which defend the Revolution settlement; it was more acceptable to men who had been reading Locke or Newton than the uncompromising dogmatism of the champions of divine right. The revolt against authority also played its part. When reason sat in judgement on every kind of sweeping claim, what chance of survival had the intransigence of divine right?

Gradually the foundations had worn away; on the eve of the Revolution men still trusted in the theory and did not suspect how insecure it had become. Then the discipline of events suddenly revealed to churchmen the true nature of the existing situation. The house of their security collapsed; almost overnight it became a ruin, cherished only by those who loved to linger in the past. Yet in the days of its usefulness it had rendered notable services to English life and thought. Behind its defences the autonomy of national institutions had been fostered until they were unassailable by any outward foe. Under its tutelage a law-abiding habit had become the settled characteristic of the English people. It can even be claimed that by a curious paradox it prepared the way for freedom of thought and made religious toleration possible.

CHAPTER IX

TOLERATION, THE TRIUMPH OF AN IDEA

THE pressure of events often decides the pattern of ideas. There are times when ancient thought-forms only survive because circumstances have not yet proved how far removed they are from actual life. At more points than one, the Restoration served to revive and maintain conceptions which had long lost touch with the realities of the existing situation. The theory of the divine right of kings is one example; another is the belief that the stability of Church and State depended on the persecution of minority religious groups. It is possible to argue that by 1660 the conditions prerequisite to toleration already existed in England. The idea had been discussed from every angle and experience had proved its need. But circumstances were not yet favourable; for nearly thirty years the debate on toleration continued, and the discussion no doubt secured at least a number of converts. Then suddenly the events of James II's reign proved how completely necessity could reconcile Englishmen to what had apparently been a most unpopular idea. The Toleration Act proclaimed the opening of a new era in the treatment of religious minorities, and Locke's famous *Letters* provided the intellectual justification of the new attitude and outlook.

For a few weeks after the return of Charles II, the nature of the ecclesiastical settlement remained uncertain. It was possible to hope that a measure of latitude would be allowed those who held unpopular opinions, and there was at least a tradition to which the advocates of leniency could appeal. The early Latitudinarians—Chillingworth and Hales and the other members of the circle at Great Tew—had been Royalist and Anglican, and yet had advocated a large measure of toleration. The Cambridge Platonists, though their chief works were published after 1660, had for some years been teaching that blend of enlightened conviction and generous forbearance which was so characteristic of their outlook.

There had also been some limited experiments in greater freedom of religious thought. By conviction Cromwell was indisposed to persecute, but circumstances thwarted his attempts to introduce any effective measure of toleration. Even his tentative experiments did not convince contemporaries of the benefits that a larger liberty would bring. Both their relative failure, and the auspices under which they were launched, tended to discredit toleration. Cromwell was regarded as a tyrant and hated as such; all that belonged to his régime or had commended itself to his judgement suffered from that very fact.

In 1660, however, it appeared for a time as though the balance of power might persuade men to adopt a policy more liberal than the views they actually held. The Presbyterians seemed to be in a strong position (though appearances deceived). They claimed credit for the ease with which the king had been restored, and the measure of influence which they apparently held seemed to justify them in demanding special consideration. But their power was a hollow shell, and they themselves began to suspect as much almost from the outset of the reign. As a result moderation—even diffidence—marked their behaviour toward the returning Episcopalians. When Sharp, the future Archbishop of St Andrew's, but then the agent in London of the Scottish Presbyterians, reported to the leading city ministers the apprehensions of the Scots regarding the course pursued in

England, he was met with evasive excuses. They pointed, he said, to 'the present necessity they lie under, and the duty they owe to the peace of the Church'.[1] When the Irish Presbyterians wished to present to the King a resolution roundly denouncing episcopacy they could find no one who would introduce them at court, and received as little encouragement from the City ministers as from anyone. More revealing still is the letter sent by Edmund Calamy, Simeon Ash and Thomas Manton to the Presbyterian ministers in Edinburgh. 'We have to do', they said, 'with men of different humours and principles; the general stream and current is for the old prelacy in all its pomp and height, and therefore it cannot be hoped for that the Presbyterial government should be owned as the public establishment of this country, while the tide runneth so strongly that way.'[2] So, with anxious hopes that a place might be found for them and for certain of their principles within an Episcopal establishment, the Presbyterians humbly looked to the king for such favours as the royal clemency might offer.

It seemed that they had good grounds for hope. The public statements of the king had suggested a real determination to avoid the unhappy expedient of persecution. The famous declaration of Breda held out strong encouragement to those of 'tender conscience', and when the Lincolnshire Quakers presented an address to the king, he assured them that 'it was not his mind that any of his subjects who lived peaceably should suffer any trouble upon account of their judgments or opinions in matters of religion, and that he had declared the same in several declarations'.[3] When

[1] Sharp to Douglas, 14 July 1660, White Kennett, *A Register and Chronicle, Ecclesiastical and Civil*, vol. 1, p. 205.

[2] Woodrow, *History of the Church of Scotland*, vol. 1, Introduction, App. no. 10.

[3] Jessey, *The Lord's Loud Call to England* (1660), p. 15.

occasion served, the king's ministers were quick to cite his efforts to promote religious peace. In one of his long-winded and sententious speeches to parliament (29 December 1660), Clarendon pointed to Charles' attempts to achieve unity, and added that 'Constantine himself hardly spent so much of his own time in private and public conferences to that purpose'.[1]

The king's advisers had shrewdly contrived that his promises were made contingent on parliamentary ratification, and it soon appeared that the eager Anglicans who made up the new parliament had no intention of giving effect to the king's promises of leniency. Yet at the very beginning of the reign even the Anglicans had been a little uncertain of their position. They had come back, but no one was quite sure with what measure of strength. As a result, many of the early proposals of Anglican spokesmen were accommodating in tone and generous in spirit.[2] Then, with amazing rapidity, they discovered how unbounded their triumph had been. Sharp, shrewdly watching the unfolding of events, reported early in the reign that 'the Episcopal party here are still increasing in number as well as confidence',[3] and soon the tide of reaction was running so strongly that nothing could check it. Clarendon, nervous for the peace and unity of the realm, tried in vain to avoid extreme courses. 'And shall we fold our arms toward one another', he asked, 'and contract our hearts with envy and malice to

[1] White Kennett, op. cit. vol. 1, p. 340.

[2] Cf. *The Declaration of the Nobility, gentry and clergy that adhered to the late King in and about the City of London*: 'we do sincerely profess that we do reflect upon our past sufferings as from the hand of God and therefore do not cherish any violent thoughts or inclinations to those who have been in any way instrumental in them. And if the indiscretion of any spirited persons transports them to any expressions contrary to this our sense, we utterly disclaim them.'

[3] Woodrow, op. cit. (Introd.), p. 49.

each other, by any sharp memory of what hath been un-
neighbourly or unkindly done heretofore?'[1] Such advice
was like straw before the fierce flames of the Anglican
revival. Every memory of the past, every circumstance in
the present, predisposed the men who now had power
against leniency toward those who had lost it. Bitterness on
account of old grievances, anxiety for the newly established
régime, a complacent attitude to their own church, and a
settled theory of what constituted the foundations of public
order—these factors, and many others, made the prospect
of toleration seem infinitely remote. When Clarendon could
declare that the Church of England was the best reformed
Church in the world, a brand plucked from the burning,
a body raised from the dead and miraculously preserved and
restored to its possessions, he was expressing that triumphant
confidence which persuaded scores of humbler Anglicans
that no concessions need be made to the shattered forces of
dissent.

But however many and however strong might be the
psychological and political forces making for repression, the
decision to persecute corresponded to a closely reasoned
body of opinion. After all, the right to persecute was disputed only by small and often negligible bodies of enthusiasts. The Anglicans who justified repression could
appeal both to the deeds and words of their opponents. It
was a leading Puritan who had assured the Long Parliament

[1] From Clarendon's speech to the two Houses of Parliament, 13
September 1660. Note the tone in which he continues: 'Whilst we
conspire together to execute faithfully this part of the Bill [an Act of
Oblivion], to put all old names and terms of distinction into utter
oblivion; let us not find new names and terms to keep up the same, or
a worse distinction. If the old reproaches of Cavalier and Roundhead
and malignant be committed to the grave, let us not find more significant
and better words to signify worse things....' White Kennett, op. cit.
vol. 1, p. 258.

that 'divisions, whether they be ecclesiastical or political, in kingdoms, cities, or families, are infallible causes of ruin to kingdoms, cities or families'.[1] After reproducing more than a score of similar denunciations, L'Estrange angrily asked why men who had expounded such opinions could dare to expect lenient treatment. 'How comes it now to be so criminal to deny these people a toleration, which they themselves account to be wholly intolerable; or with what face can they call the refusal of that liberty to themselves by the name of a persecution, which they look upon in all other cases as against the rules of government and conscience to grant?'[2] The right to persecute had always been among the prerogatives of success, but it is at least significant that men now felt it necessary to defend that ancient right.

In its simplest form, the defence of persecution appealed to current political theory. The accepted view of the relations of Church and State made it difficult for any government meekly to countenance dissent. The Church was regarded as the religious expression of the nation's life, and unity was as necessary here as it was in the political sphere. Division in the one area would inevitably foster weakness in the other. This explains the determination to bring the Nonconformists back to the Established Church. Underlying the Act of Uniformity is a simple but basic assumption: there can only be one ecclesiastical expression of the life of

[1] Calamy, *Sermon before the House of Commons*, 25 December 1644.

[2] R. L'Estrange, *The Dissenters Sayings* (the second part; 1681), p. 7. L'Estrange's triumphant conclusion is that the 'full and unanimous testimony' of the Presbyterians is against toleration, 'nay against any sort of toleration either in doctrine or in discipline, and in what measure of degree soever; as a thing utterly impious and therefore insufferable. This, methinks, should be sufficient to stop the mouth of a Presbyterian when he demands a toleration; that he himself pronounces it a wicked thing to grant it.' Ibid. p. 77.

a united nation. Consequently, outside that one church no rights can be recognized and no concessions granted. To give way at this point would inevitably foster national weakness. When Clarendon reviewed the early years of the reign of Charles II, he attributed to the king precisely this point of view. 'And then he hoped', wrote Clarendon, 'to provide...such a settlement in religion as would prevent any disorder in the state upon these pretences.'[1] It was the firm belief both of bishops and of politicians that concessions would be wrong as well as foolish.[2] It might be permissible, remarked Samuel Parker, for the king to sanction religious toleration, 'yet it is a very dangerous thing to encourage several sects of religion in the same kingdom; every one of them would wage war against another, each of them would be an enemy to the rest, and all of them to the Church established by law; it was found by the experience of all ages, that differences in religion always ended in blows...the Christian world had seldom been engaged in civil war which was not raised under a pretence of religion.'[3] In some quarters this theory reigned unchallenged to the end of the period. When the Revolution settlement was under discussion, Prideaux, who as archdeacon of Suffolk spoke out of practical experience, urged that those who attended conventicles should be registered and excluded from all government positions. His reason is illuminating: 'Nothing is more unreasonable than that those who are against the

[1] Clarendon, *Continuation*, p. 1047.

[2] Cf. Pope's *Life of Seth Ward*, p. 57, where his severity to Nonconformists is attributed exclusively to his 'love to the repose and welfare of the government'. Cf. also Cosin, *Correspondence*, vol. I, p. 93. Note also Cobbett's *Parliamentary History*, vol. IV, p. 413: in the debate on His Majesty's speech regarding the union of his Protestant subjects, one member declared that he 'never knew a toleration which did not require an army to keep all quiet'.

[3] S. Parker, *History of His Own Time*, p. 354.

government should have any hand in the management of it.'[1] Prideaux had accepted the Toleration Act; dissenters should be free to worship as they pleased, but their separation from the State Church still made them bad citizens. Thus far a conservative churchman had moved in his thinking; for most of his contemporaries this illogical compromise was no longer necessary. They had relinquished the view of Church and State which it presupposed.

The Anglican attitude to Nonconformists was put forward by an immense number of writers, and no single position commanded general assent. At the outset, there was a small but influential group who upheld establishment but favoured a relatively lenient attitude toward the dissenters. High churchmanship, in men like Thorndike, immediately proposed an alternative approach. Gradually there emerged a large body of opinion which stood, in one form or another, for the exclusive rights of the State Church, and which defended its privileges with a body of arguments which must be accepted as characteristic of Anglicanism as a whole. At the same time, it is interesting to note that the advocates of more uncompromising measures were often men like Parker and Tomkins—Episcopal chaplains with a shrewd eye for the views which would commend a rising man for high promotion. Occupying a more extreme position, and commending repression with shrill and monotonous insistence, was Sir Roger L'Estrange.

At the opening of the Restoration period, there seemed good grounds for hoping that an accommodation of religious differences could be found. Because the Presbyterians felt insecure and the Anglicans were uncertain of their strength, influential voices on both sides urged the need of a reasonable settlement. As a result, the formal discussion of toleration

[1] Humphrey Prideaux, *Letters*, p. 154.

opened in a spirit of forbearance which promised well but proved short-lived. John Gauden, bishop-elect of Exeter and a man of considerable influence, undertook to expound the meaning and consequences of the king's 'gracious declaration', and his aim in discussing religious differences was to achieve 'a happy union in Church and State'.[1] He recognized that liturgical differences kept the Protestants of England apart, and he noted with appreciation the attitude of those who looked for minor and reasonable changes and avoided extreme demands or unmeasured abuse. He believed that with a man of Baxter's mind agreement could easily be reached,[2] but he sharply rebuked those who used the prospect of concessions merely to aggravate their scrupulosity of conscience. While recognizing that changes could be made to satisfy uneasy minds, he insisted that too wide concessions would defeat their purpose and prove unsettling to the public peace. Most Englishmen, he was persuaded, wanted a liturgy: they found that it edified and instructed the people, and served as an admirable restraint against all kinds of religious extravagance.[3] Like most of his contemporaries, Gauden believed that too much latitude in belief or worship encouraged disaffection; till 'public devotion and worship' were put beyond 'eternal variations and mutual vexations' there was no prospect of prosperity or peace in England.[4] At the outset of the period, a man of established position was willing to offer minor changes while stressing the necessity of a settled form of worship. Even more important than his specific suggestions was the tone of reasonable forbearance in which he discussed a

---

[1] *Considerations touching the Liturgy of the Church of England, in reference to His Majesty's late Gracious Declaration, and in order to a happy union in Church and State* (1661).

[2] Ibid. p. 33.   [3] Ibid. pp. 9f., 22.   [4] Ibid. pp. 29–31.

subject too quickly transferred to the realm of acrimonious debate.

Even earlier a young man destined for great prominence in the Church had issued an appeal which had attracted wide attention. Stillingfleet's *Irenicum* was ostensibly a plea for a generous recognition of the rights of conscience; it was actually a strange combination of liberalism and intolerance. He admits that no single form of Church government can claim such clear authority as to silence discussion, and even if we knew the nature of Apostolic practice, changed conditions might make ancient solutions ineffective.[1] 'It would be strange that the Church should require more than Christ himself did; and make other conditions of communion than our Saviour did of discipleship. What possible reason can be assigned or given why such things should not be sufficient for communion with a church, which are sufficient for eternal salvation?'[2] According to the laws of nature, the Church must have power to preserve peace within itself, but it has 'no direct immediate power over men's opinions'.[3] Uniformity of thought is as elusive as perfection itself, and though it may be a punishable offence to advance opinions contrary to those of the Established Church, 'it is not the difference of opinion formally considered that is punishable, but the tendency to schism which lies in the divulging of it'.[4] Even schism is not necessarily evil; its character is determined by the grounds which serve to justify it. But at this point we reach the limits of Stillingfleet's liberalism. He lays down no principle which will protect the separatist from persecution. His theory of relations between Church and State rests on an extreme form of the contract theory. Except where divine precept or natural law clearly decide an issue,

---

[1] Stillingfleet, *Irenicum*, p. 152.   [2] Ibid. (Preface).
[3] Ibid. p. 108.   [4] Ibid. p. 107.

the magistrate is free to settle the proper forms of church
government and worship. Stillingfleet concedes freedom of
opinion, but withholds liberty to give outward expression
to it.[1] Consequently we already have a dualism which persists throughout a great part of the ensuing generation.
Freedom of thought is divided from freedom of action; a
man is at liberty to think as he likes provided he outwardly
conforms to the patterns of conduct prescribed by the civil
power. The reason, again, is one common to most writers
of the period: freedom of thought, when combined with
freedom of expression, disrupts the public peace, and the
magistrate can never countenance subversive forces. In the
course of his argument, Stillingfleet has advanced principles
which clearly imply the exaltation of the civil power over
the religious.[2] While apparently advocating a large measure
of religious latitude, he has laid down principles which
would serve to justify the most oppressive form of ecclesiastical régime. He recognizes the rights of the individual
conscience, but does nothing to safeguard them in case of
conflict with the civil power.

What Stillingfleet offered with one hand, he withheld
with the other, but his book occupied an important place
because it was ostensibly a plea for a more tolerant approach
to religious divisions. At this point, it is necessary to mention in passing a movement, initiated and supported by
friends of Stillingfleet, which aimed at restoring unity by
offering the dissenters comprehension within the Established
Church. Schemes of this kind were advanced from time to
time throughout the Restoration period, and usually they
commanded influential support, both clerical and lay. In
every case, the opposition could appeal to powerful prejudices, and even in the midst of anti-Roman panic the

---

[1] Stillingfleet, op. cit. pp. 39–40.   [2] Ibid. pp. 45–6.

proposals had little prospect of success. After the Revolution a final effort had the active support of Lord Nottingham on the one hand and of Bishop Burnet on the other, but Tory churchmanship, smarting from the discipline of recent political and ecclesiastical events, effectually blocked the scheme.

Meanwhile, throughout the period the general outlines of what may be described as the official Anglican position became increasingly clear. It was held with an infinite number of variations and modifications but certain points appear and reappear so often that we can assume that they formed the core of characteristic Anglican thought on the subject of toleration.

Many of the advocates of repression started with—and never got beyond—a deep-seated fear of dissenters as potential rebels. Contemporary documents of every kind bear eloquent testimony to the nervousness of all in places of responsibility. Cromwell's troopers had been disbanded and dispersed over the countryside, but might they not unite to overthrow the king? The State papers of the time are full of reports—many of them transparently absurd—of the plottings of the sectaries. 'The Schismatics', declared Parker, 'would never be quiet...they would never want the will and inclination to rebel.'[1] Dissent became identified with sedition.[2] Whenever Nonconformists gathered in noticeable numbers, the immediate inference was that 'many of them enter into plots and conspiracies to disturb the peace of the kingdom'.[3] Roger L'Estrange was convinced that

[1] Parker, *History of His Own Time*, p. 5.

[2] This is uniformly true in Cosin's letters during the early years of the period. *Correspondence*, vol. II, pp. 197–205. Cf. also *Letters to Sir J. Williamson*, vol. I, p. 93.

[3] Order in Council, 2 January 1660/1, White Kennett, *A Register and Chronicle, Civil and Ecclesiastical*, vol. I, p. 352.

the aim of the Presbyterians was 'to enslave both King and people under the masque of religion'.[1] Again and again the extravagances of the Interregnum were recalled, and cited as reasons why the dissenters must be relentlessly repressed.[2] 'All order', remarked an Anglican apologist, 'was rooted out of God's house, and the whole land made a rude chaos of confusion. There was no beauty in the holy temple, 'twas converted into a den of thieves, nay, which is worse, if possible, into a stable for horses.'[3] 'The misery of our last and wasting misery', declared another writer, 'we have not forgotten: for our land was surfeited with blood...we carried our lives in our hands and our estates were exposed to rapine. Heresies and schisms did eat like a gangrene, and religion was lost in the atheism, blasphemy, epicurism, and liberty of those looser times.'[4] The same forces, he added, still threatened the peace and stability of the country. In few books of the period was the damaging legacy of the Civil War more ably urged against the dissenters than in Parker's *A Discourse of Ecclesiastical Polity* (1669?/70). He laid the responsibility for the late troubles entirely on Puritan polity and belief, and drew the inference that sedition always grew from fanaticism. 'Indulgence to dissenting zealots', he concluded, 'does but expose the state to the perpetual squabble and wars of religion.'[5] It was consequently easy

[1] L'Estrange, *Interest Mistaken, or the Holy Cheat...*, title-page. Cf. Anthony à Wood's description of Vavasour Powell: 'an indefatigable enemy to monarchy and episcopacy.' *Fasti Oxon.* vol. II, col. 347.

[2] Cf. (Tomkins), *The Inconveniences of Toleration* (1667), pp. 28–32.

[3] Westfield, *The White Robe* (1660), Epistle to the Reader.

[4] D. Featley, *The League Illegal* (1660). Publisher's Introduction.

[5] Parker, op. cit. p. 160. Note Sir Frederick Pollock's comment that when men are discontented with the government under which they live, and the Church is inseparable from it, their discontent is directed against the Church, with sectarianism and infidelity as the results. 'It is both

for the less scrupulous Anglican champions to represent any appeal for more lenient treatment of dissent as merely a plea for dissensions in Church and State, and then triumphantly to prove how evil these actually were.[1] It was equally convenient to infer that the dissenters were maliciously stubborn people, who would respect no argument but force and respond to no discipline but persecution.[2] Such an attitude could only rest on a deliberate refusal to recognize that nonconformity was an inclusive term, and covered men of widely differing points of view.[3] It also justified the abusive tone which often did duty for more serious argument. Any man, remarked an anonymous writer, who appeals for toleration might just as well plead for drunkenness, since those who advocate the one will be guilty also of the other.[4] The practical inference drawn from all this was the value of sterner measures. If allowed any latitude, the Nonconformists will be dangerous subjects of the State; they are always unreasonable and opinionated people who must be sternly disciplined; repression will effectually persuade them to return to the national Church. There can be no danger, said L'Estrange, in subjecting so many people to

natural and convenient for churchmen to invert the real order of cause and effect, and assign the origin of every general disorder to the heresy and infidelity which is in truth only a symptom of it.' *Essays in Jurisprudence and Ethics*, p. 171.

[1] Cf. R. Perrinchief, *A Discourse of Toleration* (1667/?8), p. 10.

[2] Cf. (Turner), *Animadversions upon a late Pamphlet Entitled the Naked Penalties which a Due Reformation Requires* (1670), p. 59; Stillingfleet, *The Unreasonableness of Separation* (1680/1), p. 372; Saywell, *Evangelical and Catholic Unity Maintained in the Church of England* (1682), Preface to the Reader.

[3] As an interesting example of the tendency to include all dissenters in an undiscriminating condemnation, cf. Thorndike, *The Due Way of Composing the Differences on Foot* (1660), passim.

[4] *Toleration with its objections Fully Confuted* (1663). The author was probably Henry Savage.

persecution. 'There will not be many sufferers where there are not many offenders, and there will not be many offenders where an early severity is used.'[1]

Dissenters, of course, were of various kinds, and no seventeenth-century pamphleteer could forget Popery for very long. At times, the threat from Rome became acute, and tended to draw the divided Protestants together, but for a great part of the Restoration period Anglican writers were content to emphasize the encouragement given to Roman Catholics by the divisions for which Nonconformists were responsible. The ends pursued by both wings of dissent were regarded as actually the same.[2] It is impossible, said Stillingfleet, to eradicate Romanism where toleration is allowed,[3] because leniency always works to the advantage of Romanism.[4] In addition, of course, almost all writers were agreed that the political principles of Roman Catholics placed them beyond any pale that might be erected, but the religious aspect of the question also required consideration. It is worth noticing that with time the view increasingly prevailed that persecution (regarded as a stigma against Romanism) could not be a vice in one group and a virtue in another. If it was wrong for the Catholics to suppress

---

[1] L'Estrange, *Interest Mistaken, or The Holy Cheat* (1661), p. 148.

[2] Note the tendency to identify Nonconformists and Jesuits, cf. Hickes' sermon on 30 January 1681/2 (quoted in Figgis, *Divine Right of Kings*, p. 182). Cf. also the ballad, 'Geneva and Rome':

> 'The Bishops tell Charles we both have long nails,
> And Charles shall find it if either prevails,
> For like Sampson's foxes we're tied by the tails,
>   Which nobody can deny.'

Quoted in W. W. Wilkins, *Political Ballads*, vol. i, p. 224.

[3] Stillingfleet, *The Unreasonableness of Separation* (1680/1), Preface, p. lxxix.

[4] Saywell, *Evangelical and Catholic Unity Maintained in the Church of England* (1682), p. 131.

Protestants, it could not be right for Protestants to persecute each other.

The fear of dissent explains what is perhaps the most striking feature of the Anglican defence of repression. The tone and outlook are both those of men charged with a policeman's duties, and the paramount need of maintaining order was uppermost in many minds. It is true that on occasion a writer would appeal to the authority of Christ and his Apostles or to the example of the early Church,[1] but on the whole the argument is less theological and religious than civil and political. Fear of chaos was a legacy left by the Great Rebellion, and the need of maintaining civil order was a theme dear to every Anglican writer. The magistrate is the father of his people, and his first duty is to protect them from disturbance.[2] He must safeguard them from attacks on their faith as much as from attacks on their persons, for disturbance of religious peace will threaten the very foundations of order. Toleration encourages rebellion, and there can be no stability where the divisive tendencies of rival religious groups are not controlled.[3] The obsession of the period with the need of orderly government appears again and again. 'A bare and simple dissent' might be permissible, but 'when that dissent comes to be practical' it is 'no longer a plea of conscience but a direct conspiracy against the government...why may they not as well demand a dispensation for rebellion as for schism?'[4] Even Glanvill, a man of enlightened outlook, could combine a theoretical

[1] (Perrinchief), *Indulgence not Justified* (1668), pp. 9–30.

[2] *Toleration with its Objections Fully Confuted*, pp. 33–5.

[3] Cf. the appendix to *Fair Warning, or XXV Reasons Against Toleration.* On the destructive nature of toleration, cf. Stillingfleet, *The Unreasonableness of Separation* (Preface), p. lxxviii.

[4] L'Estrange, *The Free-born Subject; or the Englishman's Birthright* (1679), pp. 11–12.

belief in the value of toleration with an admission of the need of persecution as a bulwark of the State.[1] When the prevailing concern is a desire to preserve public order, a new importance is attached to the Church's doctrine of the obedience which subjects owe their rulers. The theory of the divine right of kings had been reinstated with enthusiasm, and from time to time an Anglican pamphleteer proved how incompatible religious liberty was with proper submission to the civil power.[2] It was consequently natural that one of the shrewdest statements of the case for repression started from the duty of proper obedience on the subject's part.[3] Beyond any other factor, conscience has proved a source of trouble to governments and a threat to the supremacy of princes. Every man's whim is cloaked with the sanctity of conscience, and when people demand the right to hold their cherished views, they defy the prince's authority and acknowledge no governor but themselves.[4] A ruler must have power to control the consciences of his subjects; government exists in order to preserve peace in the commonwealth, and this can never be secured unless religion is subject to the supreme civil power.[5] It is as necessary to control excessive zeal as it is to suppress immorality, and there is no way of controlling the turbulent emotions of men except by acknowledging the supreme power of the prince in eccle-

[1] 'To strive for toleration is to contend against all government; to allow the plea of conscience is to put an end to all laws.' Glanvill, *The Zealous and Impartial Protestant* (written 1678, publ. 1681), pp. 26–7.

[2] As in L'Estrange, *The Free-born Subject* (1679). Cf. L'Estrange's comment in *Toleration Discussed* (1663), p. 146: 'The Stress of the question, in order to a toleration, does not bear so much upon this point, whether your opinions be true or false; as whether safe or dangerous.'

[3] Parker, *A Discourse of Ecclesiastical Polity* (1669?/70).

[4] Ibid. pp. 4–7.

[5] Ibid. pp. 10, 11.

siastical affairs.[1] Given this attitude, it became an easy matter for pamphleteers to regard the law as sacrosanct in itself. It carried its own sanction; to look behind it was to show a dangerous disregard of public safety.[2] The Interregnum was seen as decisive proof of the disasters which follow from tampering with the law, and unquestioning acceptance appeared the only path of wisdom and security.[3] Such an attitude could not indefinitely survive. It was contrary to the whole genius of British constitutional development, and the experience of a few years' security showed how needless it was. Long before the end of the period, voices were raised from within the Church to protest against this blind devotion to the letter of the law. 'It is not in the laws, but in the equity and justice of them that the obligation lies, and that is the question at issue.'[4]

Often, however, the law was regarded as useful rather than sacrosanct. It might not be holy in itself, but it was a most valuable means of checking the spread of error. It was a deterrent to the rash, and a corrective to the foolish. The purpose of persecution, wrote Perrinchief, is that 'it may take off all encouragements to error, and so make men more diligent in the search for truth, when it will not be safe to deceive or be deceived'.[5] Repression may not eradicate error, but at least it will keep it from spreading.[6] An argument of this kind, it may be noted, was more subject than most to revision in the light of experience. At the beginning

[1] Ibid. pp. 25–8.
[2] Cf. L'Estrange, *Citt and Bumpkin, in a Discussion over a Pot of Ale, concerning matters of Religion and Government* (1680).
[3] Cf. Parker, op. cit. pp. 286 f.
[4] *Some Additional Remarks on the Late Book of the Reverend Dean of St Paul's by a Conformable Clergyman* (1681), p. 10.
[5] Perrinchief, *A Discourse of Toleration* (1667/?8), p. 16.
[6] (Tomkins), *The Inconveniences of Toleration* (1667), p. 24.

of the period many Anglicans were not reconciled to the prospect of dissent as a permanent element in the nation's life; by the end it had been proved that persecution would not create unity, and that 'mistaken notions' persisted in spite of the most rigorous laws.

A conspicuous feature of the debate on toleration was the attempt to draw a clear distinction between liberty of thought and freedom to give expression to it. Few Anglicans claimed that you could effectively determine a man's opinions, and the more liberal among them treated it as a mark of grace that they did not try. But it was one thing to hold to the light of conscience, and quite another so to follow its leading as no longer to conform, in conduct or in worship, to prescribed usage. Even L'Estrange admitted that it was barbarous and ridiculous to refuse liberty of conscience, but the Act of Uniformity limited men's actions, not their thoughts, and to think that conscience could expect free expression was 'not only unreasonable but utterly inconsistent both with Christianity itself and the public peace'.[1] Even Tillotson advanced the same opinion. 'I cannot but think', he declared '...that any pretence of conscience warrants any man that is not extraordinarily commissioned as the Apostles and first publishers of the Gospel were, and cannot justify that commission by miracles, as they did, to affront the established religion of a nation, though it be false, and openly to draw off men from the profession of it in contempt of the magistrate and the law.'[2]

It will be apparent at once that most of the arguments put forward are not theological or even religious in character. In so far as the safety of the State Church was involved, they were ecclesiastical, but often they were frankly concerned

[1] L'Estrange, *Toleration Discussed* (1663), p. 3.
[2] Tillotson, Sermon xxvii; cf. Similar comments in Sermon xxi.

with issues of orderly government and national stability. As regards belief, there was general agreement that the differences which divided Anglicans and Nonconformists were neither many nor serious.[1] The problem was due in part to the difficulty of admitting that a second form of worship could safely be recognized. It was a new departure; many people did not believe it was possible; even those who did, believed it would be a pernicious development. Repression, moreover, was closely related to the need for reviving ecclesiastical discipline. What was the good of excommunicating a churchman if he could immediately take refuge in a conventicle?[2] There was no widespread conviction that truth and order could be trusted to vindicate their own cause, and many believed that both would perish if not properly protected. Part of the difficulty lay in the problem of seeing how and where the limits of toleration could be established. Everyone acknowledged that you could not control a man's private convictions, and most were prepared to admit that you should not try. On the other hand, there was general agreement that order must be preserved and license restrained. Because the threat of chaos was so alarming, many people believed that freedom must be limited in the interests of order, and this became, beyond anything else, the motive of the Anglican plea for uniformity.

The discussion of toleration had, however, become a

[1] Cf. *A Sober and Seasonable Discourse*... (1681), p. 23, where the author indicates at what points Anglicans and dissenters agree or differ in doctrine. They are at one in accepting the three great creeds, and 'in all or most of the moral doctrines of our Church', but there are 'some little differences between us'—Sabbath Observance, Predestination, Free-will. When controversy arose, these 'little differences' seemed important.

[2] Thorndike, *Discourse of the Forbearance or the Penalties which a Due Reformation Requires* (1670), pp. 161, 162.

debate, and a pamphlet on one side immediately called forth
a reply on the other. The Nonconformists were quite capable
of stating their own case, but as the period advanced it
became apparent that an increasing number of thoughtful
men—inside the Established Church as well as beyond it—
were persuaded that persecution could no longer justify
itself.

The simplest of the arguments for toleration was a plea
that the Nonconformists should be judged by the principles
they actually held and not by designs arbitrarily attributed
to them by their critics. If people would only take the trouble
to discover the real dissenters behind the mythical figures so
often held up to execration, it would soon be seen that they
were not seditious schemers against the nation's peace. The
discipline of learning what the situation really was would in
itself be a most salutary check to indiscriminate abuse.[1]

Even if dissent deserved to be repressed, it was still true
that persecution was the wrong way of doing so. Of necessity it failed to secure precisely the results at which it aimed.
It could not create faith, nor could it effect moral reform.
Even if it produced conformity it won an empty victory, for
worship which does not spring from free persuasion is an
abomination in the sight of God.[2] The moral culpability of
persecution became increasingly apparent to those who felt
bound to question its success. Assent should only be given
upon conviction. Constraints on conscience amount to an
attempt to force men 'to reject all respects to the future
judgments of God', and the final results will be disastrous:

---

[1] John Owen, *A Peace Offering in an Apology and Humble Plea for Indulgence and Liberty of Conscience* (1668). *Works*, vol. XXI, pp. 403-4.
Cf. also (Croft), *Naked Truth* (Preface to the Reader).

[2] *Persecution for Religion Judged and Condemned* (a reprint in 1662 of an
earlier tract). *Tracts on Liberty of Conscience*, p. 146.

'Atheism will be the end of such an endeavour.'[1] The Gospel
cannot be enforced by persecution; it can only win its way
by 'its own piety and wisdom'.[2] It consequently follows
that the whole genius of Christianity is opposed to the persecutor's task, and the liberty of true religion is a particularly
precious witness of the Protestant Churches. The attempt
to achieve uniformity by coercion must have the most
mischievous results in any state which rests on Protestant
principles, because it alienates the best men in every party,
and antagonizes 'the generality of the nation'.[3] Even the
innate reasonableness of the average man revolts against the
anomaly of attempting to compel what can only be freely
accorded.[4] In the final analysis, uniformity is an ideal which
is doomed to frustration. Unanimity in worship has never
existed, and punishments will not create it. The suggested
goal is beyond our reach, and the means employed will never
win it for us.[5]

Repression as a political policy appealed to a certain theory
of Church and State, but the surmise was growing that that
theory is essentially unsound. It is an error to identify the
two realms, and they cannot be treated as though they were
coextensive.[6] The evidence both of Scripture and of Christian
history proves that no magistrate has received power from
God to compel acquiescence in 'spiritual causes'. The civil
power has repeatedly shown that its judgements are fallible

---

[1] John Owen, *Indulgence and Toleration Considered* (1667). *Works*,
vol. xxi, pp. 385–8.

[2] John Sturgeon, *A Plea for Toleration....* (*Tracts on Liberty of
Conscience*, pp. 323–41.)

[3] (Sir Charles Wolseley), *A Peaceable Dissertation* (1669), pp. 6–7.

[4] This argument, set forth in Sturgeon (op. cit.) is an interesting
tribute to the growing weight assigned to rational considerations.

[5] Owen, *A Peace Offering....* *Works*, vol. xxi, p. 435.

[6] Owen, *Indulgence and Toleration....* *Works*, vol. xxi, pp. 375–85.

and its insights limited or mistaken; therefore let it be
content to punish civil misdemeanours, and refrain from
claiming powers which have been withheld from it by
God.[1]

The argument from human fallibility could be developed
in more ways than one. It encouraged the claim that truth
and order could be trusted to uphold their own cause. Some,
like Stillingfleet, might still insist that religion could not be
trusted to stand alone,[2] but many believed that truth must
inevitably, and by its very nature, ultimately prevail. If error
is finally self-destructive, can we not assume that truth
possesses an inherent vitality which will overcome all
opposition?[3] It might also be assumed that, since we are so
prone to error, our imperfection would encourage an attitude of humility.[4] Consequently all laws should be so framed
that mistaken or misguided men cannot use them to impose
their own views on their fellow-men. Moreover, the argument, so frequently advanced, that national safety requires
religious uniformity, is disproved by experience. The
champions of toleration repeatedly pointed to the example
of countries where it has been tried.[5] Sir William Petty
examined in some detail the reasons for Holland's more
liberal attitude.[6] Sir William Temple, also appealing to
Dutch experience, claimed that some things by their very

[1] Cf. *Sion's Groans for her Distressed, or Sober Endeavours to Prevent
Innocent Blood* (1661). *Tracts on Liberty of Conscience and Persecution*,
pp. 349–82.

[2] Stillingfleet, *The Mischief of Separation* (1680), pp. 13–14.

[3] Owen, *A Peace Offering...*, p. 436.

[4] Cf. *Some Additional Remarks on the Late Book by the Reverend Dean of
St Paul's by a Conformable Clergyman* (1681), pp. 26–9.

[5] Cf. William Penn, *The Great Case of Liberty of Conscience Once
More Briefly Debated and Defended* (1671), pp. 39–40.

[6] Petty, *Political Arithmetic*, pp. 20–2 (in Aitken, *Later Stu-
Tracts*, pp. 1–67).

nature fall short of absolute certainty; it is therefore foolish to risk ends which can be achieved (like peace and order in the community) for goals which, like religious unanimity, lie wholly beyond our reach.[1]

It was natural that the advocates of toleration should challenge the Anglican attempt to concede liberty of belief while withholding freedom of worship. The distinction, said Owen, is unreal in itself and utterly meaningless in practice. There is no freedom of thought which does not include the right to express one's convictions, and in religion worship is merely the outward form which belief assumes.[2] If liberty is allowed in the one area, it must be granted in the other also.

The case for toleration, advocated in scores of tracts and pamphlets, found more complete expression in a number of works which should be briefly noted. William Penn, the Quaker, set forth an unusually thorough exposition of the theory of Toleration; the contributions of Croft, Burnet, and Pearse are important as indicating the point of view of liberal Anglicans, and Locke's famous *Letters* decisively closed the controversy.

Penn reduced the argument for toleration to a series of propositions. He began by asserting that persecution, by its very nature, invades the divine prerogative. The control of conscience is an incommunicable right of God; only the operation of God's Spirit can beget faith, and men who presume to regulate the beliefs of others actually claim to be infallible.[3] In the second place, the Christian religion cannot

[1] Temple, *Observations on the United Provinces* (1672). Note also *A Letter from Holland Touching Liberty of Conscience* (1688), especially pp. 1–2.

[2] Owen, *Indulgence and Toleration Considered.... Works*, vol. XXI, p. 385.

[3] Penn, *The Great Case of Liberty of Conscience....*(1671), pp. 12–14.

survive the use of force in matters of belief and worship. Christ's Kingdom is a spiritual Kingdom, and the methods of persecution are carnal. If once applied, they foster innumerable abuses, and cut off those who use them from the rewards which are the gift of true faith.[1] Moreover, the plain sense of the Scriptures is repugnant to restraint, imposition or resort to persecution.[2] Both nature and reason condemn persecution. To compel assent is to invade the liberty which is the right of every man; it robs men of the use and benefit of their natural intuition of God; it destroys all normal human affection. Even the wisest of us are fallible, and we all know that we cannot believe against our understanding. Coercion in the realm of faith makes nonsense even of the convictions we treasure most dearly, and involves the whole structure of Christian faith in collapse. Even the means employed to secure conformity are unreasonable; fines and imprisonment can never produce unity or agreement.[3] Finally, the use of force in matters of conscience is a direct threat to the very nature of government, to the means by which it is sustained and to the ends for which it exists.[4] Having established the principles on which toleration must rest, Penn was free in the remainder of his book to fortify his case by an appeal to experience.[5]

The Naked Truth—a work published anonymously by Bishop Croft of Hereford in 1675—created an immediate uproar among stricter Anglicans, but it marks the development of an outlook without which the grant of toleration would never have been possible. He placed the most

---

[1] Penn, op. cit. pp. 14–16.   [2] Ibid. p. 16.
[3] Ibid. pp. 19–23.   [4] Ibid. pp. 23–30.
[5] The Quakers, governed in their approach to the subject of toleration by their conviction regarding the inner light, contributed a large number of works to the discussion. Of these, it is only necessary to mention Isaac Penington's *Concerning Persecution*...(1661).

favourable construction on Nonconformist aims and principles; he dwelt on the variety of men and the futility of attempting to secure perfect agreement; he pointed out that Christianity is not a religion which lends itself, either by spirit or content, to coercive enforcement; he showed that ceremonies can be modified without sacrilege, and urged the value of concessions which might bring into the Church many who would be glad to accept any reasonable terms. The same general attitude is reflected in two of Burnet's many works. His *Exhortation to Peace and Unity* (1681) is an attack on 'the hot and bitter temper' of persecution, while his Preface to Lactantius' *Relation of the Death of the Primitive Persecutors* sets forth the arguments in favour of toleration. He emphasized the separate spheres of Church and State, the fallibility of men's judgement, the ability of truth to defend itself, and the corrupting effect of persecution on those who practise it.[1] Essentially similar in outlook is the series of works published by Edward Pearse in the later years of Charles II's reign. Though pleading for comprehension rather than toleration, they illustrate an attitude toward dissenters which directly contributed to the undermining of persecution.[2]

The Revolution guaranteed the acceptance of toleration as a practical feature of English political life, but its complete triumph as a theory was due to John Locke. The *Letters on Toleration* now seem tedious in their iteration of arguments which command general assent, but they only appear commonplace because Locke's immense authority firmly estab-

---

[1] Burnet, Preface to Lactantius's *Relation of the Death of the Primitive Persecutors* (Amsterdam, 1687), pp. 17–20; 12, 16, 17, 44. Cf. also his emphatic statement, *History of My Own Time*, vol. v, p. 107 (6 vols., ed. Oxford, 1823).

[2] Pearse, *The Conformist's Plea for the Nonconformist* (1681). *The Second, Third* and *Fourth Pleas* appeared in the years 1682 and 1683.

lished them among the intellectual assumptions of Western civilization. Locke's task was easier because the position which his opponents had chosen was unquestionably weak. The defence of persecution had been conducted on lines which recent events had shown to be untenable. Many of the practical objections to toleration had collapsed, and the theoretical refuge of the champions of the older approach was certainly not strong. They contended that those who would not embrace the true religion must be compelled, by moderate penalties, to consider the error of their ways. It was easy for Locke to show—and he did so repeatedly—that constraint can only produce outward conformity. It cannot secure inward conviction, and consequently all that could be punished was dissent, not 'want of consideration'. Any error which justified moderate penalties would equally warrant severe ones if initial measures failed, and no logical limits could be set to repression. Moreover, the 'true religion' can only mean in practice the faith which the magistrate himself accepts; all the attempts to avoid this conclusion ended in arguments which either begged the question or were circular in form. Again and again, Locke returned to the ineffectiveness of persecution as a means of propagating truth. The utmost it can do is to transform a man into a hypocrite. You can only believe if you see good reason to do so. There is no proper way of controlling conviction except by supplying adequate evidence on which it can rest. It is intolerable arbitrarily to dictate what others must believe.

What we actually need, declared Locke, is 'absolute liberty...equal and impartial liberty'. This unfettered freedom was hard to reconcile with certain prudential safeguards which Locke allowed, but it is with the promise of such liberty that he opened the discussion. In practice he approached the subject from a negative rather than a positive point of view. He was less convinced than most of his contemporaries of the immorality of religious error. He also had a more modest estimate of human resources for forming true judgements in religion. A constant sense of the limits of human understanding underlay all his arguments for toleration. He believed that in matters of religion there is no certain or demonstrative knowledge, and hence we must be satisfied with 'a persuasion of our own minds, short of knowledge'.[1] At the same time, he conceded that there are certain religious grounds for advocating toleration. It is, he declared, 'in the inward and full persuasion of the mind' that 'all the life and power of true religion consists.... I cannot be saved by a religion that I distrust, and by a worship that I abhor.'[2]

For at least a century past, the centre of controversy had been the right of a national Church to enforce uniformity, and the relation of the civil to the religious power had been carefully canvassed. Locke had no objection to a national establishment of religion, provided it was genuinely comprehensive, but it must be able to justify its claim to be the nation organized to promote goodness. He clearly hoped that the national religion, when recalled to the simplicities of the Gospel, would make toleration of dissenters an unreal issue, since few would remain. As to the conflict between Church and State, he would eliminate it by keeping the two spheres decisively apart. He withheld from the magistrate any right to dictate articles of belief or forms of worship, but he equally condemned those who 'upon pretence of religion' claimed special authority in civil affairs. 'I say', he added, 'these have no right to be tolerated by the magistrate.'[3]

[1] Locke, *Works*, vol. VI, p. 144.   [2] Ibid. pp. 11, 28.
[3] Ibid. p. 46.

This is not the only limitation Locke placed on the 'absolute liberty' he had promised the reader. There can be no toleration of atheists, because 'promises, covenants, and oaths, which are bonds of human society, can have no hold upon an atheist'.[1] Nor are Roman Catholics much better; their religion demands submission to a 'foreign jurisdiction', and they cannot give undivided allegiance to their own king.

The Act of Toleration (24 May 1689) ended the attempt to coerce Englishmen into religious uniformity. It provided that the persecuting acts should not apply to anyone who took the oaths of allegiance and supremacy and made the necessary declaration against trans-substantiation. It also stipulated, of course, that those who benefited from this reprieve must not hold meetings behind locked doors. Ministers were required to sign the Articles, excepting those on Church government, and special concessions were made to Anabaptists and Quakers. Roman Catholics and anti-Trinitarians were expressly excluded from the benefits of the Act. To all intents and purposes, the controversy was over. It is true that the Toleration Act did not repeal the persecuting statutes; as long as these remained the law of the land, toleration could only claim to be an exception allowed for practical purposes. But the concession was made because the persecuting spirit was dead and the theory of persecution discredited. During the coming generations, the influence of Locke made it impossible to resuscitate the old laws.

The triumph of toleration represented more than the power of certain arguments to win assent. It was the push of events that finally convinced Englishmen that persecution did not pay. Developments in the reign of James II were important, but many other factors worked to create the

[1] Locke, *Works*, vol. VI, p. 47.

situation in which the necessity of toleration could be clearly seen.

The intensity of religious feeling was steadily subsiding throughout the Restoration period. Earlier in the century every problem had had a religious aspect, and theological issues had been closely related to political developments. But the enthusiasms of the preceding years had brought reaction in their wake. A much more secular temper was beginning to prevail. Samuel Parker noted with indignation that those most eager for toleration often cared little for religion: 'a belief in the indifference, or rather imposture of all religion is now made the most effectual (not to say most fashionable) argument for liberty of conscience.'[1] Sir Charles Wolseley's discussion of the wise course for magistrates to follow[2] also illustrates the secular tone which increasingly marked much of the discussion of toleration. Theological rancour was declining and common sense finally and decisively triumphed in John Locke.

It naturally followed that persecution tended to justify itself on secular and political grounds. Political order and commercial prosperity were seen as objectives which a government might profitably pursue; men were more and more uncertain whether the magistrates could in any way regulate their neighbours' relationship to God.[3] But as a consequence it followed that persecution had to prove its actual effectiveness, and year by year doubt grew as to whether it could achieve the ends which justified its application. Once the issue had been removed from the realm of theological principle, it had to stand a pragmatic test.

[1] S. Parker, *A Discourse of Ecclesiastical Polity*, p. 167.
[2] (Sir Charles Wolseley), *A Peaceable Dissertation*, pp. 3–4.
[3] Cf. the tone of *A Letter from Holland Touching Liberty of Conscience* (1688).

As early as 1672, the king was prepared to admit failure. 'It being evident by the sad experience of twelve years that there is very little fruit of all these forcible courses',[1] it was logical to call a halt. National unity, on whose precarious position all defenders of persecution dwelt, was being jeopardized by the measures taken to preserve it.[2] An undated paper of Sir John Reresby describes the town of York as dangerously divided by religious differences.[3] The failure to achieve unity was so notable that it appears as one of the stock arguments in favour of toleration. Persecution had failed most conspicuously at precisely the point where political theory demanded success.

As the period progressed, it became clear that the Englishman's enthusiasm for persecution was rapidly declining. Parliament might still refuse to grant concessions, but steadily the popular support, without which any policy must ultimately fail, was being withdrawn. Sheldon could write to the bishops of his province that the execution of the persecuting laws was 'to the glory of God, the welfare of the Church, the praise of His Majesty and Government, and the happiness of the whole Kingdom',[4] but there is abundant evidence that the nation was less and less willing to agree. The methods used in enforcing the law were causing widespread revulsion. When John Owen protested against harshness in general and informers in particular,[5] he was not appealing to an indifferent public. John Gratton described a typical informer as 'a dark ignorant fellow, as all informers

[1] The Declaration of Indulgence, 1672. Cf. Grant Robertson, *Select Statutes, Cases, and Documents*, p. 42.

[2] This is forcibly argued in Penn's *England's Present Interest Discovered* (1675).

[3] From a paper in the Spencer MSS. Reresby, *Memoirs*, p. 264n.

[4] Quoted in Neal, *History of the Puritans*, vol. IV, p. 396.

[5] Owen, *A Word of Advice to the Citizens of London* and *The Present Distresses on Nonconformists Examined*. *Works*, vol. XXI, pp. 445–56, 473–80.

are, else they would not be informers',[1] but his language is temperate in comparison with the terms in which some of his contemporaries describe informers.[2]

The magistrates, in particular, disliked the duties thrust upon them, and were increasingly reluctant to discharge them.[3] Within ten years of the return of Charles II it was necessary to threaten justices of the peace with a fine of £100 if they neglected to enforce the persecuting laws, and when the Second Conventicle Act was passed, 'many honest men who would not be the instruments of such severities quitted the Bench'.[4] At the beginning of the period, the justice had often been as eager as anyone to harry the dissenters,[5] but the desire for revenge gradually subsided, and persecuting harmless people—however mistaken they might seem— was a task of which the man of normally decent instincts soon grew weary. The Quakers, in fact, by exhausting the malice of the justices, virtually won for the Nonconformists the right to maintain their own forms of worship.

Closely related to this was the growing respect for dissenters themselves, and, where respect is present, persecution cannot long survive. Experience was convincing the average Englishman that his Nonconformist neighbour was a decent, inoffensive member of society. By no means all dissenters were wilfully blind, and if some of them honestly held mistaken views, could they really be blamed?[6] 'They are

[1] John Gratton, *Journal*, p. 121.

[2] Cf. Burnet, *History of My Own Time* (ed. Airy), vol. 1, p. 490. Note also the extract from a contemporary tract, quoted by Geo. Fox, and reproduced in W. C. Braithwaite, *Second Period of Quakerism*, p. 78.

[3] Cf. Pearse, *The Conformist's Plea for the Nonconformist*, pp. 9–10.

[4] Neal, op. cit. vol. IV, p. 394.

[5] Cf. the examples given by John Whiting, Baxter, Martindale, Barnes, Gratton, etc.

[6] *Some Additional Remarks on the Late Book of the Reverend Dean of St Paul's by a Conformable Clergyman*, p. 29.

persons of holy lives and upright conversations, at least some of them; and I would not have a hand in persecuting or undoing them, for all the preferments this Church or this world affords.'[1] In many cases, neighbours did everything in their power to shield dissenters from the consequences of their position,[2] and before the period closes the worthiness of Nonconformists constantly appears as an argument for treating them with greater leniency.[3]

Political and economic factors also played their part. With the emergence, in embryo at least, of the two-party system, it was apparent that so large a group of citizens could not be ignored. The attempt to suppress dissent had been related to the struggle for power in the corporations,[4] but gradually the issue was lifted from the local to the national level. The Whigs were already discovering that the dissenters might be useful allies, and even the terms bandied about in the streets proved that nonconformity had been inextricably drawn into the vortex of political life.[5] During the years of Tory reaction, the dissenters suffered bitterly because of their association with the discredited leaders, but James II conferred on his country at least this benefit—that he ended the mad internecine struggle which marked the closing years of his brother's reign. The Revolution of 1688 was the joint achievement of both parties in Church and State. What neither Whig nor Tory, churchman nor dissenter, could do separately they did together. As a result, in 1689 they stood

[1] *Some Additional Remarks*..., p. 10.

[2] Cf. the particularly vivid account in Gratton, *Journal*, pp. 142–4.

[3] Cf. Pearse, op. cit. pp. 61–2. Note also H. M. Gwatkin's illuminating comments on this subject. *Cambridge Modern History* (1934 ed.), vol. v. p. 332.

[4] The Calendars of State Papers, Domestic (especially for the years 1663–4, 1667–8, 1670) contain innumerable references to the local politics of Chester, Yarmouth, Bristol, Gloucester.

[5] Cf. Luttrell, *Brief Historical Relation*, vol. i, pp. 106, 124.

as the joint custodians of power, and neither could demand that the clients of the other party should be liable to persecution. What they had won jointly, neither could appropriate to individual party ends. The last great persecution of the Nonconformists was due to political considerations, but so was the victory which they finally won.

Throughout the period Englishmen were growing more sensitive to arguments which frankly appealed to economic motives. We are repeatedly assured that persecution is bad for trade; it strikes at those sections of the community which contribute most to national prosperity; it discourages the immigration of those who have much to offer to the country, and it persuades useful members of the community to turn to a new life abroad.[1]

Persecution is only possible in a certain kind of intellectual environment. It presupposes an intensity of conviction so self-assured that truth is seen as the exclusive possession of one side and error as the characteristic mark of the other. In 1660, such an outlook prevailed in many quarters, but the forces at work throughout the period steadily corroded the confidence which maintained persecuting zeal. The authority of natural law was increasing and its mounting prestige influenced thinking on every subject, toleration included. It is a law of nature, declared Owen, to admit divergencies from uniformity;[2] 'the diversity of men's apprehension of things spiritual and supernatural'[3] merely reflects a funda-

---

[1] Cf. Owen, *Indulgence and Toleration*..., and *A Peace-offering*.... *Works*, vol. XXI, pp. 395, 439–40; (Wolseley), *A Peaceable Dissertation*, pp. 9–10; Ashley's Memorial to Charles II, Christie, *Life of Shaftesbury*, vol. II, App. I; Sir William Petty, *Political Arithmetic*, passim; *A Letter from Holland Touching Liberty of Conscience*, p. 3; Penn, *England's Present Interest Discovered*, pp. 42–5.

[2] Owen, *Indulgence and Toleration*.... *Works*, vol. XXI, p. 378.

[3] Owen, *A Peace-offering*.... *Works*, vol. XXI, p. 422.

mental element in the constitution of human society as ordered by natural law. Stillingfleet's *Irenicum* and the pamphlets of Sir Charles Wolseley reflect the same anxiety to claim the authority of natural law. An anonymous work entitled *Liberty of Conscience in its order to Universal Peace* (1681) frankly identifies 'natural religion and fundamental Christianity', and proves that both conform to the immutable laws of nature.

A part of the same change in the prevailing intellectual atmosphere was the growth of a rationalistic outlook. The claims of reason were treated with ever greater deference, and by the end of the period even common sense had established a virtual tyranny over religious thought. Many men had contributed to this result; few had expressed it more forcibly than Glanvill. 'To be confident in opinions', he declared, 'is ill manners and immodest.... This is that spirit of immorality that saith unto dissenters, "Stand off, I am more orthodox than thou art"; a vanity more capital than error.'[1] When such views were current, the assurance which claims possession of the truth and presumes by persecution to force others to accept it could only appear the height of opinionated arrogance. An anticipation of the cool and disengaged propriety of eighteenth-century enlightenment was already abroad. To such a mentality, the harrying of minor sects—or even the persecution of important religious minorities—was not the occupation of self-respecting men. In such an atmosphere a new belief in the value of toleration could rapidly gain ground. On the eve of the Revolution, Reresby, a typical Anglican squire, could affirm that 'most men were now convinced that liberty of conscience was a thing of advantage to the nation'.[2]

---

[1] Glanvill, *Scepsis Scientifica* (1665), pp. 199–200 (Owen's edition).
[2] Reresby, *Memoirs*, p. 393.

CHAPTER X

CONCLUSION

CENTURY by century the complexion of religious thought changes, and every period has its distinctive quality. But the transition from the seventeenth century to the eighteenth represents a modification more complete and more important than the differences of emphasis which normally distinguish one period from the next. In the forty years which followed the Restoration, a change took place of quite unusual significance. The men who represented Anglicanism when Charles II came back to his throne had clear affinities with the past. Thorndike and Hammond had been trained in the school of Hooker and Andrewes, but Hooker, as Dr Tillyard has shown,[1] reflects the outlook of the Elizabethan age. His view of the world traced its origin back beyond the Renaissance, through the Middle Ages to thought-forms yet more ancient. But at the end of the century, the men whose works were moulding religious thought were indebted to Newton for their understanding of the world and to Locke for their interpretation of man's relation to it. Their outlook was, in embryo at least, the outlook of the modern age. These forty years have usually been neglected; the religious leaders were for the most part mediocre men, and great writers few and far between, but the works of men of second-rate ability mark a change of first-rate importance.

As the character of religious thought altered, the ascendancy of reason became steadily more pronounced. This was the most striking single feature of the period from 1660 to

[1] E. M. W. Tillyard, *The Elizabethan World Picture* (London, 1943), p. 10.

1700, and this essay has referred to it again and again. The importance of reason was not a new discovery of the Restoration age. In Anglican theology there was a strain of very ancient lineage which emphasized the rôle of the intellect in religion, and in the earlier part of the seventeenth century men like Chillingworth and Hales had protested in the name of reason against both dogmatism and irrationality. But the great religious struggle of the century had been fought in a spirit very different from that of the circle at Great Tew. The Puritans had magnified certain exceedingly important elements in Christian thought and experience, but their theology increasingly sacrificed the qualities of balance and proportion, and invited a reaction all the more severe because political power was also at stake. Certain excesses of the sects inspired a deep-seated dread of fanaticism in all its forms. The overthrow of the Puritans meant the repudiation of many of their most characteristic attitudes, and the reaction found its clearest expression in the exaltation of reason. This seemed the surest safeguard against 'enthusiasm', and men of widely varying points of view united to affirm the rights and prerogatives of the intellect. In time this unanimity gave way to uniformity. The Cambridge Platonists had been as ready to dwell on the need of reason as were the later Latitudinarians, but their characteristic qualifications gradually slipped into obscurity and were forgotten. As a result, the emphasis on reason acquired a new quality as well as a new predominance. It was defined in a new way, but it was also approached in a new spirit. The claims of reason more and more approximated to the standards of common sense. What it gained in scope it lost in depth and comprehensiveness. Chillingworth, Whichcote and Toland all agreed that reason is important, but the differences in tone are profound. The change in the character of religious thought in the later seventeenth. century resulted in the arid intellectualism of the succeeding age. The Restoration period saw the steady acceptance of the claims of reason; of greater importance is the fact that reason proved to be a circumscribing as well as a liberating force.

As the period wore on, the whole approach to religious knowledge gradually altered. The Puritans had not ignored the part the imagination plays, but there was a widespread belief that they had abused it. 'Enthusiasm' was the arch-sin of 'fanatics', and the imagination was branded as an irrational force. Intuition also was ignored. Locke excluded it from the earlier sections of his *Essay*; then, in defiance of consistency, he returned to it in Book IV of his most famous work.[1] The results are seen in the subsequent course of philosophy, but the ordinary person was satisfied with the attitude which Locke had originally adopted. The witness of religious experience was less and less understood, and consequently more and more ignored. The results are most clearly seen in the limited and unimaginative outlook of William Paley.

A period marked by the steadily increasing prestige of reason was not disposed to view with any favour the claims of authority. It listened with suspicion to the voice of tradition and the claims of dogmatic systems. This was natural; in the theological warfare of recent years, the appeal to authority had been a common weapon, but it had often been unscrupulously used. The striking lack of historical insight which marked the close of the seventeenth century made it all the harder to deal justly with the past. Moreover, the confident faith in reason made the testimony of any previous period seem comparatively unimportant. The protest against any disposition to impose by fiat a system of belief was necessary and salutary, but the age of Locke and

[1] N. Kemp Smith, op. cit. pp. 27f.

Toland did not see that new forms of authority were creeping in to displace the old. The authority of common sense, in particular, threatened to become a tyranny scarcely less exacting than the methods previously used to secure conformity. There gradually emerged what can only be described as the cult of plausibility. The end of the seventeenth century invested with a new authority whatever was simple, reasonable, well-balanced and well-bred.

The pre-eminent position of the Bible remained apparently unchallenged. Actually the corrosives of the new outlook affected it in less obvious but almost equally important ways. At the end of the period, men spoke of its authority with a reverence seemingly as great as that of the Puritans themselves, but the reader is left with an uncomfortable suspicion that they protested too much. An earlier age had believed without question that the Scriptures were a final and absolute standard of truth. All other issues were tested by reference to that sovereign norm. At the end of the seventeenth century, most writers make the same profession, but they vindicated the Scriptures by referring them to another standard—that of reason. 'Reason', said Locke, 'must be our last judge and guide in everything.'[1] He and his contemporaries agreed that the Scriptures accorded with the canons of sound reason; the fact remains that the Bible was no longer the final and absolute standard. However it might stand the test, it had been brought to the bar of another court. With regard to miracles, also, the same process was at work. They were still cited as conclusive proofs of the truth of the Christian revelation, but they were first shown to be part of a comprehensively reasonable interpretation of the world.

Miracles were discussed with reference to the reign of law, and this points to the change, which, more than any other,

[1] Locke, *Essay*, IV, 19, 14.

marks this period as decisively important in the history of modern thought. Intelligent and progressive men could not ignore the findings of the new science. The Newtonian view of the world increasingly gained ground. Englishmen noted with delight that a fellow-countryman had unfolded for them the mysteries of the universe, and in Addison we clearly see the complacent satisfaction with which educated Englishmen were adjusting their thinking to the newly discovered facts. As Professor Raven has pointed out, the seventeenth century held out high hopes that the insights of science and religion would be brought to fruitful reconciliation.[1] The promise was not fulfilled. The succeeding generation was unequal to the task of integrating the new and the old. Our period ends with the curious spectacle of men who accepted with no sense of incongruity the ancient stories of Genesis and the recent discoveries of Newton.

The earlier part of the seventeenth century had been an age of bitter struggle, and the Restoration period valued stability above most things. Security could best be secured by repressing those who might disturb it, and consequently the Nonconformists were persecuted. In the years immediately following 1660, there were few in position of authority who would have countenanced the view that minorities should not be suppressed. Whether the issue was seen from the political or the religious side, there was virtually complete agreement that toleration was both inexpedient and wrong. By 1688, the discipline of events had for the first time convinced those who might have withheld toleration that they ought to grant it. This momentous change was possible because the lessons of experience reinforced a theory which was rapidly gaining acceptance. As a result, toleration was established within the bounds which political security allowed. Atheists and Roman

[1] C. E. Raven, *Science, Religion and the Future*, pp. 28–9.

Catholics were still barred from its full benefits, but only because in both cases their views were regarded as potentially disruptive of the stability of the State. Locke's first letter on Toleration was the cogent summary of the case against religious persecution, and it remained the classic justification of the Revolution Settlement. But it is worth noting that the terms in which toleration was defined further illustrate the changes in English religious thought. The repression of minorities had become indefensible because the majority had lost much of the confidence which persecution presupposes. Part of Locke's contribution to the thought of his age was a new recognition of the limitations to which our knowledge is subject. It was now possible to grant toleration, not so much because you had gained a new respect for the integrity and sincerity of others, as because any vehement certainties were thoroughly suspect.

The closing years of the seventeenth century had no place for arrogance or dogmatism, but they opened an era uniquely confident and self-assured. Enthusiasm was suppressed and passion carefully controlled, but this made it all the easier to believe in the neatly ordered regularity of life. Man was a noble creature (though never in an extravagant way); the universe was marvellously contrived (though not as yet so vast as to dwarf man by its immensity); the political order was securely established, and liberty (reasonably limited) was a part of the firm structure of society. God, the ultimate ground of this stability, remained discreetly in the back-ground as a kind of honorary president of the universe that He had made. The influences which had recently been shaping the character of religious thought had combined to create a mood of dangerously complacent satisfaction, and Addison, the spokesman of the coming age, could invite his readers 'to consider the world in its most agreeable lights'.

BIBLIOGRAPHY

(NOTE. A bibliography of this kind is necessarily selective. The nature of seventeenth-century religious literature—much of it in pamphlet form, but with very lengthy titles—would otherwise expand the bibliography to intolerable dimensions. Only works actually referred to in the text have been listed, and titles have in all cases been quoted in the shortest form.)

I. PRIMARY OR CONTEMPORARY WORKS

AITKEN, G. A. (editor). *Later Stuart Tracts*. London, 1903.

Allegiance—*The Case of Allegiance in our Present Circumstances Consider'd, In a Letter from a Minister in the City to a Minister in the Country*. London, 1689.

(ALLESTREE, R.). *The Whole Duty of Man*. London, ed. of 1735.

AUBREY, J. *Brief Lives, Chiefly of Contemporaries* (ed. by A. Clark). 2 vols. Oxford, 1898.

BARKER, EDM. *Votum Pro Caesare*. London, 1660.

Memoirs of the Life of Mr. Ambrose Barnes, 1627–1710. (Surtees Society, vol. 50.)

BARROW, ISAAC. *Works* (ed. by J. H. Hamilton). 3 vols. London, 1861.

BAXTER, R. *Reliquiae Baxterianae* (ed. by M. Sylvester). London, 1696.

—— *Practical Works*. 4 vols. London, 1854.

BENTLEY, R. *Eight Sermons Preached at the Hon. Robert Boyle's Lecture, in the First Year*, MDCXCII. (*The Confutation of Atheism*.) Cambridge, 1724 (5th ed.).

BIRCH, T. *Life of Dr John Tillotson* (ed. of 1820). Prefaced to *Works* of Archbishop Tillotson. 10 vols.

BLOUNT, C. *Anima Mundi*. London, 1679.

BOHUN, E. *Non-Resistance or Passive Obedience noway concerned in the Controversies now Depending*. London, 1689.

BOULTON, R. *Life of the Hon. Robert Boyle*. London, 1725.

BOYLE, R. *Works*. 5 vols. London, 1725.

BRABOURNE, THEOPHILUS. *A Defence of the King's Authority and Supremacy....* London, 1660.

The Autobiography of Sir John Bramston. (Camden Society.) London, 1845.

A Brief History of the Succession of the Crown of England. London, 1688/9. (Reprinted in *The Harleian Miscellany*, vol. 1, London, 1744.)

BUNYAN, J. *Works* (ed. by H. Stebbing). 4 vols. London, 1859.

BURNET, G. *Some Unpublished Letters of Gilbert Burnet, the Historian* (ed. by H. C. Foxcroft). Camden Miscellany, vol. XI.

—— *Exhortation to Peace and Unity.* London, 1681.

—— *A Sermon Preached in the Chapel of St. James Before His Highness the Prince of Orange*, 23 December 1688. London, 1689.

—— A Relation of the Death of the Primitive Persecutors. Written originally in Latin by L. C. F. Lactantius, Englished by Gilbert Burnet, To which he hath made a large Preface concerning Persecution. *Burnet's Tracts*, vol. II. 1689.

—— *Pastoral Letter*—concerning the Oaths of Allegiance and Supremacy, 1689.

—— *A Sermon Preached at the Funeral of the Hon. Robert Boyle*, 7 January 1691/2. London, 1692.

—— *Discourse on the late Hon. Mr. Boyle.* London, 1692.

—— *Four Discourses to the Clergy of The Diocese of Sarum.* London, 1694.

—— *A Sermon Preached at the Funeral of the Most Reverend Father in God, John by the Divine Providence Lord Archbishop of Canterbury...*, 30 November 1694. London, 1695.

—— *History of My Own Time.* 6 vols. Oxford, 1823; (ed. by O. Airy) 2 vols. Oxford, 1897.

—— *The Beginnings and Advances of a Spiritual Life* (in Scugal's *Life of God in the Soul of Man*).

BUTLER, J. *Works* (ed. by W. E. Gladstone). 2 vols. Oxford, 1896.

CALAMY, E. *An Abridgement of Mr Baxter's History of his Life and Times, with an Account of the Ministers, etc., who were Ejected After the Restoration.* 2nd ed. 2 vols. London, 1713.

CALAMY, E. *The Nonconformist's Memorial* (abridged, corrected, etc., by Samuel Palmer). 2nd ed. 3 vols. London, 1802.

CAMPAGNAC, E. T. (ed.). *The Cambridge Platonists*. Oxford, 1901.

CARTWRIGHT. *The Diary of Thomas Cartwright, Bishop of Chester*. (Camden Society.) London, 1843.

The Case Stated Touching the Sovereign's Prerogative and the People's Liberty. London, 1660.

CLARENDON. *Life and Continuation*. 2 vols. Oxford, 1857.

Cobbett's Parliamentary History of England, vol. IV. London (T. Hansard), 1808.

COLLINS, A. *A Discourse of Free Thinking*. London, 1713.

Considerations touching the Liturgy of the Church of England, in reference to His Majesty's late Gracious Declaration, and in order to a happy union in Church and State. London, 1661.

The Correspondence of John Cosin, Lord Bishop of Durham. (Surtees Society, vols. 52 and 55.)

COWLEY, A. *Poetical Works*.

(CROFT, H.). *The Naked Truth, or the True State of the Primitive Church*. London, 1675.

CUDWORTH, R. *True Intellectual System of the Universe*. 1678.

A Defence of the Profession which the Right Reverend Father in God, John, late Lord Bishop of Chichester, made upon his death-bed; Concerning Passive Obedience and the new Oaths. London, 1690.

A Discourse Concerning the Unreasonableness of a New Separation, on Account of the Oaths, With an Answer to the History of Passive Obedience so far as relates to them. London, 1689.

EDWARDS, JOHN. *The Preacher*. London: vol. I, 1705; vol. II, 1706; vol. III, 1709.

EVELYN, JOHN. *Diary*. (Everyman's Library.) 2 vols.

Fair Warning, or XXV Reasons Against Toleration. 1663.

FEATLEY. *The League Illegal*. London, 1660.

FILMER, R. *Patriarcha* (ed. by Henry Morley). London, 1884.

Life of Thomas Firmin. London (1698).

FOWLER, E. *Principles and Practices of Certain Moderate Divines of the Church of England, Abusively Called Latitudinarians.* . . . London, 1670.

GAUDEN, JOHN. *Considerations Touching the Liturgy of the Church of England* . . . . London, 1661.

GLANVILL, JOSEPH. *Plus Ultra.* London.

—— *Saducismus Triumphantus.*

—— *The Vanity of Dogmatizing.* London, 1660.

—— *Scepsis Scientifica.* 1665.

—— λογουθρησκεία, *or a Seasonable Recommendation and Defence of Reason in the Affairs of Religion* . . . . 1670.

—— *Essays Upon Several Important Subjects in Philosophy and Religion.* London, 1676.

—— *Seasonable Reflections and Discourses, in order to the conviction and Cure of the Scoffing and Infidelity of a Degenerate Age.* 1676.

—— *The Zealous and Impartial Protestant* (written 1678). 1681.

The Remains of Dennis Granville, D.D., Dean and Archdeacon of Durham. (Surtees Society.) 2 vols. 1860 and 1865.

GRATTON, J. *A Journal of the Life of that ancient servant of Christ, John Gratton.* Stanford, N.Y. 1805.

GREY, A. *Debates of the House of Commons, 1667 to 1694.* 10 vols. London, 1763.

The Autobiography of Anne Lady Halkett. (Camden Society.) London, 1865.

HALYBURTON. *Natural Religion Insufficient.* 1714.

The Hatton Correspondence. (Camden Society.) 2 vols. London, 1878.

HICKES, GEORGE. *Jovian, or an Answer to Julian the Apostate.* London, 1683.

JESSEY. *The Lord's Loud Call to England.* London, 1660.

JOHNSON, S. *Julian the Apostate.* London, 1682.

The Diary of the Rev. Ralph Josselin, 1616–1683. (Camden Society.) London, 1908.

KENNETT, BISHOP WHITE. *History of England.* 2nd ed. London, 1719.

—— *Register and Chronicle, Ecclesiastical and Civil.* London, 1728.

L'ESTRANGE, R. *Interest Mistaken, or The Holy Cheat.* 1661.

L'ESTRANGE, R. *Toleration Discussed.* 1663.

—— *The Free-born Subject.* 1679.

—— *Citt and Bumpkin.* 1680.

—— *The Dissenters Sayings (second part).* 1681.

A Letter from a Gentleman in the City to a Gentleman in the Country, about the Odiousness of Persecution. London, 1687.

A Letter Out of Suffolk to a Friend in London. 1695.

LOCKE, J. *Letter Concerning Toleration.* London, 1689.

—— *A Second Letter Concerning Toleration.* London, 1690.

—— *A Third Letter For Toleration.* London, 1692.

—— *The Reasonableness of Christianity.* London, 1695.

—— *A Letter to the Bishop of Worcester Concerning Some Passages Relating to Mr. Locke's Essay of Human Understanding in a Late Discourse of his Lordship's in Vindication of the Trinity.* London, 1697.

—— *Works,* 8th ed. 4 vols. London, 1777.

—— *Two Treatises of Government* (ed. by Henry Morley). London, 1884.

—— *Essay Concerning Human Understanding* (ed. by A. S. Pringle-Pattison). Oxford, 1924.

LUTTRELL, N. *Brief Historical Relation of State Affairs.* 6 vols. Oxford, 1857.

The Life of Adam Martindale. Written by himself. (Chetham Society.) 1845.

MARVELL, A. *Works.* 4 vols. 1872–5.

—— *Poems and Letters of* (ed. by H. M. Margoliouth). 2 vols. Oxford, 1927.

MORE, HENRY. *Philosophical Writings.*

—— *The Theological Works of the Most Pious and Learned Henry More.* London, 1708.

—— *A Collection of Several Philosophical Writings of Dr. Henry More,* 4th ed. London, 1712.

The Diary of the Rev. Henry Newcombe. (Chetham Society.) 1849.

The Autobiography of Henry Newcombe. 2 vols. (Chetham Society.) 1852.

NEWTON, I. *Opera.*

NICOLSON. *Epistolatory Correspondence* (ed. by John Nichols). 2 vols. London, 1809.

NORTH, THE HON. R. *The Lives of the Norths* (ed. by A. Jessop). 3 vols. London, 1890.

OWEN, JOHN. *A Peace Offering in an Apology and Humble Plea for Indulgence and Liberty of Conscience.*

—— *Indulgence and Toleration Considered.*

—— *The Present Distresses on Nonconformists Examined.*

—— *A Word of Advice to the Citizens of London.*

—— *Vindication of the Nonconformists from the Charge of Schism.*

—— *Works*, 24 vols. Edinburgh, 1851–62.

The Judgment and Decree of the University of Oxford. Oxford, 1683.

PARKER, S. *A Discourse of Ecclesiastical Polity.* 1669?/70.

—— *History of His Own Time* (trans. by T. Newlin). London, 1727.

PATRICK, S. *A Friendly Debate Between a Conformist and a Nonconformist.* 3rd ed. London, 1669.

—— *Autobiography.* Oxford, 1839.

'S.P.' (SIMON PATRICK?). *A Brief Account of the New Sect of Latitude men; Together With Some Reflections on the New Philosophy.* London, 1662.

PEARSE, E. *The Conformist's Plea for the Nonconformist.* 1681.

—— *The Second, Third* and *Fourth Pleas.* 1682–3.

PENN, WILLIAM. *The Great Case of Liberty of Conscience.* London, 1671.

—— *England's Present Interest Discovered.* 1675.

PEPYS, SAMUEL. *Diary* (ed. by H. B. Wheatley). 9 vols. London, 1893f.

PERRINCHIEF, R. *A Discourse of Toleration.* London, 1667/?8.

—— *Indulgence Not Justified.* London, 1668.

PETTY, SIR WM. *Political Arithmetic.* London, 1690.

POPE, DR WALTER. *Life of Seth Ward, Bishop of Salisbury.* London, 1697.

Prerogative—The Case Stated, Touching the Sovereign's Prerogative and the People's Liberty. London, 1660.

The Letters of Humphrey Prideaux...to John Ellis. (Camden Society.) London, 1875.

Royal Proclamations, 1660–4. London.

RAY, JOHN. *The Wisdom of God, Manifested in the Works of Creation* (ed. of 1768).

The Memoirs of Sir John Reresby. London, 1875.

The Last Speech and Behaviour of William, late Lord Russell. London, 1683.

Sanderson, R. *Works.* 6 vols. Oxford, 1854.

(SAVAGE, H.). *Toleration with its Objections Fully Confuted.* 1663.

The Savile Correspondence. Letters to and from Henry Savile.... (Camden Society.) 1858.

SAYWELL. *Evangelical and Catholic Unity Maintained in the Church of England.* London, 1682.

SHERLOCK, W. *The Case of the Allegiance Due to Sovereign Powers.* London, 1691.

(SHOWER, B.). *An Antidote Against Poison.* London, 1683.

The Last Speech of Algernon Sidney. London, 1683.

SMITH, JOHN. *Select Discourses* (ed. by H. G. Williams). Cambridge, 1859.

Some Additional Remarks upon the Late Book of the Reverend Dean of St. Paul's, by a Conformable Clergyman. 1681.

Some Free Reflections upon Occasion of the Public Discourse About Liberty of Conscience. London, 1687.

SOUTH, ROBERT. *Sermons.* 3rd ed. 6 vols. London, 1704.

SPRAT, T. *History of the Royal Society* (ed. of 1702).

STILLINGFLEET, E. *Irenicum.* London, 1660.

—— *Originis Sacrae.* 3rd ed. London, 1666.

—— *The Mischief of Separation.* London, 1680.

—— *The Unreasonableness of Separation.* London, 1680/1.

—— *A Rational Account of the Grounds of the Protestant Religion. Works* (1709), vol. v.

The True Protestant Subject. London, 1680.

Succession—*A Brief History of the Succession of the Crown of England.* London, 1689. (Reprinted in the Harleian Miscellany, vol. I, 1744.)

Autobiography and Anecdotes by William Taswell. Camden Miscellany, vol. II. London, 1853.

TEMPLE, SIR WILLIAM. *Observations on the United Provinces.* London, 1672.

—— *A Letter from Holland Touching Liberty of Conscience.* 1688.

THORNDIKE, H. *The Due Way of Composing the Differences on Foot.* London, 1660.

—— *Discourse of the Forbearance of the Penalties which a Due Reformation Requires.* 1670.

The Charge of Socinianism Against Dr. Tillotson. London, 1695.

TILLOTSON, J. *A Sermon Preached at the Funeral of Dr. Benjamin Whichcote.* London, 1683.

—— *Works.* 3 vols. London, 1735.

TOLAND, JOHN. *Christianity Not Mysterious.* London, 1695.

(TOMKINS, T.) *The Inconveniences of Toleration.* London, 1667.

Trelawney Papers. Camden Miscellany, vol. II. London, 1853.

(TURNER). *Animadversions upon a late Pamphlet Entitled the Naked Penalties which a Due Reformation Requires.* 1670.

TURNER, F. *Animadversions Upon a late Pamphlet entitled The Naked Truth.* London, 1676.

WALTON, IZAAK. *Life of Sanderson*, in Sanderson's *Works*, vol. VI.

WARD, SETH. *Against Resistance of Lawful Powers.* London, 1661.

WESTFIELD. *The White Robe.* London, 1660.

WHICHCOTE, B. *Select Sermons.* London, 1698.

—— *Moral and Religious Aphorisms...to which are added Eight Letters which passed between Dr. Whichcote...and Dr. Tuckney....* London, 1753.

—— *Moral and Religious Aphorisms.* London, 1930.

WHITING, J. *Persecution Exposed, in some Memoirs relating to the Sufferings of John Whiting.* London, 1715.

Letters to Sir Joseph Williamson. (Camden Society.) 2 vols. London, 1874.

(WOLSELEY, SIR CHARLES). *Liberty of Conscience upon its true and proper Grounds asserted and vindicated.* London, 1668.

—— *Liberty of Conscience the Magistrate's Interest.* London, 1668.

—— *A Peaceable Dissertation.* 1669

WOOD, A. *Athenae Oxonienses.* 2 vols. London, 1721.

—— *Life and Times*, vols. I–III. Oxford Historical Society, 1891–4.

WOODCOCK. *Extracts from the Papers of Thomas Woodcock.* Camden Miscellany, vol. XI.

II. Secondary Works

Abbey, C. J. and Overton, J. H. *The English Church in the Eighteenth Century*. 2 vols. London, 1878.

Acton. *Lectures on Modern History*. London, 1906.

Alexander, S. *Locke*. London, n.d.

Austin, E. M. *Ethics of the Cambridge Platonists*. Philadelphia, 1935.

Bastide, C. *Anglo-French Entente in the Seventeenth Century*. London, 1914.

Blaxland, B. *The Struggle With Puritanism*. London, 1910.

Bourne, H. R. Fox. *Life of John Locke*. 2 vols. London, 1876.

Braithwaite, W. C. *The Beginnings of Quakerism*. London, 1912.

—— *The Second Period of Quakerism*. London, 1919.

Brett, G. S. *Newton's Place in the History of Religious Thought* in *The History of Science and Society*. Baltimore, 1928.

Burtt, E. A. *The Metaphysical Foundations of Modern Physical Science*. London, 1925.

Cardwell, E. *Documentary Annals of the Reformed Church of England*. 2 vols. London, 1839.

—— *History of Conferences and Other Proceedings Connected with the Revision of the Book of Common Prayer*. London, 1840.

—— *Synodalia, a Collection of Articles of Religion, Canons and Proceedings of Convocations of Canterbury*. 2 vols. London, 1842.

Cassirer, E. *Die Platonische Renaissance in England und die Schule von Cambridge*. Leipzig, 1932.

Clark, G. N. *The Seventeenth Century*. Oxford, 1929.

—— *The Later Stuarts*. Oxford, 1934.

—— *Science and Social Welfare in the Age of Newton*. Oxford, 1937.

Clarke and Foxcroft. *Life of Gilbert Burnet*. Cambridge, 1911.

Cooper. *Annals of the University of Cambridge*. 5 vols. 1842–53.

Dalrymple, J. *Memoirs of Great Britain and Ireland*. 3 vols. London, 1790.

DE BOER. *The Theory of Knowledge of the Cambridge Platonists.* Madras, 1931.

DE PAULEY, W. C. *The Candle of the Lord.* London, 1937.

D'OYLY, G. *Life of William Sancroft.* 2 vols. London, 1821.

EVE, A. S. *The Mind of Newton.* (In the *University of Toronto Quarterly*, vol. II, no. 2.)

FEILING, K. *A History of the Tory Party, 1640–1714.* Oxford, 1924.

FIGGIS, J. N. *The Divine Right of Kings.* 2nd ed. Cambridge, 1914.

FORSTER. *Sir John Eliot.* 2 vols. London, 1864.

FOXCROFT, H. C. *The Life and Letters of Sir George Savile, First Marquis of Halifax.* 2 vols. London, 1898.

—— *Supplement to Burnet's History of My Own Time.* Oxford, 1902.

FRANKS, R. S. *History of the Doctrine of the Work of Christ.* 2 vols. London, n.d.

GIBSON, J. *Locke's Theory of Knowledge....* Cambridge, 1917.

GREENSLET, F. *Joseph Glanvill.* New York, 1900.

GWATKIN, H. M. *Toleration in England.* (In *Cambridge Modern History*, vol. V, ch. XI.)

HALLER, W. *The Rise of Puritanism.* New York, 1938.

HARRIS, W. *Memoirs of Thomas Manton.* London, 1725.

HAWKINS, L. M. *Allegiance in Church and State.* London, 1928.

HODGSON, L. *The Doctrine of the Trinity.* New York, 1944.

HUNT, J. *Religious Thought in England.* 3 vols. London, 1870.

HUTTON, W. H. *A History of the English Church from the Accession of Charles I to the Death of Anne.* London, 1903.

INGE, W. R. *Christian Mysticism.* London, 1899.

—— *The Platonic Tradition in English Religious Thought.* London, 1917.

JEBB, R. C. *Bentley.* London, 1882.

KEMP, J. E. (ed.). *The Classic Preachers of the English Church.* London, 1877.

KITCHIN, G. *Roger L'Estrange.* London, 1913.

LATHBURY, T. *A History of the Non-jurors.* London, 1845.

LECKY, W. E. H. *A History of England in the Eighteenth Century*, vol. I. London, 1878.

LODGE, R. *The History of England from the Restoration to the Death of William III* (new impression). London, 1918.

MACKINTOSH, SIR JAMES. *History of the Revolution in England, 1688*. London, 1834.

McLACHLAN, H. *The Religious Opinions of Milton, Locke and Newton*. Manchester, 1941.

MARKOWER, F. *The Constitutional History of the Church of England*. London, 1895.

MATTHEWS, A. G. *Calamy Revised*. Oxford, 1933.

MITCHELL, W. F. *English Pulpit Oratory from Andrewes to Tillotson*. London, 1932.

MOFFATT, J. (ed.). *The Golden Book of Tillotson*. London, 1926.

MORE, L. T. *Isaac Newton*. New York, 1934.

MUIRHEAD, J. H. *The Platonic Tradition in Anglo-Saxon Philosophy*. London, 1931.

NOTESTEIN, W. *History of Witchcraft in England from 1558 to 1718*. New Haven, 1911.

OGG, D. *England in the Reign of Charles II*. 2 vols. Oxford, 1934.

OMAN, JOHN. *The Problem of Faith and Freedom in the Last Two Centuries*. London, 1906.

ORME, W. *Life of Richard Baxter*. (In vol. I of the *Practical Works of Richard Baxter*.) London, 1830.

OVERTON, J. H. *Life in the English Church, 1660-1714*. London, 1885.

—— *The Non-jurors*. London, 1902.

PATTISON, MARK. *Essays*. Oxford, 1889.

PAWSON, G. P. H. *The Cambridge Platonists*. London, 1930.

PLUMPTRE, E. H. *The Life of Thomas Ken*. 2 vols. London, 1890.

POLLOCK, SIR F. *Essays in Jurisprudence and Ethics*. London, 1882.

POLLOCK, SIR JOHN. *The Popish Plot*. 2nd ed. Cambridge, 1944.

PORTUS, G. V. *Caritas Anglicana, or an Historical Inquiry into those Religious and Philanthropical Societies that Flourished between 1678 and 1740*. London, 1912.

POWICKE, F. J. *The Cambridge Platonists*. London, 1926.

PRINGLE-PATTISON, A. S. *Preface to Locke's Essay Concerning Human Understanding*. Oxford, 1924.

RANKE, L. VON. *History of England, principally in the Seventeenth Century*. 6 vols. Oxford, 1875.

RAVEN, C. E. *John Ray, Naturalist*. Cambridge, 1942.

—— *Science, Religion and the Future*. Cambridge, 1943.

SCHLATTER, R. D. *Social Ideas of Religious Leaders, 1660 to 1688*. Oxford, 1940.

SEATON, A. A. *The Theory of Toleration under the Later Stuarts*. Cambridge, 1911.

SMITH, N. KEMP. *John Locke*. Manchester, 1933.

SMYTH, C. H. *The Art of Preaching*. London, 1940.

SORLEY, W. R. *History of English Philosophy*. Cambridge, 1920.

STEPHEN, LESLIE. *English Thought in the Eighteenth Century*. 2 vols. London, 1876.

—— *English Literature and Society in the Eighteenth Century*. 1904.

STOUGHTON, J. *The Ecclesiastical History of England*. Rev. ed. London, 1881.

SULLIVAN, J. W. N. *Isaac Newton*. London, 1927.

SYKES, N. *Church and State in England in the Eighteenth Century*. Cambridge, 1934.

TENNANT, F. R. *Miracle*. Cambridge, 1925.

—— *Philosophical Theology*. 2 vols. Cambridge, 1926, 1930.

TREVELYAN, G. M. *England Under the Stuarts*. London, 1904.

—— *The English Revolution*. London, 1938.

TROELTSCH, E. *The Social Teaching of the Christian Churches* (trans. by O. Wyon). 2 vols. London, 1931.

TULLOCH, J. *Rational Theology and Christian Philosophy in England in the Seventeenth Century*. 2nd ed. 2 vols. Edinburgh, 1874.

VAN DUSEN, H. P. *Church and State in the Modern World*. New York, 1937.

WESTCOTT, B. F. *Essays in the History of Religious Thought in the West*. London, 1891.

WHITING, C. E. *Studies in English Puritanism from the Restoration to the Revolution, 1660–1688*. London, 1931.

WILLEY, B. *The Seventeenth Century Background*. London, 1934.

INDEX

Rel